The Metaverse

The Metaverse: A Critical Introduction provides a clear, concise, and well-grounded introduction to the concept of the Metaverse, its history, the technology, the opportunities, the challenges, and how it is having an impact on almost every facet of society. The book serves as a stand-alone introduction to the Metaverse and as an introduction to the range of topics that will be covered by the specialist volumes in The Metaverse Series.

Key Features:

- a concise history of the Metaverse idea and related implementations to date;
- an examination of what the Metaverse actually is;
- an introduction to the fundamental technologies used in the Metaverse;
- an overview of how the different uses and aspects of the Metaverse are having an impact on our lives across multiple disciplines and social contexts;
- a consideration of the opportunities and challenges of the evolving Metaverse; and
- a sense of how the Metaverse may mature over the coming decades.

This book is a primer and Metaverse reader, drawing on academic research and practical and commercial experiences and taking inspiration from the science fiction origins and treatments of the Metaverse. The book explores the use of the increasing number of virtual worlds and proto-Metaverses which have existed since the late 1990s and includes a critical consideration of recent developments in cryptoworlds and mixed reality. The aim is to provide professional and lay readers, researchers, academics, and students with an indispensable guide to what counts as a metaverse, the opportunities, and challenges, and how the future of the coming Metaverse can best be guided.

The Metaverse Series

The Metaverse: A Critical Introduction
David Burden & Maggi Savin-Baden
A well-grounded introduction to the concept of the Metaverse, its history, the technology, the opportunities, the challenges and how it is having an impact almost every facet of society.

The Metaverse for Learning and Education
Maggi Savin-Baden & David Burden
A clear and concise guide for practitioners and other interested readers in how the Metaverse and related technologies can be best used to create and deliver innovative learning and education, and how the delivery of learning and education in the Metaverse might evolve.

The Metaverse for Psychotherapy: A Practitioner's Guide to Effective Mental Health Treatment
Bruce Bassi
A guide for clinicians and other interested readers in how the Metaverse and related technologies can be best used to deliver effective psychotherapy and how the delivery of psychotherapy in the Metaverse might evolve.

Cities in the Metaverse: Digital Twins, Society, Avatars, and Economics on the New Frontier
Andrew Hudson-Smith, Valerio Signorelli, and Duncan Wilson
Cities in the Metaverse delves into the possibilities and challenges of a future where we can interact with each other in virtual spaces, create digital twins of real-world cities, and even build new worlds based on AI.

The Military Metaverse: The Opportunities and Challenges for Global Security
Andy Fawkes and David Burden
The Military Metaverse explores the impact that the Metaverse is having today on how the world's militaries procure, maintain, train, plan, and fight, and how the Metaverse presents new challenges and potentially even a new environment for future conflicts.

The Metaverse and Religion
Eric Trozzo
The Metaverse and Religion provides a balanced consideration to ways that the Metaverse poses challenges to conventional conceptions of religion, exploring the new understandings of religion that may be opened up, and how it might be used by religious movements.

For more information and further titles in this series please visit: https: //www. routledge.com/The-Metaverse/book-series/

The Metaverse
A Critical Introduction

David Burden and Maggi Savin-Baden

CRC Press
Taylor & Francis Group
Boca Raton London New York

CRC Press is an imprint of the
Taylor & Francis Group, an **informa** business

A CHAPMAN & HALL BOOK

First edition published 2024
by CRC Press
2385 NW Executive Center Drive, Suite 320, Boca Raton FL 33431
and by CRC Press

4 Park Square, Milton Park, Abingdon, Oxon, OX14 4RN

CRC Press is an imprint of Taylor & Francis Group, LLC

ISBN: 9781032497891 (hbk)
ISBN: 9781032497884 (pbk)
ISBN: 9781003395461 (ebk)

DOI: 10.1201/9781003395461

Typeset in Palatino
by KnowledgeWorks Global Ltd.

The essential lesson that we have abstracted from our experiences with Habitat is that a cyberspace is defined more by the interactions among the actors within it than by the technology with which it is implemented. ... At the core of our vision is the idea that cyberspace is necessarily a multiple-participant environment ... Beyond a foundation[al] set of communications capabilities, the technology used to present this environment to its participants, while sexy and interesting, is a peripheral concern.

Chip Morningstar and F. Randall Farmer
The Lessons of Lucasfilm's Habitat
The First International Conference on Cyberspace
University of Texas at Austin
May 1990

To my daughters, Jo and Ruth, so they no

longer have such a hard time in explaining

exactly what it is their Dad does!

And from us both to all the people and

avatars we have met, worked with, and talked

to during our years in virtual worlds.

Contents

About the Authors

David Burden created his first virtual world in 1996 and has spent most of the time since working in virtual spaces and with virtual humans for a variety of clients through his company Daden Limited. His first presentation on the Metaverse was in 2008. David and Maggi co-wrote the book *Virtual Humans* for Routledge in 2019 and also worked together on the book *Digital Afterlife* in 2020.

Maggi Savin-Baden is a research Professor at Blackfriars Hall, University of Oxford. She has researched and evaluated staff and student experience of learning for over 20 years and has a strong publication record of over 70 research publications and has completed 25 books. Her research and writing reflect her interests on the impact of innovative learning, digital fluency, digital afterlife, and the postdigital, and she has worked with David on a number of research projects since 2008.

Acknowledgements

Our sincerest thanks to Randi Slack at CRC/Taylor and Francis for being so positive when we suggested the idea of not one but a whole series of books on the Metaverse, and who has been so supportive of us both since our initial work on *Virtual Humans*. Any mistakes and errors are ours; we are, after all, still only physical humans.

Introduction

The term "Metaverse" was first coined in Neal Stephenson's 1992 novel *Snow Crash* (Stephenson, 1992) to describe an on-line, three-dimensional (3D) digital world which acted as an extension of people's physical lives. However, much of what we now think of as a metaverse was present in the fantasy-style virtual world of Vernor Vinge's True Names (Vinge, 2015), first published in 1981. Some of the first practical Metaverse-like environments were the text-based multi-user dungeons (MUDs) and object-orientated MUDs (MOOs). But it was the first 3D social virtual worlds such as Active Worlds, and particularly Second Life, which began to show that something like the Stephenson's vision could be built in reality. As this generation of proto-metaverses began to flounder in the early 2010s, the arrival of the Oculus virtual reality (VR) headsets prompted further interest in immersive spaces. Mark Zuckerberg's renaming of Facebook's holding company as Meta seemed to confirm that the Metaverse was still a current vision.

Many of the recent publications on the Metaverse take a technological or financial approach, are focused on the profiteering of Blockchain and non-fungible token (NFT)-based worlds, or have a relatively uncritical approach to the topic. Faced with such sources, and with the considerable hyperbole of commentaries on platforms such as X/Twitter and Medium, it can be difficult for those unfamiliar with the evolution of the Metaverse over the last two decades to appreciate the essential elements of the Metaverse idea, and to understand the potential pitfalls as well as the opportunities that the Metaverse may offer.

To provide some vital initial context, Chapter 1 examines the history of the metaverse, from its origins in science fiction, and the text-based MUDs and MOOs of the 1980s, through the 2D and 3D social virtual worlds of the late 1990s and early 2000s, and then on to the headset-based VR wave of the 2010s and finally the cryptoworlds of the 2020s.

Chapter 2 considers some of the competing definitions of the metaverse and presents ten axioms for what a fully realised Metaverse should demonstrate. It concludes with an examination of what it is particularly about the VR experience that makes it so different from other Internet-based experiences.

With a clearer understanding of what constitutes a metaverse, Chapter 3 considers the use and impact of the metaverse across a broad range of commercial and societal endeavours including business, collaboration, training and education, economics, marketing, entertainment, gaming, arts, and defence, drawing examples from over 20 years' worth of metaversal activity.

Chapter 4 looks at the technologies that underpin the metaverse, presenting them in a hopefully non-technical way, and identifying which are core to the metaverse concept and which are optional.

DOI: 10.1201/9781003395461-1

Chapter 5 considers some of the broader issues and dichotomies that emerge when considering the metaverse and the personal, social, and global challenges and related opportunities, which any ultimate Metaverse would need to address.

Chapter 6 brings the foregoing analysis together, looking at the short-, medium-, and long-term challenges to the Metaverse, before considering seven different scenarios for the future of the Metaverse.

As we were writing the book, there was something of a shift in terminology in some quarters, away from "metaverse" and towards "spatial computing". We have stayed with metaverse for two reasons. First, metaverse as a term has been around for a long time as the dominant term for the sort of spaces we are talking about, and we expect that it will dominate and outlive spatial computing in most people's minds – despite the latter actually having the longer heritage. Second, and more importantly, spatial computing is a very technology-centric term, and, as we hope this book will show, the future virtual spaces that we are talking about will be far more about the people and the communities within it. If the metaverse really delivers, the technology should just fade into the background.

There are two other considerations that have informed our writing of this book – and could be taken as biases. First, we were both highly active in Second Life during the 2000s/early 2010s, and this has undoubtedly shaped many of our views on what the Metaverse could, and even should be, as well as how we feel Second Life and OpenSim compare to other more recent platforms and initiatives. Second, we feel that the term "Metaverse" should be kept for the highest common denominator model of what the virtual realm should be like, not for its lowest common denominator implementations.

The intention is for this book to be a practical guide to the concept of the Metaverse, drawing on academic research and practical and commercial experiences. The aim is to give the reader a better understanding of what is meant by the Metaverse, how far it is in its evolution, and what the benefits and challenges of the Metaverse could be.

WEBSITE AND MICROVERSE

We have created a website to support this book with additional information, links (including all URL references), and updates at http://www.themetaverseseries.info/. We are also practising what we preach and so have created a 3D microverse accessible from that site and within a web browser which provides a "data garden" approach (see Chapter 3) to the content of the book and is a place where hopefully we'll be able to meet up with readers and discuss the Metaverse in a metaverse!

Key Terms

Any discussion of the metaverse won't get far without mentioning some of the key technologies and concepts related to it. Whilst this book (and particularly Chapter 4) will describe these technologies in more detail, a summary of each is provided (see Tables 0.1 and 0.2) for the benefit of the reader less familiar with this area and to clarify how the terms are used in this book.

TABLE 0.1

Definition of Key Terms

Term	Definition
Augmented reality (AR)	Augmented reality overlays digital information onto a viewscreen (typically a smartphone, but possibly a heads-up-display or a set of glasses) and supplements reality, rather than replacing it.
DesktopVR	DesktopVR refers to VR experiences delivered using a conventional 2D computer screen (desktop, laptop, tablet, or mobile), in either first person (the view out of the avatar's eyes) or third person (an "over the shoulder" view which includes the back of the avatar). A combination of mouse, keyboard, joystick, and touchscreen are used for control and interaction.
Head-mounted display VR (HMD-VR)	HMD-VR is VR delivered through a head-mounted display (HMD) which fully covers the user's field of view, completely blocking out the physical world. Hand controllers and/or ordinary body movement are used for control and interaction.
Head-mounted display XR (HMD-XR)	An HMD capable of delivering both VR and MR experiences.
Mixed reality (MR)	Mixed reality overlays 3D digital visualisations onto a head-mounted screen or see-through visor, where the digital information is "aware" of the physical geometry of the world and the user's movement in it and can respond to both.
Virtual reality (VR)	A 3D spatial, subjective, synthetic digital environment, which can be accessed through a smartphone, tablet or conventional computer (DesktopVR), or a head-mounted display (HMD-VR). VR completely replaces physical reality in the user's view (and even other senses).
Virtual world (VW)	A VR environment which provides a space for users to interact, to have agency and (ideally) some ability to shape the world. Note that in this book, "virtual world" and "metaverse" tend to be used interchangeably since the term "metaverse", as commonly used, is now wide enough to encompass almost all virtual worlds, and some virtual worlds show more metaversal features than some other environments that are being described as metaverses!
Extended reality (XR)	Extended reality is the umbrella term used for all the technologies that create immersive experiences in which users interact with digital content which augment or replace the perceived physical world. As such it includes VR, MR and AR.

As mentioned above, the following convention has been adopted within this book to discriminate between different uses of the word "metaverse". An actual definition of "metaverse" will be considered in Chapter 2.

TABLE 0.2

Metaverse Usage

Term	Usage
metaverse (lower case m)	A persistent digital synthetic environment populated by a large number of avatars who have agency and can interact, for collaboration, work, recreation, learning, relationships, and/or play; and which may be accessible through a range of technologies including VR, MR, and possibly AR.
Metaverse (upper case M)	An ultimate manifestation of the metaverse concept, covering all metaversal features in a globally used and accessible system, which may be a singular metaverse, or a network of interconnected individual metaverses – i.e. a multiverse.
metaversal	Exhibiting some or all of the features of a metaverse.
multiverse/Multiverse	A network of interconnected individual metaverses. It may be that the Metaverse is actually a Multiverse – the capitalisation is again reserved for the fully developed manifestation.
proto-Metaverse	A metaverse which shows many or most of the metaversal features but which is not fully enough developed to warrant the term Metaverse.

FULL DISCLOSURE

Both David and Maggi have actively worked in the metaverse space for around 20 years, both independently, through multiple universities, and through David's company Daden Limited. Where projects that they worked on are mentioned in the text, an endnote will be included noting their involvement.

NOTE: When virtual worlds and metaversal platforms are first introduced in the text, they will normally be followed by the date of their public launch, e.g. Second Life (2003), and, where relevant, a URL. Any citation to a relevant paper or other reference then follows.

References

Stephenson, N. (1992). *Snow Crash*. Bantam Books.
Vinge, V. (2015). *True Names and the opening of the cyberspace frontier*. Tor Books.

1

A History of the Metaverse

Introduction

This chapter provides an overview of the history of the Metaverse, both as an idea and as a series of evolving virtual worlds and extended reality experiences and technologies. It examines how some of the early text-based social spaces could be considered as proto-metaverses before looking at the graphical two-dimensional (2D) and three-dimensional (3D) social virtual worlds that evolved during the 1990s and 2000s. The chapter then describes how, from 2013, the concept of the Metaverse became dominated by the new generation of headset-mounted VR displays (HMD-VR) and the rise of popular 3D game worlds, before examining the impact of Meta's decision to back the metaverse concept, and then the rise of the blockchain and cryptocurrency-based virtual worlds. It also briefly considers the developments in augmented reality (AR) and mixed reality (MR) that are a part of the metaverse. The chapter closes by examining how the Metaverse has been represented in fictional works.

The Beginning

The term "Metaverse" was famously coined by Neal Stephenson in Snow Crash (Stephenson, 1992). The Metaverse described there shows most of the features that are now expected of a metaverse. It is multi-user, social, interactive, inhabited by human- and artificial intelligence (AI)-driven avatars, and provides an environment where people can pretty much do what they want to do. Notably, the world is based on a spatial arrangement – that of a straight road around the equator of a virtual globe, and where land prices depend on the distance along and from the road. The Metaverse is accessed through an HMD-VR display fed optically rather than digitally from a portable computer.

However, the concept of a metaverse pre-dates Stephenson. Whilst the seminal *Neuromancer* (Gibson, 1984) and many other cyberpunk works featured a very abstract representation of cyberspace, the fantasy-style virtual

DOI: 10.1201/9781003395461-2

world of Vernor Vinge's *True Names* (Vinge, 2015), first published in 1981, has many metaversal elements with its protagonists meeting in their own rooms in a virtual castle and travelling the virtual world.

MUDs and MOOs and Habitat

In practical terms, the roots of the metaverse concept can be found in the multi-user dungeons (MUDs) and multi-user object-orientated dungeons (MOOs) of the late twentieth century. MUDs and MOOs, such as *MUD* (1978) (Bartle, 2004) and *LamdaMOO* (1990) (Schiano & White, 1998), offered a far broader range of environments than the dungeon moniker suggests. Since everything in them is described in text, a starship or alien world can be "rendered" in just a single sentence. As long as users engage with the experience, the immersion can be psychologically and emotionally strong. Whilst engagement with these worlds was usually a positive experience, instances such as the digital rape documented in *My Tiny Life* (Dibbel, 1994) provided an early warning of the potential pitfalls of the Metaverse.

The move from text to 2D graphics came most notably from *Habitat* (1986), a 2D virtual world with simple and blocky graphics created by Chip Morningstar and F. Randall Farmer (Morningstar & Farmer, 2008). *Habitat* was inspired by, amongst other things, the virtual world described in *True Names*. Habitat included 20,000 locations, avatars that could move around, gesture, interact with objects, and text chat with each other. The world also had its own economy. Initially built for the Quantum Link dial-up system, *Habitat* was later ported to Compuserve. In a paper they presented in 1990, Morningstar and Farmer tellingly noted that:

> The essential lesson that we have abstracted from our experiences with Habitat is that a cyberspace is defined more by the interactions among the actors within it than by the technology with which it is implemented. While we find much of the work presently being done on elaborate interface technologies – DataGloves, head-mounted displays, special-purpose rendering engines, and so on – both exciting and promising, the almost mystical euphoria that currently seems to surround all this hardware is, in our opinion, both excessive and somewhat misplaced. We can't help having a nagging sense that it's all a bit of a distraction from the really pressing issues. At the core of our vision is the idea that cyberspace is necessarily a multiple-participant environment … Beyond a foundational set of communications capabilities, the technology used to present this environment to its participants, while sexy and interesting, is a peripheral concern.
>
> **(Morningstar & Farmer, 2008).**

Replace "cyberspace" with "metaverse", and the statement is probably as true today as it was over 30 years ago.

Moving onto the Internet and into 3D

Whilst defence, enterprise, and even consumer HMD-VR was around by the late 1990s (for instance, the Virtuality Entertainment installations in Piccadilly Circus and at the Dave & Buster's bar chain) (Virtual Reality Society, n.d.), it was not until the advent of the Web and the broader uptake of the Internet that readily accessible virtual worlds became feasible. Virtual reality markup language (VRML) (https://www.w3.org/MarkUp/VRML/) was an early hypertext markup language (HTML) style standard that let developers use a text editor to create pages of VRML that would render as full 3D DesktopVR virtual environments within a PC viewer application or even a browser plug-in.

A number of companies started to take advantage of the Internet as a way of delivering multi-user virtual worlds, either into the browser or more commonly to a downloadable application. Two key worlds were:

- *Worlds Chat* (1994), developed by Worlds Inc. and probably the first 3D virtual world, although it was little more than sliding simple 3D avatar objects around within a 3D space and engaging in text-chat; and

- *Worlds Away* (1996), which shares some history with Habitat and had a similar but improved 2D graphical interface and ran across the Internet rather than a network like Compuserve (Brenchley, 2023).

The Children of Snow Crash

Legend has it that when *Snow Crash* came out, several entrepreneurs placed it down on the table in front of investors or their teams and said "we're going to build this". Perhaps more realistically, it became a reference point for those developing the first 3D virtual worlds (Au, 2023). One of the earliest, and most complete in vision, was *Active Worlds* (1995, https://www.activeworlds.com/). By today's standards, the graphics are quite basic (but beyond the 8-bit graphics of early video games), but it had a contiguous geographic world where you could buy a plot of land, and similar to *Snow Crash*, land prices were related to the distance from the centre and to the closest teleporting "railway" station. Avatar clothing could be bought, and buildings were built from a collection of simple shapes and components acquired through the in-world marketplace. Crucially, *Active Worlds* had a scripting language, which not only allowed in-world scripting but also limited interfacing to applications on the Internet. *Active Worlds* is still operational nearly 30 years later.

David built his first metaverse house around 1999 at a place called Retsmah Crossing in *Active Worlds* (see Figure 1.1). Like many metaverse houses, before and since, it followed an "ocean living" aesthetic of open plan layout, glass walls and chrome finishes. Using scripting, David then built a simple non-player avatar that would respond to commands, could navigate its way around the local area, and even play hide-and-seek.

FIGURE 1.1
David and his house at Retsmah Crossing in Active Worlds.

Whilst simpler in graphics (far closer to the 8-bit model) and with a fixed 2.5D/isomorphic perspective, *Habbo Hotel* (2000, https://www.habbo.com/) attracted a large user base and was seen as being one of the most popular teen-orientated social virtual worlds with 273 million registered users in 2013 (Mäntymäki & Salo, 2013), although this had fallen to four million by 2018 (Leotoddy, 2019). Whilst it lacked many metaverse features beyond avatar outfits, room decoration, and text-chat, it was a popular place to hang out and chat. Like many other social worlds, it suffered from problems of abusive and exploitative behaviour, resulting in a month-long "mute" of chat on the system in 2012 following a Channel 4 report into the use of the world by paedophiles (Bryce, 2020).

A different world entirely was *There.com* (2003, https://www.prod.there.com/) – see Figure 1.2. This featured (then) state-of-the-art graphics and beautifully rendered environments but never had the usage levels of a world like Habbo Hotel. Users had to be approved to create and sell assets in the world. *There.com* closed in 2010, and Márquez (2013) has an interesting study on what happened to its residents, called "Thereians" afterwards, and which is probably representative of other closed virtual worlds. Márquez identifies how the Thereians used social media to maintain the social connectivity that they had created, and explored the transference of their identities, groups, and activities to other social virtual worlds, such as *Second Life*. *There.com* itself re-opened in 2012.

FIGURE 1.2
David's favourite *There.com* moments were riding his hoverboard around the crater edge of Nene Peak and then surfing down its steep slopes to a brilliantly glistening sea.

Second Life and OpenSim

Second Life (2003, www.secondlife.com), also known just as SL, is the creation of Philip Rosedale and Linden Lab. *Second Life* reflected many of the same ideas as Active Worlds but delivered a more complete execution. It is worth spending some time looking at *Second Life* as it is still one of the best implementations of a proto-Metaverse environment (Au, 2023; Lamb, 2022).

EXPERIENCING SECOND LIFE

So what is the *Second Life* experience like? This description is largely based on *Second Life* c.2008, but whilst some of the details may have changed, the basic experience hasn't. It is also generally applicable to other virtual worlds and proto-metaverses.

You sign up for an account on the *Second Life* website and download the Viewer application. In the early days, Linden Lab made only a small selection of avatar/account last names available, but users were free to choose their first name. This had the benefit of both giving SL avatars fanciful yet consistent names and of generating additional bonds when you found someone with the same surname. For the record, David is Corro Moseley (chosen partly as he lives in Moseley, Birmingham in the United Kingdom) and Maggi is Second Wind.

When you first log in to the Viewer, you get to design your avatar – body shape, face, skin, hair, clothes, etc. This can be changed at any time, and you can store as many avatar looks as you want (business, party, beachwear, animal, robot, etc.). When you first arrive in *Second Life*, you are placed at a Welcome Center (Figure 1.3). This can be a chaotic place, as newbie avatars (like you) are struggling to control their avatars, whilst old-pros are trying to entice you to their shop or bar, or potentially acting in an anti-social manner – so-called "grief-ers". Volunteer greeters may be on hand to help you. There are some notice panels to explain how to move, navigate, interact, and chat, and at various times, there have been simple practical exercises that you need to graduate in before you move on. When working commercially with *Second Life*, developers could route their clients directly to private

FIGURE 1.3
A *Second Life* welcome area, c.2006.

arrivals areas and design whatever onboarding was required. Once you've mastered the basics; that's it, you're on your own, and *Second Life* or Linden Lab isn't going to tell you what to do next!

Many new users start with a spot of sightseeing. The Viewer will show you the whole world map; how many people are on each sim; and a list of searchable, popular, and promoted places. You might want to check out the shops, or a museum, a wilderness area, or a clone/tribute to a physical world city or location. You might want to try flying, sailing, or skydiving; play a game (on a board or tabletop RPG style); or visit a genre-themed area based on Star Trek, Lord of the Rings, or a myriad of other themes – all fan built and ideal for virtual LARPing. Or you might want to take a class or just hang out in a club or a bar. Just click on the map or a location button, and you are instantly teleported to the new location. On arrival, there may well be a greeter to welcome you – often an automated robot, sometimes a human. You can wander around, interact with things, and do whatever you want to do. Some land in SL is set to private, so you'll often see a big yellow grid as you approach a new parcel of land to tell you that you are not allowed in. *Second Life* is big, so walking takes some time, and teleporting misses the view, so there is *lots* of flying in SL. No need for a plane, just jump up into the air, Superman-style (angel wings were briefly *de rigueur* in the early days).

You'll fairly soon realise that your newbie clothes make you stand out. So, use your credit card on the *Second Life* website to buy some Linden Dollars (L$, in 2023 1$ was worth about 320 L$), and then either walk into a shop or use the Viewer-based Amazon-style marketplace to buy some new clothes (typical prices range from L$50 to L$1000 for anything from a new hair style or dress or suit to a whole new body shape and skin texture –prices depend on the quality).

Soon, you might get bored with passively consuming *Second Life* and want to start building. Find yourself a Sandbox (a public area to practice building in, wiped automatically every so often), look at the Wiki tutorials, and rez (make appear) your first 1-m wooden looking cube. Stretch it, colour it, and twist it. Then, add a sphere, then a cone, and so on, joining them into groups and groups of groups. At any stage, save a copy into your inventory ready to be rezzed elsewhere later. If you're already familiar with 3D build tools such as Blender, then you can import your existing objects directly into *Second Life*. You can learn basic scripting at the same time, just add a script to change the object's colour, make it jump into the air as someone approaches, or read out live stock market prices, and customise the script as much as you want.

FIGURE 1.4
A virtual seminar in *Second Life*, c.2014.

Whilst most people tend to be in *Second Life* to play, certainly in the early 2000s, lots of people were there to work, and it's still heavily used as a place to teach and learn (Figure 1.4). *Second Life* meetings can be held in locations that reflect the topic under discussion and become rich interactions through the combined use of voice and text chat, with people rezzing objects to help explain or explore issues. People naturally position themselves as they might be in a real meeting, standing by friends, moving closer to see things, their avatars even lolling forward if their owner isn't engaged! All of which gives far more cues to remember the meeting than yet another screen of webcam videos.

As you spend more time in *Second Life*, you'll probably want a home. Premium accounts now come with a plot of land and a cookie-cutter house. If you want something more personal, use your Linden Dollars to buy a parcel of land (1024 m^2 is a good size to start, currently around L$ 550 depending on the location) either directly from Linden Lab or an estate manager (in which case, it will cost more but might come with a home and even condominium style rental conditions!). You can then terraform your land (within limits), adding a hill or pond, buy (or make) flowers and trees and even bird, bees, and other animals. Likewise, you can buy or build your house or commission an architect to build it for you. A trip to the marketplace can see it furnished in almost any style you can think of, and scripting means that things work – lights, doors, video screens, audio system, robot butlers, etc. Of course, you don't actually *need* a house, and there is no rain or cold in *Second Life*, but users do seem to like that sense of a home base, somewhere to tinker and meet friends – but that can be as simple as a fire pit or as fanciful as a cloud in the sky if you want!

With a permanent base, you can then really start to think about how you want to use *Second Life*. Have friends over for parties or late-night philosophical chats around your virtual fire? Use those newfound crafting skills to sell your own range of clothes or vehicles or your scripting skills to sell widgets that take data from the Web and display it in 3D in innovative ways. Bring students in for classes – in dedicated educational spaces or using *Second Life* as one huge language/anthropology/ geography/sociology field trip. Create some incredibly new form of art that takes advantage of (essentially) user-controllable gravity and visibility, stunning lighting effects, and an audience that can fly. It may be a hackneyed phrase, but in *Second Life*, and in the Metaverse when it comes, the only limit is indeed your imagination.

As with *Active Worlds*, *Second Life* is based around a map (Figure 1.5), and initially all the land was part of a single continent, which over time has been joined by other continents and thousands of island clusters. The *Second Life* land model is based around plots 256 m × 256 m in size (called "sims" or "regions"), and users can buy parcels of land as small or as large as they want. Currently (as of 2023), premium users (paying US$99 a year) get a land grant of 1024 m² (including a house) as part of their package, and full island regions cost a US$349 set up fee and US$209 monthly maintenance. However, there is no need to own land to enjoy *Second Life*, and basic accounts are free. Users can sublet sims, and many early SL businesses were effective property development and real estate management businesses, buying a blank sim; improving it by adding roads, parks, houses, shops, marinas, etc.; and then selling plots (with or without houses) to individual users. Initially, *Second Life* had a reputation management system, reminiscent of the Whuffie in *Down and Out in the Magic Kingdom* (Doctorow, 2003), so users could vote any avatar they met up or down based on their interactions, but this was abandoned relatively early on (Au, 2009).

Second Life has its own currency – the Linden Dollar (L$) – which has always been freely exchangeable with the US$ (in both directions) at a fluctuating exchange rate. Indeed, Au (2023) credits it with being an essential part of the rise of Bitcoin and the whole cryptocurrency movement. Several papers (e.g. Chambers, 2011; Ernstberger, 2009) have been written on *Second Life*'s economic model and economy management, and it has never suffered from the speculation associated with cryptocurrencies. Castronova's original 2002

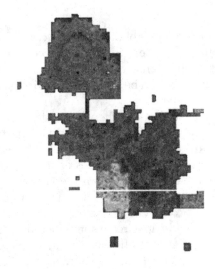

FIGURE 1.5
The *Second Life* Map, 2006. Each small square is a 256 m × 256 m "sim".

paper on virtual economies (Castronova, 2002) is also relevant and raises the important issues as to who has jurisdiction over these new economies. Linden Lab only takes a cut when you convert from L$ to US$ – there is no internal income take for the L$ that people earn and keep or spend in *Second Life* other than through land rental payments and Marketplace fees. Linden Lab only charges a 10% commission on SL Marketplace sales (Second Life Marketplace, n.d.), compared to a typical 30% on other platforms (Ball, 2022), and even 60% on *Fortnite* (Au, 2023) – and the use of the Marketplace is optional. At various times, there have been taxes on "prims" (effectively the number of 3D objects a user has, weighted by their complexity), and this has typically been bound up in the land charges. The ability to readily convert from L$ to US$ is key as it means that if a person sets up a business in SL (renting land, designing clothing, writing scripts, etc.), then they can convert their earnings into physical-world cash and actually make a physical-world living. According to Au (2023), the gross income to content creators in *Second Life* is roughly equal to Linden Lab's gross revenues from the platform.

In 2022, *Second Life* had a virtual economy with an annual GDP of US$650 million on 345 million virtual transactions (Linden Lab, 2022). In 2020, around 1600 people were making over US$10,000 a year from user-generated content (UGC) sales in *Second Life*, compared to around 1050 on *Roblox*, but by that time, *Second Life* had only around 600,000 monthly active users compared to 250 million in *Roblox* (Au, 2023). *Second Life* content developers cashed out around US$80 million from the virtual to the physical world economy in the 12 months to June 2021 (Galov, 2023).

In the early days, *Second Life* only had text-chat, and there was a huge furore in 2007 when it was announced that voice chat would be introduced as that would immediately "dox" (i.e. reveal) people in terms of their physical world gender, possibly age and nationality and even background and social class (Krotoski, 2009). Avatar gender fluidity was (and is) common, and many users have ungendered avatars (e.g. robots, abstract shapes, even domestic appliances, etc.), and there is a sizeable population of furries (anthropomorphic animal avatars) in *Second Life* (Brookey & Cannon, 2009). One survey (Bell et al., 2009) found that 11% of physical world males used a female avatar in SL, whilst only 5% of physical world females used male avatars. Of the sample, 51% reported as female and 43% as male in the physical world. The survey also found that 23% of respondents had changed the gender of their avatars at some point. This freedom to assume and explore any identity is perhaps one of the key facets and benefits of a social virtual world. Both *Coming of Age in Second Life: An Anthropologist Explores the Virtually Human* (Boellstorff, 2015) and *Virtual Environments and Cultures: A Collection of Social Anthropological Research in Virtual Cultures and Landscapes* (Frömming, 2013) are excellent anthropological studies of the early *Second Life* population.

Although there was a notable performance by Grammy award-winning singer-songwriter Suzanne Vega in SL in 2006 (Wired, 2006) (and see Figure 1.6 for an early use of SL by the BBC), and many working artists have continued to use *Second Life* as a performance platform (Au, 2023), it is perhaps the in-world art scene that is the most vibrant and original. High points have included the aerial dance/multi-media shows of the ZeroG SkyDancers (Au, 2013), a performance of Pink Floyd's The Wall (Hayes, 2008), Joff Chafer of Coventry University's mixed reality pieces (Fewster et al., 2011), the SL Shakespeare Company and the Avatar Repertory Theater, the towering human sculptures of Starax Statosky (Sichelseifert, 2009a), and the contemplative landscapes of AM Radio (Sichelseifert, 2009b), whose work *The Faraway* was later recreated by the artist's son in *Fortnite* (Au, 2023).

Almost as soon as the rapid consumer growth of *Second Life* started, it grew from about 100,000 registered accounts in December 2005 to two million in

FIGURE 1.6
BBC Radio 1 streamed a music festival into *Second Life* in 2006.

December 2006 to 11 million in December 2007 (Voyager, 2023), physical world businesses started to take an interest. From 2006 to around 2009, the media was full of stories of companies like IBM, Nike, Visa, L'Oreal, General Motors, Intel, and American Apparel setting up shops in *Second Life* (Barnes & Mattsson, 2011). There were even embassies from Sweden (Bengtsson, 2011), Estonia (Estonia, 2007), and the Maldives (Sydney Morning Herald, 2007). The 2007 Davos summit was streamed into *Second Life*, with one session being held in-world by Reuters (Hounshell, 2007). The world also became a base for multi-national protest – such as the protests about the Burmese government (Borgen, 2007), as well as for global fund-raising events, such as the annual Walk for Life (American Cancer Society, n.d.). Even politicians have made an appearance (SpeedMatters, 2007), and election campaign events have also been held there – such as those for Le Pen and Sarkozy in the 2007 French presidential elections (Kar-Gupta, 2007).

Note, though, how many of these references are to 2007. Since much of the early corporate involvement was driven mainly by marketing and public relations (David worked on projects for General Motors, Visa, and Red Nose Day), as it became clear that consumer interest in SL, and social virtual worlds in general, was fading and that they weren't going to be "the next big thing", much of that marketing and enterprise activity disappeared.

One of the key reasons for the decline was that many users just couldn't work out what *Second Life* was *for*. They approached it like a computer game and expected it to have goals and objectives – but *Second Life* isn't like that (despite some late attempts by Linden Lab to retrospectively add such features with Quests and Linden Realms) (Uccie, 2014). Au (2023) also explains how other factors from internal management issues, technical decisions, and the emerging challenges from smartphones all contributed to *Second Life's* retrenchment.

However, others, particularly in the education and training community, had found out what a versatile platform *Second Life* was for their own uses. Building in *Second Life* is really just toy building-blocks on steroids – although mastery takes a while – and so any tutor could teach themselves the basics, read the wiki, or attend an in-world class (this all started pre-You Tube!). Scripting in *Second Life* uses Linden Scripting Language, and whilst it has its own quirks, it is similar in complexity to Javascript – so again something that a keen teacher could use to develop basic functionality. A 2009 survey by Virtual World Watch found that around 50 higher education institutions in the United Kingdom were using *Second Life* (Kirriemuir, 2009a), and their annual Snapshots provided a good survey of the wide range of ways in which virtual worlds, predominantly *Second Life*, were being used in education at the time (Kirriemuir, 2009b). In 2009, the United Kingdom's Joint Information Systems Committee (JISC), an independent not-for-profit charity funded mainly by the government and universities, which advises on and manages shared IT for UK Higher Education, published a guide to *"Getting Started with Second Life"* (Savin-Baden et al., 2009), and the Open University ran two ReLive conferences on education in virtual worlds (in 2009 and 2011). The Virtual Worlds Education Consortium (https://www.vweconsortium. org/), the latest organisation to support educators in virtual worlds, with its main base in *Second Life*, was established only in 2021.

Linden Lab provided an educational discount for sims used by schools and colleges, but when this was withdrawn in 2010, many of these institutions started to leave. Many turned instead to developing in *OpenSim* (2007, http://opensimulator.org/) – which is further described below. Others developed bespoke immersive environment applications using Unreal and Unity – although these have never had the flexibility that tutor (and even student) authoring brings.

It wasn't just the education sector that saw the benefits of *Second Life*. There were a large number of medical training projects, for example, at Imperial College; St. George's Hospital[1] (Figure 1.7); Cornell and Idaho State University (Stott, 2007); Ohio State University (DigitalUnionOSU, 2008); and the University of Calgary and SAIT Polytechnic, Calgary (Kopp & Burkle, 2010); on projects ranging from paramedic and nursing training to virtual laboratories and fly-throughs of human anatomy. New York City's Office of Emergency Management delivered hurricane relief centre training in a virtual copy of a New York public school[2] (Brouchoud, 2011). Consultants Booz Allen Hamilton and the Texas Woman's University assessed training based on Federal Emergency Management Agency models for tornado response

FIGURE 1.7
An early paramedic training simulation at St. George's, London, in SL, 2008.

(Taylor-Nelms & Hill, 2014), and Miami University Oxford and the University of Cincinnati trained nurses in triage for radioactive and explosive disasters (Farra et al., 2013). Hsu et al. (2013) provide a useful overview of Disaster Preparedness and Response Training projects in *Second Life* and other platforms. Even the military (e.g. Pey, 2020) and, according to the Snowden Papers, the intelligence community were in *Second Life* (NSA, 2008).

There was a brief plan by Linden Lab to create stand-alone or intranet-based enterprise servers for *Second Life* (Korolov, 2010). This never came to fruition as a Linden Lab project, but exactly that functionality was soon available from *OpenSim*.

OpenSim is essentially a reverse engineered version of *Second Life* (Figure 1.8). Linden Lab had always had quite an open approach to code, and the core "Viewer" code that users use to access *Second Life* had already been made available so that developers could create customer third-party viewers (TPVs) supporting additional functionality. *OpenSim* took this one stage further and developed a version of the *Second Life* server code that works in almost exactly the same way as the official code, even to the extent of being able to use the *Second Life* viewer to access it, but which people can run on their own servers, and even connect to other people's *OpenSim* servers to create a "hyper-grid".

One of the biggest advantages of *OpenSim* is that users can save the whole of a sim's set up – all its builds and scripts – as a single OpenSimulator Archives (OAR) file. This can then be uploaded to a new server, so sims can be easily distributed, archived, or duplicated (useful for scaling training exercises as a typical sim could only support around 50 users).

FIGURE 1.8
A refugee camp built on *OpenSim* for humanitarian relief training.

Just as *Second Life* has continued as a useful platform despite the desertions of the 2010s, so too *OpenSim* is still a vibrant community. In 2023, Hypergrid Business (which has been tracking *OpenSim, Second Life,* and other metaverse activities for over 15 years) logged 427 *OpenSim* grids (i.e. publicly accessible and typically more than one sim), of which about 317 were connected to the Hypergrid (Hypergrid Business, 2023). And this does not count any *OpenSim* instances being run purely for private use.

In many ways, the *OpenSim* Hypergrid (http://opensimulator.org/wiki/ Hypergrid) may be the closest thing to an open Metaverse that currently exists. It is based on open-source code; each grid is privately run and hosted; and anyone can run and host a grid, or buy a sim, or land on a sim on a grid. Being based on *Second Life,* the build tools are all built into the viewer and include a powerful scripting engine with read/write access to the web. And the hypergrid protocol, which enables the connectivity between the grid, supports teleporting and agent (i.e. user) transfers from grid to grid (Lopes, 2011).

The subsequent work of Linden Lab (on *Project Sansar*) and Philip Rosedale (on *High Fidelity*) will be discussed later in this chapter – as well as considering *Second Life*'s current state of health.

Second Life Alternatives

Second Life wasn't the only proto-metaverse available during the early 2000s. *Open Wonderland* (2010) (Kaplan & Yankelovich, 2011), which had its origins in Sun Microsystems, was based on an open-source coding model and let developers build their own stand-alone virtual worlds. Technically complex, *Open Wonderland* was an early pioneer of some novel features, such as windows and doors between worlds where someone could look through from one world to another, step through, and then look back to the world they'd just come from.

Twinity (2008) was one of the first real attempts at a digital twin. It let users explore replicas of London, Berlin, and several other cities; buy virtual apartments in them; and then go clubbing or shopping in suitably themed spaces (Schultz, 2018). However, these virtual cities didn't include a single shopfront or facia – it is assumed so as to avoid brand infringement (Figure 1.9). As Schultz reports, *Twinity* eventually even had to abandon the digital city twin model for legal and financial reasons.

Other virtual environments of the time included:

- *Croquet* (2004) (Smith et al., 2003), later evolving into *Open Croquet* and then *Qwaq*, and which had some novel collaboration tools but very blocky avatars. The technology has more recently been used by *Virtend* (2022, https://www.3dicc.com/product-details/), a business collaboration focused virtual world, and Croquet itself released a Microverse World Builder using the latest release of the core

FIGURE 1.9
Exploring a virtual Berlin in Twinity.

Croquet Microverse open source project in 2022 (https://croquet.io/) (Croquet, 2022);

- *Kaneva* (2006) (Forbes, 2007) was a glossier virtual world than *Second Life*, with a far smoother interface and some early automated avatars for roles like greeters, but less focus on user content creation;
- *Forterra's OLIVE* (c.2006) (Badger, 2008) was one of the early enterprises-focused training and collaboration platforms and shared the same technical base as *There.com*. There were even plans to deploy it within the intelligence community (NSA, 2008);
- *Vastpark* (2007) from Australia, as well as being a virtual world (with local hosting capabilities), was leading an early attempt to develop portable avatars with their OpenAvatar project (Hypergrid Business, 2011);
- *Sony Home* (2008) (Takashi, 2010) was Sony's attempt to bring virtual worlds to the masses via its PlayStation console. Launched in 2008, it had amassed over 17 million users by the end of 2010 but was closed in 2015. As with *Kaneva*, the focus was more on good-looking graphics and ease of use rather than UGC;
- *Blue Mars* (2009) (Sherstyuk et al., 2010) was another high-gloss virtual world, built on the then state-of-the-art CryEngine, but with a wider range of UGC tools. Although the public world closed in 2012, one of its legacies was the Chatscript chatbot engine that was built by Bruce Wilcox to drive the in-world avatars, and which has been subsequently used in a wide variety of chatbot projects, including two Loebner Prize wins (an annual public Turing Test) (Wilcox & Wilcox, 2013); and
- *AvayaLive Engage* (c.2012) (Camilleri et al., 2013) was similar to Forterra's *OLIVE*, being aimed at more enterprise use of virtual worlds for collaboration, education, and training.

In addition to these purpose-built social virtual worlds, users were also finding out how to subvert multi-user games (especially multi-user online role playing games – MMORPGs) such as *Runescape* (2001), *World of Warcraft* (2004), and even *Club Penguin* (2005) in order to use them as places to hang out, chat, collaborate, and even teach and learn (e.g. Marsh, 2016).

One notable early development in social virtual worlds was Google's ill-fated *Lively* (2008) (Huvila, 2015). Launched on 8 July 2008, *Lively* was fairly innovative in terms of being accessed through the browser rather than from a downloaded application. Each user was given a small island on which they could then place objects and upload textures (images) – as with almost any virtual world. But this was aimed at the mass market, so thousands of people started using it, and the most popular sites were listed on a league table. The only problem was that a large number of the worlds were full of pornographic

FIGURE 1.10
Building a business presence in Cloud Party.

images. Without adequate moderation in place, Google announced *Lively*'s closure on 19 November 2008, only four months after its launch. It is interesting to speculate what if *Lively* had lived (Burden, 2011). Would there be a *Lively* tab alongside Images and Maps for every Google search taking users to a list of informative and engaging virtual world sites where they could explore the topic of their search in a completely different, and possibly more memorable and engaging way? Will there ever be such a feature?

A very similar world was *Cloud Party* (2011) – again majoring on delivering a build-and-visit experience directly into the browser (Figure 1.10). *Cloud Party* was founded in 2011, bought by Yahoo in 2014, and closed the same year (Etherington, 2014)!

Virtual worlds weren't only of interest to consumers and educators. Despite some early experimentation directly in virtual worlds by the military (much shown at the briefly annual Federal Virtual Worlds Conference organised by the US Government's Federal Virtual World Consortium; Harris, 2010), military simulation has tended to follow an independent track. Whilst combat aircraft and medical training were a constant driver for much HMD-VR hardware development (e.g. Simons & Melzer, 2003), it was the land army requirement for large rural or urban spaces in which to hold virtual exercises that was closer to that of virtual worlds. Bohemia Interactive's *Virtual Battle Systems* (VBS) series launched in 2003 is a good example of what was being created and used and was itself developed from the *Flashpoint* (2001) series of consumer video games. With each iteration (as of 2023, it's at VBS4), graphics and capability have improved to the point where there is now a whole-earth model, and it can even reproduce seasonal and weather effects such as rain, mud, fog, and snow (https://bisimulations.com/products/vbs4). Flight simulators (such as the *Microsoft Flight Simulator* series) have seen a similar rate of evolution from the wireframe graphics of the 1971 original to the whole-earth model of the 2020 edition (https://www.flightsimulator.com/), and indeed Ball (2022) sees *Flight Simulator* as helping to position Microsoft in a strong position for the future of the Metaverse.

The Arrival of Oculus

In 2013, the virtual world space changed forever with the launch of the Oculus DK1 virtual reality (VR) HMD (Kumparak, 2014) (Figure 1.11). Whilst the resolution was usable, if not stunning, the key advance was that HMD-VR was now affordable to the keen enthusiast, it was no longer the plaything of defence, medicine, and aerospace. DK1 on its own only offered 3 degrees

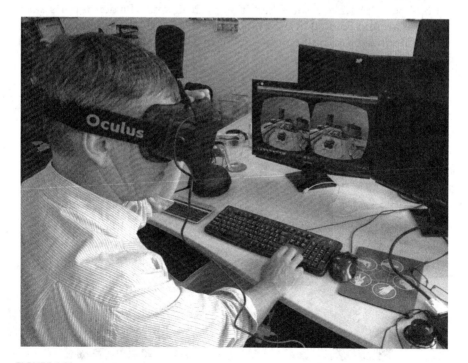

FIGURE 1.11
David using Oculus DK1 to explore a virtual copy of Birmingham's Centenary Square built in Unity.

of freedom (3DOF) (i.e. it responded to you turning your head, but not to any lateral movement), but a desk sensor added the lateral movement to give 6 degrees of freedom (6DOF) – but only when close to the sensor. In DK2 (released 2014), there were two sensors, but tracking was still only for a limited space. HTC's Vive was first to deliver easy whole-room tracking in 2016 (Robertson, 2016) – enabling the user to naturally walk around in a physical space in order to explore a VR environment.

However, both Oculus Rift and HTC Vive headsets needed a powerful PC to drive them – adding at least $1000 to around a US$599 headset cost, and making setup a moderate nightmare. An alternative approach was to use a mobile phone as the processing and display device, splitting its screen to give left- and right eye-views, and placing it in a simple head-mounted case with a couple of lenses to complete the system. Samsung Gear VR was a typical high-end version (Rundle, 2015), and the briefly ubiquitous Google Cardboard was a low-end version (e.g. Fabola et al., 2015) (Figure 1.12). In between were dozens of plastic clones that soon ended up in remainder bins as people's early VR experiences failed to live up to the promise.

Sony was again the only console manufacturer to really engage with VR, releasing the PlayStation VR headset in 2016 (Habgood et al., 2017), and reportedly achieving five million sales by the end of 2020 (Hayden, 2023a). An updated PSVR2 was launched in early 2023, and Hayden reports sales of that at around 550,000 in the first six weeks after the launch. In July 2023, Sony announced a $2 million investment in XR and metaverse research and development (Kolo, 2023).

FIGURE 1.12
Trying out a Google Cardboard.

Nintendo actually had a VR headset back in 1994 – the Virtual Boy – which failed to gain any real traction (Boyer, 2009). In 2019, Nintendo launched Labo VR, essentially Google cardboard for their Switch console, and the third-party Orzly VR headset provides a cheap but more robust headset when using the Switch in VR mode. In 2023, there was still speculation on a native Nintendo VR headset (e.g. Hayden, 2023b).

Facebook bought Oculus in 2014 (Dredge, 2014), but the next big step forward was in 2019 with the release of the Oculus Quest – a fully contained, 6DOF, room-scale VR headset for £399, which no longer needed to be connected to a high-end PC or required additional room sensors. Now, almost anyone who could afford a smartphone could also buy a decent VR headset. In 2020, the Quest 2 was launched, and by 2023, Oculus/Meta had reportedly sold nearly 20 million Quest headsets (Heath, 2023). The Quest 3, which added a state-of-the-art mixed-reality capability, was launched in October 2023.

HMD-VR Virtual Worlds

Whilst most of the applications released for the Quest have been video games or 360-degree video cultural and geographical tours, there have been a number of interesting virtual world type applications.

The most common category is probably that of meeting and collaboration applications. Examples include *Glue* (c.2017, https://glue.work/), *MeetInVR* (2020, https://www.meetinvr.com/), and *Arthur* (2021, https://www.arthur. digital/). These typically have a corporate, business-like feel and support a limited number of location styles, limited avatar choices, and limited object placement/import, but a reasonable set of collaboration tools such as virtual whiteboards, PowerPoint screens, browser displays, Google Docs integration, voice and text-chat, 3D emoticons, screen share, and even webcams.

In terms of environments aimed at consumer socialising, *VRChat* (2014) (https://hello.vrchat.com/) is probably most popular with concurrency rates comparable to the most popular online games (Au, 2022a) but has a pretty extreme aesthetic (Figure 1.13), as does *Cryptovoxels* (2018) (https://www. voxels.com/). The positive side of this is that the creativity in *VRChat* rivals *Second Life* in its hey-day (Au, 2023), and the negative side are the reports on grooming, exploitation, and significant child-safeguarding issues (Crawford & Smith, 2022).

More restrained but equally creative was *AltSpaceVR* (2015), which hosted a virtual Burning Man festival each year and was probably the closest of the current crop to the *Second Life* feel. In its original 2015 iteration, *AltSpaceVR* had an innovative feature called "enclosures" allowing the user to write code to define the 3D contents of that space – even pulling in web data to visualise in the display (see Figure 1.14). For larger spaces, developers used Unity to build an environment and then uploaded it to *AltSpaceVR* (a common approach in

FIGURE 1.13
Non-human avatars are very common in VRChat.

many worlds). *AltSpaceVR* briefly folded and was then bought and relaunched by Microsoft, all in 2017, but then closed in 2023 (Hayden, 2023c). However, some of its technology found its way into Microsoft's Mesh 3D collaboration environment, launched as part of Teams in 2021 (Warren, 2021).

There have also been a number of VR applications aimed specifically at training and education. One of the better examples is *Engage* (2017) (https://engagevr.io/), which whilst not (yet) supporting in-world building or

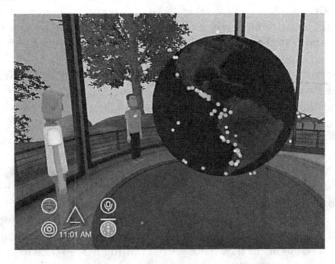

FIGURE 1.14
David's Earthquake Globe using US Geophysical Survey data in the original AltSpaceVR.

scripting does allow object import and placement and has a good set of collaboration tools. One of its unique features is to record a lecture, meeting, or lesson as a data file, rather than as a video, so that when replayed, it moves all the avatars around you as they moved during the event – even yours! So, you can have the weird sensation of standing there as your "live" avatar watching your "recorded" avatar move and talk and interact within the space – a real out-of-body experience.

Other current social VR applications of note include:

- *Virbela* (c.2012, www.virbela.com) – a conference-focused platform with a large virtual campus and a variety of lecture theatres and meeting rooms. The avatars are too small and cartoony for many people's taste (see Figure 1.15), but they do help ensure that the service runs on PCs with lower specifications. Enterprises can have their own private *Virbela* worlds;

- *Rec Room* (2016, https://recroom.com/) – a wonderful application full of different "physical" games made virtual to play with your friends, including frisbee golf, dodgeball, paintballing, and even rock climbing. During the COVID lockdown, it was a great way to host virtual team-building sessions. *Rec Room* has an in-world system to allow players to build and script their own "rooms" and games;

- *Vark* (2018, https://corp.vark.co.jp/) – a Japanese VR application in whose original version anime-style virtual popstars gave virtual performances, but all the other attendees were "ghosted" so it seemed like you're getting a personal performance; and

FIGURE 1.15
Arriving at the Virbela campus.

- *Spatial* (2020, https://www.spatial.io/) which in 2021 pivoted away from an initial business focus to more of a social and entertainment focus.

Whilst all of the applications above are promoted for use with HMD-VR headsets, most of them also have a DesktopVR version available. Anecdotal evidence (e.g. by watching how people move in the spaces) and game metrics (e.g. only one third of VRChat users used HMD-VR in 2019; Au, 2022a) suggest that most users are accessing these worlds via their PC/phone, not via an HMD, although there is some evidence that HMD-VR use is growing (Au, 2023). This is somewhat ironic given the column-inches (and investment) that some of these worlds have attracted, whilst *Second Life* seems to be ignored because it doesn't have an official HMD-VR implementation.

3D Massively Multi-Player On-Line Games

Just as an earlier generation found new ways to use massively multi-player online (MMO) platforms such as *World of Warcraft*, so in the 2010s, people began to use *Minecraft* (2011, https://www.minecraft.net/) for education (Bar-El & Ringland, 2021), geography (Lecordix et al., 2018), code visualisation (Balogh & Beszedes, 2013), and even religious services and virtual Sunday Schools[3] (CofE, 2020; Jeremy, 2021). *Minecraft* offers a variety of world-building, scripting, marketplace, and collaboration tools to help in the building of UGC and even allows people to run their own servers. In January 2023, *Minecraft* had around 176 million monthly active users (MAUs) (Sharma, 2023).

Roblox (2006, https://www.roblox.com/) has also seen significant use in education, again being enabled by easy-to-use building, scripting, and sharing tools (Han et al., 2023). *Roblox* has also been used by several high-profile brands such as Walmart (Blackwood, 2023) and Nike (Utoyo et al., 2022) for marketing campaigns. Whilst *Roblox* supports UGC and does have a developer community, that community, as previously mentioned, is not making as much income as the developer community in *Second Life*. In 2023, *Roblox* had around 214 million MAUs (Ruby, 2023).

The other popular MMO at the time of writing is *Fortnite* (2017, https://www.fortnite.com/). Whilst it arguably has better graphics, the game tightly binds the players into a battle royale model, so there was initially less creativity and non-gaming use than in worlds such as *Roblox* and *Minecraft*. In 2018, Epic released *Fortnite: Creative*, providing players with an editor to create their own game experiences, and in 2023, Unreal Editor for Fortnite (UEFN) allowed Epic's core Unreal game engine to be used by developers to create *Fortnite* experiences (Franey, 2023). Garst (2023) reports that Fortnite users "spend roughly 40% of their total playtime exploring experiences inside the game's Creative mode, including custom user-created games, training modes and branded experiences". A number of high-profile brands and personalities have been active on *Fortnite*, including Ariana Grande, Travis Scott (Regan, 2021), Marvel, and the NFL (Goodman, 2023). In March 2023, *Fortnite* announced that it had reached 70 million MAUs (Jacob, 2023), and in mid-2023, it announced that it was going to give 40% of its net revenue to creators (Peters, 2023).

The science-fiction-orientated MMOs such as *EVE Online* (2003), *Elite Dangerous* (2014), *No Man's Sky* (2016), *Dual Universe* (2022), and blockchain-based *Million on Mars* (2022) also have metaversal elements.

The platform that has always had potential to be a virtual world but has never delivered is *Google Earth* (2001, https://earth.google.com/web/). Even though there has been steady development in the 3D modelling of cities and global landmarks, it stubbornly remains a solo experience. The VR version is currently (2024) only available on the HTC Vive and Oculus Rift rather than on the more popular Quest, although a 2023 announcement by Google suggests that this may change, and there are emerging third-party solutions such as the Wooorld (sic) MR app (Bezmalinovic, 2023).

Facebook Takes an Interest

Facebook's acquisition of Oculus, and in particular Mark Zuckerberg's presentation at Facebook Connect on 28 October 2021 (and which was live streamed into the *Oculus Horizons Spaces* virtual world) and the announcement of the name change of Facebook's holding company to Meta, returned the concept of the Metaverse to the public (or at least geek) consciousness. However, there was really little there that wasn't being talked about ten years ago, and much that already existed in *Second Life* 15 years ago. Zuckerberg also talked about the Metaverse as being the "replacement" for the mobile internet – something that will be challenged in Chapter 3 given the inconvenience of HMDs. Some of the more interesting announcements of (then) future developments, which are equally applicable to other virtual world platforms, included: making PCs and smartphones applications usable from their digital twins inside of VR (elements now in *Apple Vision Pro*, *Somnium Space*, and *Immersed*), headsets that detect facial expression and eye movement for more natural avatar interaction (in *Apple Vision Pro*, *Quest Pro*, and others), and detecting hand movement and gesture using electromyography (EMG)-based neurotech devices (something pioneered by Thalmic Labs MYO back in 2016) (Burden, 2021). Their new Codec "photo-realistic" avatars were previewed in Zuckerberg's interview on the Metaverse with Lex Fridman (Fridman, 2023), but set against a black backdrop and only showing head-and-shoulders still had an uncanny valley feeling.

Meta's intent appears to grow the current "home" that a user has in their Quest (from where they choose applications), along with the "Spaces" community viewing app into a more fully rounded multi-user social virtual world called *Horizon Worlds* (2021, https://www.meta.com/en-gb/experiences/2532035600194083/), which includes both build tools and a Scratch-type visual scripting language (https://scratch.mit.edu/about). *Horizon Worlds* usage was stated by Meta to be around 200,000 MAUs in October 2022, more recent data not being readily available (Tassi, 2022).

The announcements in 2022/2023 that Meta was laying off 15,000 staff seem to put their whole Metaverse strategy in doubt, but whilst Reality Labs (the part of Meta developing metaverse applications) seems not to have been as badly hit as other parts of the company, Meta's "recent flip-flopping from focusing on its 'metaverse' initiatives to artificial intelligence has put a major onus on the Reality Labs division" (Barr, 2023).

Beyond the West

Although most of the worlds discussed so far have come out of Western culture, there is also a strong metaversal movement in other parts of the globe. *Vark* from Japan has already been mentioned, and *Zepeto* (2018, https://web.zepeto.me/en) is a South Korean world. Also from South Korea, Krafton, owners of the popular *PUBG: Battlegrounds* game (similar to *Fortnite*), are launching *Overdare*, a *Roblox*-like NFT-driven metaverse in 2024 (Irwin, 2023). South Korea's Ministry of Science and ICT has even created a "metaverse alliance" (Kim, 2021). *GOXR* and *PartyOn* (both from XRSpace – https://www.xrspace.io/us) are Taiwanese worlds. The Chinese VR market has been estimated by some as accounting for over 40% of the global market and involves the key Chinese technology firms of Baidu, Alibaba, and Tencent (Kurzydlowski, 2021). ByteDance, the Chinese owners of TikTok, bought Pico, one of the leading HMD-VR manufacturers in 2021 (Kharpal, 2021). In the Middle East, Dubai has launched its own metaverse strategy, the UAE has opened a metaverse incubator, and the NEOM future city has a metaverse element to support collaboration during its build phase (*MIT Sloan Management Review*, 2023). So, whatever happens in the West, it seems that metaverse developments are likely to continue elsewhere on the globe.

Crypto Virtual Worlds

Another significant change to the virtual world space in the last few years has been the rise of blockchain-based virtual worlds – the "cryptoverse" (Au, 2023). *Somnium Space* (2018, https://somniumspace.com/) was one of the first platforms, offering a lot of *Second Life* style features and a similar land model, and is planning its own HMD-VR headset for 2024. Others include

Decentraland (2020, https://decentraland.org/) and *Cryptoverse* (2022, https://www.cryptoverse.vip/).

The big difference with *Second Life* era worlds is that all transactions and ownership are tracked through blockchains, and land and assets are bought using cryptocurrency – and as a result, prices can be excessively high and are subject to the vagaries of cryptocurrency speculation. As a result, virtual assets effectively become non-fungible tokens (NFTs) – and with the recent craze around NFTs further pushing prices beyond the reach of most ordinary users. For instance, on *Decentraland* land, prices are around $40–$300 per square metre, and a new dress costs $2–$20. In contrast, in *Second Life*, land prices are around $0.0016 per square metre, and a dress costs around $0.30–$2 (all prices are as of July 2023).

These costs don't help with generating high user engagement. *Decentraland* reported only around 57,000 MAUs in September 2022 (Decentraland, 2022), and Au reports that *Somnium Space's* peak concurrency for Steam users (so may not capture all users) over 12 months was only 16 users (Au, 2022b). Symptomatic of this lack of traction the *Alloverse* cryptoworld (2020) closed in 2023 stating that "our coffers are now empty, and … we are taking a break on commercial operations" but that they would "transition from an 'open core' commercial company with an open source center, into a fully open source project" (Bengtsson, 2023). In contrast, *Second Life* had a concurrency of around 30–50,000 in 2022 (Galov, 2023), *VRChat* had a concurrency of around 65,000 in late 2022 (Virtual Girl Nem, 2022), and *Rec Room* hit three million MAUs in mid-2022 (Lang, 2022).

There may well be a place for the blockchain technology behind these worlds, as will be discussed in Chapter 4, but at the moment, they could be seen to be doing more to frustrate the development of the Metaverse than to encourage it. Interestingly, in their 2024 Manifesto, *Decentraland* recognises the need to look at "diversifying payment methods, improving educational resources, and avoiding crypto slang" and to "Imagine a platform that welcomes users unfamiliar with the crypto ecosystem; with just your standard social profiles, you can jump into *Decentraland* and make your account—no digital wallet creation necessary, it's all handled for you behind the scenes" (Decentraland, 2024).

A Third Life?

What has been fascinating is that whilst all the hyperbole has been around HMD-VR, then Meta/Facebook and then cryptoworlds, *Second Life* and *OpenSim* have just carried on regardless – as the numbers just shown attest. When the Oculus DK1 was released, a "Third Party Viewer" (TPV) called CtrlAltStudio was soon created for *Second Life* (and *OpenSim*) which ran on the DK1 so that you could experience *Second Life* in full HMD-VR (see

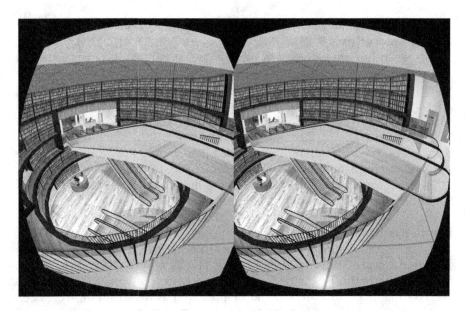

FIGURE 1.16
Viewing the Virtual Library of Birmingham build in *Second Life* in VR, with an Oculus DK1 – it can be done!

Figure 1.16) – but it wasn't a route that was followed by Linden Lab. However, the CtrlAltStudio viewer was updated to work with Oculus DK2 and Oculus Rift CV1, and the Firestorm TPV currently offers a VR Mod (Tate, 2022), so "VR versions of *Second Life* and *OpenSim* viewers still exist and are in daily use" (Tate, 2024), giving the lie to the belief that *Second Life* and *OpenSim* aren't "proper" VR applications.

Once Philip Rosedale left Linden Lab in 2010, the new owners seemed to think that the future lay in a more consumer-friendly virtual world application, which was launched as *Project Sansar* (2017, https://www.sansar.com/). It certainly had better graphics but had moved to the "room" model and away from the contiguous virtual world of *Second Life*. It was sold in 2020 so that Linden Lab could (re)focus on *Second Life* and was sold on again in 2022. It has now pivoted to being a virtual events platform, announcing a partnership in 2022 to make the application and events available through LG Smart TVs (Cimerman, 2022) and in 2023 a further partnership with *Somnium Space* to develop interoperability between the two platforms (SomniumSpace, 2023).

Philip Rosedale meanwhile set up *High Fidelity* (2016, https://www.high-fidelity.com/) to work on leading edge virtual world technologies. *High Fidelity* was very much a coders platform, but the naturalness of the avatars, driven by real-time facial and limb position capture, resulted in some excellent life-like demo videos and virtual presentations (e.g. High Fidelity, 2017). Like *Sansar*, *High Fidelity* wasn't a great success, and in 2019, it pivoted to be a spatial audio-driven meetings platform (Au, 2021).

In 2022, High Fidelity Inc. became an investor in Linden Lab (and hence *Second Life*), and Philip Rosedale returned as a strategic advisor to Linden Lab (Pey, 2022). Whilst there has been nothing public about HMD-VR for *Second Life*, or a whole Second-Life refresh, or perhaps even a Third Life, a mobile client was announced in 2023 and is currently in a Private Alpha with *Second Life* Premium Plus residents (Axon, 2023). *Second Life* (and *OpenSim*) still seems to offer a more complete Metaverse experience than probably any other platform, as will be discussed further in Chapter 2.

VIRTUAL WORLDS DATABASE

David maintains a database of the key current and past virtual world applications that can be accessed via the Metaverse Series at http://www.themetaverseseries.info/. This summarises their key features and capabilities and provides direct links to each world or application.

Using the Web

Whilst Meta has attracted much of the media attention, potentially more interesting developments have been taking place elsewhere. The WebGL standard (https://get.webgl.org/) was officially approved in 2011 and provides a way to define 3D graphics, including DesktopVR immersive environments, with Javascript in an ordinary web page. The next crucial ingredient has been the WebXR (https://immersiveweb.dev/ and https://www.w3.org/TR/webxr/) standard (developed out of WebVR – https://webvr.info/) and was launched in 2018. This enables a WebGL web page/application to sense if it's running in a VR headset, and if so, it offers the user the ability to launch the full HMD-VR experience directly from a web page in a browser.

This combination of technologies significantly enhances the accessibility of both DesktopVR and HMD-VR experiences and from an open-source base. Inviting a user into a virtual world becomes as simple as sending them a link to click on, or embedding it in a web page, and then they can be straight into the DesktopVR experience in the browser on their laptop (or even smartphone or tablet), or into the HMD-VR experience if wearing their headset – without any software downloads or even sign-ups. There'll be more on these technologies in Chapter 4.

The important result is that these technologies are being used by a new generation of web-delivered social virtual worlds – notably *Mozilla Hubs*[4] (2018, https://hubs.mozilla.com/) (Fodor, 2020) (see Figure 1.17) and Virbela's *Frame* (2020, https://learn.framevr.io/) (see Figure 1.18), as well as in crypto-worlds such as *Hyperfy* (2022, https://hyperfy.io/) (Metamike, 2023). *Hubs* and

FIGURE 1.17
David's Virtual Environment Design Space (VEDS) in Mozilla Hubs.

Frame both provide a set of template spaces that users can use and customise, or they can import their own. Both also offer a range of collaboration tools – although *Frame* has the edge here. *Hubs* has a better set of build tools, but they exist in a separate, but still web delivered, app called *Spoke*. Both have initially taken a "widget" approach to developing functionality, enabling builders to drop in features such as particle emitters, sound sources, and "interactables", which could be linked together. At the end of 2023, *Frame* started to release

FIGURE 1.18
A team meeting in FrameVR, with webcams showing the physical users.

proper scripting based on the *Wonderland* game engine but as of early 2024 only allowed one script per "world", and the scripts had a far steeper learning curve than Linden Scripting Language. They also introduced ChatGPT style AI-driven non-player character (NPC) avatars that could be defined by a simple backstory. However, neither (as of early 2024) supports user marketplaces, an economy or even a persistent communal world space, both being fully wedded to the "room" model (see Chapter 3). *Mozilla Hubs* is though fully Open Source, so developers can not only host their own *Hubs* servers (https://hubs.mozilla.com/docs/hubs-cloud-intro.html) but also customise the source code to add new interactivity features (Benetou, n.d.; Freeman, 2020).

Technologies such as WebGL/WebXR can also be used with any standard software development environment to develop immersive applications with high levels of functionality and rich levels of interactivity. The major game engines such as Unity and Unreal (both used by developers to create not only games but also training and educational applications and even virtual worlds) allow projects to be exported as WebGL/WebXR applications so that they will run in the browser.

Whilst WebGL/WebXR hold out significant promise, the current worlds implemented with them lack many of the key features of the Metaverse, or even a proper social virtual world – but a move towards more web-delivered virtual worlds and metaversal spaces and applications seems likely and would significantly enhance the accessibility of the metaverse experience.

Augmented and Mixed Reality (AR and MR)

Books such as *Rainbow's End* (Vinge, 2007) have painted as compelling a vision of AR as *Snow Crash* has of VR and the Metaverse. As Zuckerberg's 2021 Connexions presentation showed, there is certainly some overlap between the Metaverse and AR/MR technology. Despite the brief flirtation with Google Glass (launched in 2013), and now Facebook's Ray-Ban Meta Smart Glasses, consumer AR was first made accessible by the camera, display, and processing capabilities of the smartphone. *Pokemon Go* (2016, https://pokemongolive.com/) is probably still the defining consumer application for location-based AR, beyond the simple AR filters for Snapchat and Messenger. However, in these AR applications, the Pokemon (or other) image is really just a 2D graphic pasted over the 2D camera image; the Pokemon character is not displayed in the context of the physical world around it, and so will happily hang in mid-air or underwater. *Pokemon Go* is still managing around 79 million MAUs (Krawanski, 2023). Companies such as Ikea have also been using AR to help customers visualise home improvements (Ozturkcan, 2021), and there are many other marketing, education, and training uses of AR (Parekh et al., 2020).

With MR, the augmenting objects are full 3D virtual objects and are placed so that they are fixed in, and can even respond to, the physical environment around them. For instance, a box of virtual building blocks opened out over a physical table would see the blocks bounce across the table, and many fall onto the floor. Microsoft released the Hololens (https://www.microsoft.com/en-us/hololens) in 2016, and Hololens 2 was released in 2019, but the US$3790 price-tag limits any consumer uptake. Magic Leap (https://www.magicleap.com/) was finally launched in 2018, after several years of hype, with their own Version 2 in 2022, and with similar pricing.

The downside of the Hololens 1 was the narrow field of view (FOV) of only 30° horizontal and increased to 43° in Hololens 2, marginally more than Magic Leap 1's 40° (Heaney, 2019). This compares to a human's physical world c.120° binocular FOV and c.200° peripheral FOV (Wang & Cooper, 2022). As a result, only a small part of the user's visual field experiences the MR effect. Meta's Quest Pro headset (US$1500 plus extras) offers both VR and MR modes, and with greater field of view – although using a video pass-through approach rather than projecting onto a visor, so reducing resolution – but reception has been poor (e.g. Robertson, 2022). Meta's new consumer Quest 3 VR headset (US$500) includes full-colour pass-through and an MR experience that is arguably better than that of the Hololens or Magic Leap (Figure 1.19) – and with a wide field of view (McMillan & Moore-Colyer, 2023). Apple made its entry into the VR/

FIGURE 1.19
First Encounters – the Quest 3 Mixed Reality welcome game in David's study.

MR space with the Vision Pro in 2024. Whilst potentially a direct competitor to Meta's Quest Pro – but according to reviewers far better implemented (Porter, 2024) – its price tag of US$3499 will keep it out of reach of most users.

Quite how MR will enable metaverses to bleed into the physical world, and what the consumer use cases are, remain the subject of much discussion and will be further explored in later chapters. The Quest 3 is perhaps the MR industries "Oculus DK1" moment – providing an affordable and high performing device with which to experiment and create new applications and experiences to further define what the Metaverse is capable of.

The Metaverse in Popular Culture

Having started in popular culture, it is no surprise that the idea of a metaverse, or at least the concept of a well-developed social virtual world, has been utilised by a number of books, movies, TV series, and even radio shows, some predating even *Snow Crash*. Of particular note are:

- *True Names* (Vinge, 2015), as mentioned, first published in 1981 and featuring a fantasy-style virtual world where anonymity is a vital concern in order to hide from "the Feds";
- *Star Trek: The Next Generation* (Roddenberry, 1987), often featured the "holodeck", a kind of reverse MR where virtual spaces appeared to become physically real;
- *The Matrix* (Wachowskis, 1999) – the *sina qua non* of virtual world films, where the population of the earth exists without their knowledge in a virtual world in order to generate energy for the AI overlords;
- *Rainbow's End* (Vinge, 2007) – the augmented/mixed reality equivalent of *Snow Crash* where MR headsets can completely repaint the physical reality that the users experience;
- *Permutation City* (Egan, 2008), in which many of the characters are Copies, run in virtual simulations. One of its most interesting ideas is that those simulations might be running at incredibly slow speeds, for example, one computer instruction a second, so that whilst life would seem "normal" inside the simulation, outside time would be passing a thousand or millions times faster – great for exploring the stars;
- *PlanetB* (Broughton et al., 2009), a BBC Radio drama series set in a very *Second Life* type world, and featuring "rogues" – computer-controlled avatars that are developing a life independent of human operators;
- *Caprica* (Aubuchon & Moore, 2010), which features a character who seems to be inspired by Linden Lab's Philip Rosedale, and whose V-world virtual world is home to the first virtual humans generated from the digital traces of physical humans;

- *Ready Player One* (Cline, 2011), a book and film where the characters hunt for clues in a cross between a video game and *Second Life* in order to become its owners;
- *Black Mirror* (Brooker, 2011) includes several episodes that feature virtual worlds and virtual and mixed reality including *San Junipero* about the dead and elderly living in a virtual world, *Men Against Fire* where MR repaints opponents in a manner similar to Rainbow's End, *USS Callister* with a virtual spaceship crewed by avatar clones of real people and *Striking Vipers* where virtual experiences start to bleed through into the physical world;
- *Kiss Me First* (Moggach, 2013), a book and Channel 4 TV Series, where a young woman agrees to impersonate a dying woman. In the TV series, much of the action is moved from the text-based chat room of the book to a *Second Life*-like virtual world;
- *Fall; or, Dodge in Hell* (Stephenson, 2020), the *Snow Crash* authors' sequel to *Reamde*, where the creator of a fantasy MMORPG world is uploaded to a computer after his death and "thinks" a new fantasy virtual world into being, which then receives the minds of others who have died and been uploaded;
- *Upload* (Daniels, 2010), an American sitcom based in a virtual world hotel to which all the guests have been uploaded just before their death, and from where they have limited communications with their loved ones back in the physical world; and
- *When the Sparrow Falls* (Sharpson, 2021), where most of the Earth's population has been "contraned" so that their consciousness can be transferred to a virtual realm – or vice-versa, and people move fluidly between existing in the physical and virtual worlds.

The cluster of fictional works appearing around the first wave of social virtual worlds in 2004–2010 is quite noticeable.

Summary

This chapter has hopefully shown that prior to the emergence of Oculus and Facebook/Meta, there was already a lot of experience of building, using, and living in metaverse-type worlds, something which many of the current generation of users, developers, and commentators of metaverses seem unaware of. To emphasise this, Figure 1.20 shows the number of entries on Google Scholar mentioning "metaverse" since 1992.

Despite several decades of work towards the Metaverse, there has arguably been very little concrete progress since *Second Life* and *OpenSim*. Whilst its graphics *may* look basic in comparison to today's high-end games, the

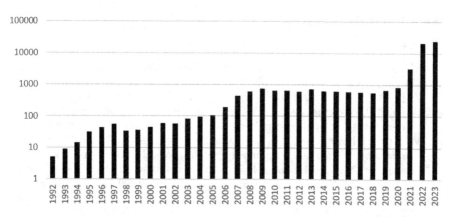

FIGURE 1.20
Google Scholar "metaverse" entries since (after Childs, 2023, and updated to 2023 by the original author).

functionality of *Second Life*, and in particular the in-world building and scripting and fully functioning marketplace and economy, and the contiguous landscape model are still far closer to that original *Snow Crash* vision than any world since. The current crop of worlds is either primarily focused on games (e.g. *Fortnite, Roblox, Rec Room*), playing it safe with room-based models, object placement, and out-of-world editing (e.g. *VRChat*, most business/collaboration worlds), or they are caught up in the blockchain hyperbole (e.g. *Decentraland, Somnium Space, Cryptovoxels*). The two bright spots are the continuing developments of consumer HMD-VR headsets and the ability to deliver virtual world experiences to the browser using WebGL and WebXR – as in *Hubs* and particularly *Frames*.

Given the couple of decades of history in developing virtual worlds and proto-metaverses, the next chapter will try to define, in the light of that, what the Metaverse is, or at least what the Metaverse could or should be.

Notes

1 Full disclosure, both Maggi and David were involved in this project.
2 Full disclosure, David was involved in this project.
3 Full Disclosure: The Revd. Jo Burden mentioned in the Church of England reference is David's daughter – an early introduction to Second Life as a child obviously paid off!
4 On 15 February 2024, just as the manuscript for this book was being submitted, Mozilla announced that Hubs would close on 31 May 2024 (Lardinois, 2024). Since Hubs is already open-source, it may be that the technology has a life after Mozilla, and the Hubs team hopes that it "can have a vibrant life outside of Mozilla", and so all references to Hubs have been left intact (https://hubs.mozilla.com/labs/sunset/).

References

American Cancer Society. (n.d.). *The society in Second Life*. American Cancer Society. https://www.cancer.org/involved/volunteer/society-second-life.html

Au, W. J. (2009). *The making of Second Life: Notes from the new world*. Collins Business.

Au, W. J. (2013). *Who wants a sneak preview of SkyDance V in SL tomorrow?* New World Notes. https://nwn.blogs.com/nwn/2013/01/skydancers-sl-art-preview.html

Au, W. J. (2021). *Philip Rosedale on Clubhouse bringing High Fidelity's metaverse-driven spatial audio to the massive audio chat app*. New World Notes. https://nwn.blogs.com/nwn/2021/08/clubhouse-high-fidelity-spatial-audio-philip-rosedale.html

Au, W. J. (2022a). *VRChat user concurrency hit nearly 90,000 last New Year's Eve!* New World Notes. https://nwn.blogs.com/nwn/2022/01/vrchat-concurrency-2021.html

Au, W. J. (2022b). *Metaverse real estate "boom" actually has all the makings of a bubble*. New World Notes. https://nwn.blogs.com/nwn/2022/02/metaverse-real-estate-boom-bust-sandbox-somnium-space-cryptovoxels.html

Au, W. J. (2023). *Making a metaverse that matters: From Snow Crash & Second Life to a virtual world worth fighting for*. John Wiley & Sons.

Aubuchon, R., & Moore, R. D. (Creators). (2010). *Caprica* [TV series]. Syfy.

Axon, S. (2023, March 16). 20 years later, Second Life is launching on mobile. *Ars Technica*. https://arstechnica.com/gaming/2023/03/20-years-later-second-life-is-launching-on-mobile/

Badger, C. (2008). *Recipe for success with enterprise virtual worlds*. Forterra Systems, Inc. http://www.cedma-europe.org/newsletter%20articles/TrainingOutsourcing/Recipe%20for%20Success%20with%20Enterprise%20Virtual%20Worlds%20(Dec%202008).pdf

Ball, M. (2022). *The metaverse: And how it will revolutionize everything*. Liveright Publishing.

Balogh, G., & Beszedes, A. (2013, September). CodeMetrpolis—A Minecraft based collaboration tool for developers. *2013 First IEEE Working conference on software visualization (VISSOFT)* (pp. 1–4). IEEE. http://www.inf.u-szeged.hu/~beszedes/research/paper34.pdf

Bar-El, D., & Ringland, K. (2021, September). Teachers designing lessons with a digital sandbox game: The case of Minecraft education edition. *European conference on games based learning*. Academic Conferences International Limited. https://www.researchgate.net/profile/David-Bar-El/publication/354563191_Teachers_Designing_Lessons_with_a_Digital_Sandbox_Game_The_Case_of_Minecraft_Education_Edition/links/61404e89a29a250dbf6d8ad5/Teachers-Designing-Lessons-with-a-Digital-Sandbox-Game-The-Case-of-Minecraft-Education-Edition.pdf

Barnes, S. J., & Mattsson, J. (2011). Exploring the fit of real brands in the Second Life 1 virtual world. *Journal of Marketing Management, 27*(9–10), 934–958.

Barr, K. (2023, April 19). Meta layoffs begin and even the game developers aren't safe. *Gizmodo*. https://gizmodo.com/meta-layoffs-begin-game-developers-metaverse-1850353319

Bartle, R. A. (2004). *Designing virtual worlds*. New Riders.

Bell, M. W., Castronova, E., & Wagner, G. G. (2009). *Surveying the virtual world: A large scale survey in Second Life using the Virtual Data Collection Interface (VDCI)*. https://www.econstor.eu/bitstream/10419/129253/1/diw_datadoc_2009-044.pdf

Benetou, F. (n.d.). *Mozilla Hubs.* Fabien Benetou's PIM. https://fabien.benetou.fr/Tools/Hubs

Bengtsson, N. (2023). *Commercial operations taking a break.* Alloverse. https://alloverse.com/2023/06/08/commercial-operations-taking-a-break/

Bengtsson, S. (2011). Virtual nation branding: The Swedish embassy in second life. *Journal of Virtual Worlds Research, 4*(2). https://www.learntechlib.org/p/178165/article_178165.pdf

Bezmalinovic, T. (2023, May 27). We are one step closer to a Google Earth VR for standalone headsets. *MIXED Reality News.* https://mixed-news.com/en/photorealistic-3d-tiles-standalone-google-earth-vr/

Blackwood, G. (2023). Roblox and Meta Verch: A case study of Walmart's Roblox games. *M/C Journal, 26*(3). https://www.journal.media-culture.org.au/index.php/mcjournal/article/view/2958

Boellstorff, T. (2015). *Coming of age in Second Life: An anthropologist explores the virtually human.* Princeton University Press.

Borgen, C. (2007). *Zick on Second Life and cyber-activism.* OpinioJuris. http://opiniojuris.org/2007/10/21/zick-on-second-life-and-cyber-activism/

Boyer, S. (2009). *A virtual failure: Evaluating the success of Nintendo's Virtual Boy. The Velvet Light Trap, 64,* 23–33.

Brenchley, K. (2023, April 23). Meta isn't building the first 'Verse. *Medium.* https://medium.datadriveninvestor.com/meta-isnt-building-the-first-verse-d0ea7725717c

Brooker, C. (2011). *Black mirror* [TV series]. Channel 4.

Brookey, R. A., & Cannon, K. L. (2009). Sex lives in second life. *Critical Studies in Media Communication, 26*(2), 145–164.

Brouchoud, J. (2011). *Portfolio—Simulation training—Hurricane shelter…* Flickr. https://www.flickr.com/photos/crescendo/albums/72157625910273942

Broughton, M., Dromgoole, J., Hoyle, S., & Robinson, J. (Creators), & Dromgoole, J. (Producer). (2009). *Planet B* [Radio series]. BBC.

Bryce, A. (2020, July 28). I logged back into Habbo Hotel for its 20th anniversary. *Vice.* https://www.vice.com/en/article/jgxvkk/habbo-hotel-20-years-old-online-game

Burden, D. J. H. (2011). *Virtual worlds—A future history.* Slideshare. https://www.slideshare.net/davidburden/virtual-worlds-a-future-history

Burden, D. J. H. (2021, October 29). Facebook (aka Meta) Connect2021. *Daden's Blog.* https://dadenblog.blogspot.com/2021/10/facebook-aka-meta-connect2021.html

Camilleri, V., de Freitas, S., Montebello, M., & McDonagh-Smith, P. (2013). A case study inside virtual worlds: Use of analytics for immersive spaces. *Proceedings of the third international conference on learning analytics and knowledge* (pp. 230–234). Association for Computing Machinery. https://www.researchgate.net/profile/Vanessa-Camilleri/publication/257765038_A_case_study_inside_virtual_worlds_Use_of_analytics_for_immersive_spaces/links/0c960525d3d2155886000000/A-case-study-inside-virtual-worlds-Use-of-analytics-for-immersive-spaces.pdf

Castronova, E. (2002). *On virtual economies* (Cesifo Working Paper No. 752). CESifo. https://papers.ssrn.com/sol3/delivery.cfm/SSRN_ID338500_code021011590.pdf?abstractid=338500

Chambers, C. (2011). How virtual are virtual economies? An exploration into the legal, social and economic nature of virtual world economies. *Computer Law & Security Review, 27*(4), 377–384. https://doi.org/10.1016/j.clsr.2011.05.007

Childs, M. (2023). *Pedagogy and curriculum research cluster poster session.* Durham University School of Education.

Cimerman, A. (2022, December 27). Source Digital announced the world's first meta-verse experience for LG smart TVs. *Metaverse Post*. https://mpost.io/source-dig-ital-announced-the-worlds-first-metaverse-experience-for-lg-smart-tvs/

Cline, E. (2011). *Ready player one*. Crown Publishing Group.

CofE. (2020). *Curate takes worship into whole new dimension—With children's services in Minecraft*. Church of England. https://www.churchofengland.org/news-and-media/stories-and-features/curate-takes-worship-whole-new-dimension-childrens-services

Crawford, A., & Smith, T. (2022, February 23). Metaverse app allows kids into virtual strip clubs. *BBC News*. https://www.bbc.co.uk/news/technology-60415317

Croquet. (2022, November 10). Croquet announces availability of Microverse World Builder. *PR Newswire*. https://www.prnewswire.com/news-releases/croquet-announces-availability-of-microverse-world-builder-301673922.html

Daniels, G. (2010). *Upload* [TV series]. Deedle-Dee Productions. https://www.imdb.com/title/tt7826376/

Decentraland. (2022, October 11). How many DAU does Decentraland have? *Decentraland*. https://decentraland.org/blog/announcements/how-many-dau-does-decentraland-have

Decentraland. (2024, January 29). Decentraland 2024 manifesto: Forging foundations for the future. *Decentraland*. https://decentraland.org/blog/announcements/decentraland-2024-manifesto-forging-foundations-for-the-future?utm_source=decentraland.beehiiv.com&utm_medium=newsletter&utm_campaign=weekly-newsletter-february-1

Dibbel, J. (1994). A rape in cyberspace or how an evil clown, a Haitian trickster spirit, two wizards, and a cast of dozens turned a database into a society. *The New York University Annual Survey of American Law*, 1994: 471–500. http://www.juliandib-bell.com/articles/a-rape-in-cyberspace/

DigitalUnionOSU. (2008, November 5). *The Second Life project: An interview with Douglas Danforth* [Video]. YouTube. https://www.youtube.com/watch?v=vEk48Sc9UaM&ab_channel=DigitalUnionOSU

Doctorow, C. (2003). *Down and out in the magic kingdom*. Turtleback Books.

Dredge, S. (2014, July 22). Facebook closes its $2bn Oculus Rift acquisition. What next? *The Guardian*. https://www.theguardian.com/technology/2014/jul/22/facebook-oculus-rift-acquisition-virtual-reality

Egan, G. (2008). *Permutation city*. Gollancz.

Ernstberger, P. (2009). *Linden Dollar and virtual monetary policy*. University of Bayreuth. https://citeseerx.ist.psu.edu/viewdoc/download?repid=rep1&type=pdf&doi=10.1.1.555.9589

Estonia. (2007). *Estonia opens embassy in virtual world Second Life*. Estonia Ministry of Foreign Affairs. https://vm.ee/en/news/estonia-opens-embassy-virtual-world-second-life

Etherington. (2014). *Yahoo acquires virtual world gaming startup Cloud Party, will shut it down*. TechCrunch. https://techcrunch.com/2014/01/24/yahoo-acquires-will-shut-down-browser-based-virtual-world-gaming-startup-cloud-party/

Fabola, A., Miller, A., & Fawcett, R. (2015). Exploring the past with Google Cardboard. *2015 Digital heritage* (Vol. 1, pp. 277–284). IEEE. https://research-repository.st-andrews.ac.uk/bitstream/handle/10023/12489/DigitalHeritage2015_sub-mission_98.pdf

Farra, S., Miller, E., Timm, N., & Schafer, J. (2013). Improved training for disasters using 3-D virtual reality simulation. *Western Journal of Nursing Research, 35*(5), 655–671. https://citeseerx.ist.psu.edu/document?repid=rep1&type=pdf&doi=6 97106d9fe9bc81b48a0936cd0ddbcff2cad12e4

Fewster, R., Wood, D., & Chafer, J. (2011). Staging Second Life in real and virtual spaces. *Teaching through multi-user virtual environments: Applying dynamic elements to the modern classroom* (pp. 217–235). IGI Global.

Fodor, G. (2020, April 19). The secret Mozilla Hubs master plan. *Medium.* https://gfodor.medium.com/the-secret-mozilla-hubs-master-plan-2c1364033bec

Forbes. (2007, December 7). Rocking the virtual world. *Forbes.* https://www.forbes.com/forbes/2007/1224/103.html?sh=18eed1735a55

Franey, J. (2023). *How to get Fortnite Creative 2.0 and what is it for?* Games Radar. https://www.gamesradar.com/fortnite-creative-20/

Freeman, C. (2020, December 3). *Creating a custom Mozilla Hubs client* [Video]. YouTube. https://www.youtube.com/watch?v=E71SLxpEWzE&ab_channel=Colinfreeman

Fridman, L. (Host). (2023). *Mark Zuckerberg: First interview in the Metaverse* (Lex Fridman Podcast #398) [Video]. YouTube. https://www.youtube.com/watch?v=MVYrJJNdrEg&ab_channel=LexFridman

Frömming, U. U. (2013). *Virtual environments and cultures: A collection of social anthropological research in virtual cultures and landscapes.* Peter Lang GmbH.

Galov, N. (2023, March 6). 18 Second Life facts in 2023: What it means to live in a virtual world. *Web Tribunal.* https://webtribunal.net/blog/second-life-facts/#gref

Garst, A. (2023, May 9). How Epic Games is revamping the ecosystem of Fortnite Creative to sweeten the deal for in-game creators. *Digiday.* https://digiday.com/marketing/how-epic-games-is-revamping-the-ecosystem-of-fortnite-creative-to-sweeten-the-deal-for-in-game-creators/

Gibson, W. (1984). *Neuromancer.* Ace.

Goodman, K. (2023). *How Fortnite weaves brands into the game & makes billions.* Weird Marketing Tales. https://weirdmarketingtales.com/fortnite-integrates-brands-makes-billions/

Habgood, M. J., Wilson, D., Moore, D., & Alapont, S. (2017). HCI lessons from PlayStation VR. *Extended abstracts publication of the annual symposium on computer-human interaction in play* (pp. 125–135). http://shura.shu.ac.uk/16656/3/Habgood%2520HCI%2520lessons%2520from%2520playstation%2520VR%2520%2528AM%2529.pdf

Han, J., Liu, G., & Gao, Y. (2023). Learners in the Metaverse: A systematic review on the use of Roblox in learning. *Education Sciences, 13*(3), 296. https://www.mdpi.com/2227-7102/13/3/296

Harris, C. (2010). *Government consortium to investigate virtual world best practices.* Government Technology. https://www.govtech.com/dc/articles/government-consortium-to-investigate-virtual-world.html

Hayden, S. (2023a). *PSVR 2 outsold original PSVR in first 6 weeks, Sony confirms.* Road to VR. https://www.roadtovr.com/psvr-2-sales-figures-units-sony/

Hayden, S. (2023b). *Why Nintendo hasn't made a real VR headset yet.* Road to VR. https://www.roadtovr.com/nintendo-missing-real-vr-headset/

Hayden, S. (2023c). *Microsoft is shutting down pioneering social VR platform 'AltspaceVR' tomorrow.* Road to VR. https://www.roadtovr.com/microsoft-social-vr-xr-interface-layoffs.

Hayes, G. (2008). *Photostream*. Flickr. https://www.flickr.com/photos/garyhayes/2793935191/

Heaney, D. (2019). *HoloLens 2's field of view revealed*. Upload VR. https://www.uploadvr.com/hololens-2-field-of-view/

Heath, A. (2023, February 28). This is Meta's AR/VR hardware roadmap for the next four years. *The Verge*. https://www.theverge.com/2023/2/28/23619730/meta-vr-oculus-ar-glasses-smartwatch-plans

High Fidelity. (2017, June 12). *Highlights: The state of VR with Robert Scoble and Philip Rosedale* [Video]. YouTube. https://www.youtube.com/watch?v=9wCz52lq9CE&ab_channel=HighFidelity

Hounshell, B. (2007). *Second Life does Davos*. Foreign Policy. https://foreignpolicy.com/2007/01/22/second-life-does-davos/

Hsu, E. B., Li, Y., Bayram, J. D., Levinson, D., Yang, S., & Monahan, C. (2013). State of virtual reality based disaster preparedness and response training. *PLoS Currents*, 5. https://www.ncbi.nlm.nih.gov/pmc/articles/PMC3644293/

Huvila, I. (2015). We've got a better situation: The life and afterlife of virtual communities of Google Lively. *Journal of Documentation*, 71, 526–549. http://dx.doi.org/10.1108/JD-09-2013-0116.

Hypergrid Business. (2011). *VastPark launches open source avatar kit*. Hypergrid Business. https://www.hypergridbusiness.com/2011/06/vastpark-launches-open-source-avatar-kit/

Hypergrid Business. (2023). *Statistics » Active OpenSim Grids*. Hypergrid Business. https://www.hypergridbusiness.com/statistics/active-grids/

Irwin, K. (2023). *PUBG creator Krafton unveils 'overdare' NFT game with AI creation tools*. Decrypt. https://decrypt.co/197345/pubg-creator-krafton-unveils-overdare-nft-game-ai-creation-tools

Jacob. (2023, March 28). Fortnite has 70 million monthly active players in 2023. *Fortnite News*. https://fortnitenews.com/fortnite-has-70-million-monthly-active-players-in-2023/

Jeremy, W. (2021). *Welcome to Minecraft Church*. Church Mission Society. https://pioneer.churchmissionsociety.org/2021/03/welcome-to-minecraft-church

Kaplan, J., & Yankelovich, N. (2011). Open wonderland: An extensible virtual world architecture. *IEEE Internet Computing*, 15(5), 38–45.

Kar-Gupta, S. (2007, March 26). French politics heads to 'Second Life'. *NBC News*. https://www.nbcnews.com/id/wbna17796832

Kharpal, A. (2021, August 30). TikTok owner ByteDance takes first step into virtual reality with latest acquisition. *CNBC*. https://www.cnbc.com/2021/08/30/tiktok-owner-bytedance-acquires-pico-and-takes-first-step-into-virtual-reality.html

Kim, S. (2021, November 2). South Korea's Approach to the Metaverse. *The Diplomat*. https://thediplomat.com/2021/11/south-koreas-approach-to-the-metaverse/

Kirriemuir, J. (2009a). *Learning through falling: Second Life in UK academia*. Slideshare. https://www.slideshare.net/silversprite/learning-through-falling-second-life-in-uk-academia

Kirriemuir, J. (2009b). *Virtual world activity in UK universities and colleges. An academic year of expectation?* Virtual World Watch. https://www.silversprite.com/ss/wp-content/uploads/2014/10/snapshot-seven.pdf

Kolo, K. (2023). *Sony investing $2B into XR (metaverse) research and development*. VR/AR Association. https://www.thevrara.com/blog2/2023/7/14/sony-investing-2b-into-xr-metaverse-research-and-development

Kopp, G., & Burkle, M. (2010). Using second life for just-in-time training: Building teaching frameworks in virtual worlds. *International Journal of Advanced Corporate Learning (IJAC)*, *3*(3), 19–25. https://www.researchgate.net/publication/45523975_Using_Second_Life_for_Just-in-Time_Training_Building_Teaching_Frameworks_in_Virtual_Worlds

Korolov, M. (2010). *Second Life discontinues enterprise platform*. Hypergrid Business. https://www.hypergridbusiness.com/2010/08/second-life-discontinues-enterprise-platform/

Krawanski, F. (2023, November 30). How many people play Pokemon Go? Pokemon Go player count. *Dexerto*. https://www.dexerto.com/pokemon/how-many-people-play-pokemon-go-pokemon-go-player-count-2132719/

Krotoski, A. (2009). *PhD Study 3 Intro Draft 1: On the implications of voice in Second Life*. Alek Krotoski. http://alekskrotoski.com/post/phd-study-3-intro-draft-1-on-the-implications-of-voice-in-second

Kumparak, G. (2014, March 27). A brief history of Oculus. *TechCrunch*. https://techcrunch.com/2014/03/26/a-brief-history-of-oculus/

Kurzydlowski, C. (2021). *The VR market in China: Moving toward the metaverse*. The China Guys. https://thechinaguys.com/china-virtual-reality-market/

Lamb, H. (2022, April 13). *What can the Metaverse learn from Second Life? E&T Engineering and Technology*. https://eandt.theiet.org/content/articles/2022/04/what-can-the-metaverse-learn-from-second-life/

Lang, B. (2022). *Virtual social platform 'Rec Room' hits 3 million monthly active VR users*. Road to VR. https://www.roadtovr.com/rec-room-monthly-active-vr-users-3-million-peak/

Lardinois, F. (2024, February 13). Mozilla downsizes as it refocuses on Firefox and AI: Read the memo. *TechCrunch*. https://techcrunch.com/2024/02/13/mozilla-downsizes-as-it-refocuses-on-firefox-and-ai-read-the-memo/

Lecordix, F., Fremont, D., Jilani, M., Séguin, E., & Kriat, S. (2018). Minecraft® on Demand—A new IGN service which combines game and 3D cartography. *Proceedings of the ICA* (Vol. 1, pp. 1–5). Copernicus GmbH. https://ica-proc.copernicus.org/articles/1/65/2018/ica-proc-1-65-2018.pdf

Leotoddy. (2019). *Habbo Statistics 2018—Habbo*. Puhekupla. https://puhekupla.com/news/habbo-statistics-2018-habbo

Linden Lab. (2022). *High Fidelity invests in Second Life*. Linden Lab. https://lindenlab.com/press-release/high-fidelity-invests-in-second-life

Lopes, C. (2011). Hypergrid: Architecture and protocol for virtual world interoperability. *IEEE Internet Computing*, *15*(5), 22–29. https://web.archive.org/web/20150426153421/https://dl.dropboxusercontent.com/u/18483217/hypergrid-draft.pdf

Mäntymäki, M., & Salo, J. (2013). Purchasing behavior in social virtual worlds: An examination of Habbo Hotel. *International Journal of Information Management*, *33*(2), 282–290.

Márquez, I. V. (2013). What happens when a cyberworld ends? The case of There.com. *Proceedings of DiGRA 2013: DeFragging game studies*, Atlanta, GA. http://www.digra.org/wp-content/uploads/digital-library/paper_280.pdf

Marsh, J. (2016). The relationship between online and offline play: Friendship and exclusion. *Children's games in the new media age* (pp. 109–132). Routledge. https://eprints.whiterose.ac.uk/79790/1/9781409450245_J.Marsh.pdf

McMillan, M., & Moore-Colyer, R. (2023, March 29). *Meta Quest 3 release date, price, specs and latest news*. Tom's Guide. https://www.tomsguide.com/news/oculus-quest-3-release-date-rumors-specs-news

Metamike. (2023). *Hyperfy: An extensible WebXR virtual world platform for creators and professionals.* HackMD.io. https://hackmd.io/@metamike/hyperfy

MIT Sloan Management Review. (2023). *The Middle East is unlocking the potential of virtual worlds.* MIT Sloan Management Review. https://www.mitsloanme.com/article/the-middle-east-is-unlocking-the-potential-of-virtual-worlds/

Moggach, L. (2013). *Kiss Me First.* Picador.

Morningstar, C., & Farmer, F. R. (2008). The lessons of Lucasfilm's Habitat. *Journal for Virtual Worlds Research, 1*(1). https://jvwr-ojs-utexas.tdl.org/jvwr/index.php/jvwr/article/download/287/241

NSA. (2008). *Exploiting terrorist use of games & virtual environments.* Guardian/NSA. https://www.theguardian.com/world/interactive/2013/dec/09/nsa-files-games-virtual-environments-paper-pdf

Ozturkcan, S. (2021). Service innovation: Using augmented reality in the IKEA Place app. *Journal of Information Technology Teaching Cases, 11*(1), 8–13. https://journals.sagepub.com/doi/pdf/10.1177/2043886920947110

Parekh, P., Patel, S., Patel, N., & Shah, M. (2020). Systematic review and meta-analysis of augmented reality in medicine, retail, and games. *Visual Computing for Industry, Biomedicine, and Art, 3,* 1–20. https://link.springer.com/article/10.1186/s42492-020-00057-7

Peters, J. (2023, May 22). Epic is going to give 40 percent of Fortnite's net revenues back to creators. *The Verge.* https://www.theverge.com/2023/3/22/23645633/fortnite-creator-economy-2-0-epic-games-editor-state-of-unreal-2023-gdc

Pey, I. (2020). *Coalition Island: Looking at the US Military's use of Second Life.* Modemworld.me. https://modemworld.me/2020/06/28/coalition-island-looking-at-the-us-militarys-use-of-second-life/

Pey, I. (2022). *High Fidelity, Linden Lab, and the Return of Philip Rosedale—Updated.* Modemworld.me. https://modemworld.me/2022/01/13/high-fidelity-linden-lab-and-the-return-of-philip-rosedale/

Porter, J. (2024). Everything we know about Apple's Vision Pro headset. *The Verge.* https://www.theverge.com/23689334/apple-mixed-reality-headset-augmented-virtual-reality-ar-vr-rumors-specs-features

Regan, T. (2021). *From 'Fortnite' to 'Roblox': The best in-game concerts ever, ranked.* NME. https://www.nme.com/features/gaming-features/fortnite-roblox-best-in-game-concerts-2021-3021418

Robertson, A. (2016, April 5). HTC Vive review. *The Verge.* https://www.theverge.com/2016/4/5/11358618/htc-vive-vr-review

Robertson, A. (2022, November 22). Meta Quest Pro review: Get me out of here. *The Verge.* https://www.theverge.com/23451629/meta-quest-pro-vr-headset-horizon-review

Roddenberry, G. (Creator & Executive Producer). (1987). *Star Trek: Next generation* [TV series]. CBS Television.

Ruby, D. (2023). *Roblox Statistics 2023—Demographics & financials.* Demand Sage. https://www.demandsage.com/how-many-people-play-roblox/

Rundle, M. (2015, December 2). Samsung's Gear VR is out now in the UK. *Wired.* https://www.wired.co.uk/article/gear-vr-uk-launch

Savin-Baden, M., Tombs, C., Poulton, T., & Kavia, S. (2009). *Getting started with Second Life.* JISC.

Schiano, D. J., & White, S. (1998). The first noble truth of cyberspace: People are people (even when they MOO). *Proceedings of the SIGCHI conference on human factors in computing systems* (pp. 352–359). Association for Computing Machinery.

Schultz, R. (2018). *Twinity: A brief introduction*. Ryan Schultz. https://ryanschultz.com/2018/05/10/twinity-a-brief-introduction/

Second Life Marketplace. (n.d.). *Second Life marketplace fee and listing policies*. Second Life Marketplace. https://marketplace.secondlife.com/listing_guidelines

Sharma, A. (2023). *How many people play Minecraft? 2023 player count*. Charlie Intel. https://www.charlieintel.com/minecraft/how-many-people-play-minecraft-2022-player-count-195437/

Sharpson, N. (2021). *When the sparrow falls*. Solaris.

Sherstyuk, A., Olle, S., & Sink, J. (2010). *Blue Mars chronicles: building for millions*. *ACM SIGGRAPH ASIA 2010 Sketches*. https://citeseerx.ist.psu.edu/document?repid=rep1&type=pdf&doi=551d876235a939c1707009219fe675bc156dd645

Sichelseifert. (2009a). *Starax Statosky: Second Life Giotto*. Second Life Masterpieces. https://sichelseifert.wordpress.com/2009/01/05/starax-statosky-second-life-giotto/

Sichelseifert. (2009b). *The Landscapes Master: AM Radio*. Second Life Masterpieces. https://sichelseifert.wordpress.com/2009/01/19/the-landscapes-master-am-radio/

Simons, R., & Melzer, J. E. (2003, September). HMD-based training for the US Army's AVCATT—A collective aviation training simulator. *Helmet- and head-mounted displays VIII: Technologies and applications* (Vol. 5079, pp. 1–6). SPIE.

Smith, D. A., Kay, A., Raab, A., & Reed, D. P. (2003). Croquet—A collaboration system architecture. *First conference on creating, connecting and collaborating through computing* (pp. 2–9). IEEE. https://citeseerx.ist.psu.edu/document?repid=rep1&type=pdf&doi=2d294e41d2d49881591a8dceb55c3199b6947a4d

SomniumSpace. (2023, July 31). Somnium Space announces strategic investment in Sansar to achieve full cross-platform interoperability. *Medium*. https://somniumspace.medium.com/somnium-space-announces-strategic-investment-in-sansar-to-achieve-full-cross-platform-716a7bedd780

Speed Matters. (2007, February 9). Second Life offers a new platform for politicians. *Speed Matters*. https://speedmatters.org/news/secondlifeoffersanewplatform forpoliticians

Stephenson, N. (1992). *Snow Crash*. Bantam Books.

Stephenson, N. (2020). *Fall; or, Dodge in Hell*. William Morrow & Company.

Stott, D. (2007). Learning the second way. *BMJ, 335*(7630), 1122–1123.

Sydney Morning Herald. (2007, May 23). Maldives opens first virtual embassy on Second Life. *Sydney Morning Herald*. https://www.smh.com.au/national/maldives-opens-first-virtual-embassy-on-second-life-20070523-gdq7im.html

Takashi, D. (2010, December 10). Sony's Home virtual world hits 17M users and finds a business model in virtual goods. *VentureBeat*. https://venturebeat.com/games/sonys-home-virtual-world-hits-17m-users-and-finds-a-business-model-in-virtual-goods/

Tassi, P. (2022, October 17). Meta's 'Horizon Worlds' has somehow lost 100,000 players in eight months. *Forbes*. https://www.forbes.com/sites/paultassi/2022/10/17/metas-horizon-worlds-has-somehow-lost-100000-players-in-eight-months/?sh=6502e7ed2a1b

Tate, A. (2022, February 20). History of Second Life and OpenSim VR viewers. *Austin Tate's Blog*. https://blog.inf.ed.ac.uk/atate/2022/02/20/vr-viewers/

Tate, A. (2024, January 15). [Email to David Burden]. Copy in possession of David Burden.

Taylor-Nelms, L., & Hill, V. (2014). Assessing 3D virtual world disaster training through adult learning theory. *International Journal of Serious Games*, 1(4). https://citeseerx.ist.psu.edu/document?repid=rep1&type=pdf&doi=9ef3e246c95ece34d0eb5065b6939ed259c6942c

Uccie. (2014). *Linden Realms: Two perspectives*. The Poultry Report. https://poultryreport.wordpress.com/2014/02/18/linden-realms-two-perspectives/

Utoyo, A. W., Warbung, T., Bonafix, N., Aprilia, H. D., & Oei, J. (2022). Branding in metaverse: Why big brand advertising in metaverse. *Proceedings of open society conference perspective and impact of metaverse on sustainable development goals*. Online International Conferences. https://repository.unmul.ac.id/bitstream/handle/123456789/46298/BUKU-PROSIDING-OSC-2022_FIX.pdf?sequence=1&isAllowed=y#page=347

Vinge, V. (2007). *Rainbows end*. Tor Books.

Vinge, V. (2015). *True Names and the opening of the cyberspace frontier*. Tor Books.

Virtual Girl Nem. (2022, May 22). VRChat breaks records with 92,000 simultaneous users! "Metaverse" user count surges over 5 times due to COVID-19 and Quest 2. *Medium*. https://medium.com/@nemchan_nel/vrchat-breaks-records-with-92-000-simultaneous-users-9464a33f3561

Virtual Reality Society. (n.d.). *Virtuality—A new reality of promise, two decades too soon*. Virtual Reality Society. https://www.vrs.org.uk/dr-jonathan-walden-virtuality-new-reality-promise-two-decades-soon/

Voyager, D. (2023). *Second Life stats*. Daniel Voyager. https://danielvoyager.wordpress.com/sl-stats/

Wachowskis. (1999). *The Matrix* [Film]. Warner Bros.

Wang, M., & Cooper, E. A. (2022). Perceptual guidelines for optimizing field of view in stereoscopic augmented reality displays. *ACM Transactions on Applied Perception*, 19(4), 1–23. https://dl.acm.org/doi/pdf/10.1145/3554921

Warren, T. (2021, May 2). Microsoft Mesh feels like the virtual future of Microsoft Teams meetings. *The Verge*. https://www.theverge.com/22308883/microsoft-mesh-virtual-reality-augmented-reality-hololens-vr-headsets-features

Wilcox, B., & Wilcox, S. (2013). Making it real: Loebner-winning chatbot design. *Arbor*, 189(764), a086. https://citeseerx.ist.psu.edu/document?repid=rep1&type=pdf&doi=b4008a89363730219e36ac563d9c8d74fcb15be1

Wired. (2006, August 15). Second Life rocks (literally). *Wired*. https://www.wired.com/2006/08/second-life-rocks-literally/

2

What Is the Metaverse?

Introduction

There are a lot of different ways in which developers (and users and authors) are interpreting the word "metaverse". This chapter examines some of the current definitions, as well as considering how the "3D Internet" and Web3 concepts relate to the Metaverse. Whilst simple definitions of the metaverse may be useful for marketing, they can hinder a deeper exploration of what a Metaverse might actually be, and what its implications are, so the chapter instead presents 10 axioms in order to define the Metaverse – considering the Metaverse in terms of its most complete and developed form. The chapter illustrates how some current platforms measure up against the axioms and examines *Second Life*'s standing (and that of *OpenSim*) as the most complete current model of a Metaverse. In the second part of the chapter, the focus shifts to explaining what it is that is notably different about the virtual reality (VR) experience in psychological terms, and how this gives additional power to the metaverse concept.

Competing Views of the Metaverse

As noted in the Introduction, one of the issues about discussing the metaverse is that there is no real agreement as to what it is. Table 2.1 presents several recent definitions and descriptions of the metaverse.

Figure 2.1 represents these definitions as a word cloud. About the only word common to most of the definitions is "virtual". The idea that the metaverse will actually be a multiverse – a network of metaversal spaces – is echoed in almost half of them. The linkage between the virtual world and the physical world is emphasised by Hackl, the International Telecommunications Union (ITU), and Narula. Interestingly, it's both Hackl and the ITU that get down into the technicalities including concepts such as blockchain, 5G, and digital twins. Several take the "next generation of the Internet" approach that will be challenged below.

DOI: 10.1201/9781003395461-3

TABLE 2.1

Definitions of the Metaverse

Source	Definition
Au (2023)	"The Metaverse is a vast, immersive virtual world simultaneously accessible by millions of people through highly customisable avatars and powerful experience creation tools integrated with the off-line world through its virtual economy and external technology".
Ball (2022)	"A massively scaled and interoperable network of real time rendered 3-D virtual worlds that can be experienced synchronously and persistently by an effectively unlimited number of users with an individual sense of presence, and with continuity of data, such as identity, history, entitlements, objects, communications, and payments".
Deloitte (Greig, n.d.)	"In the simplest terms, the metaverse is the internet, but in 3D…It's a form of digital interaction where connected, virtual experiences can either simulate the real world or imagine worlds beyond it. Many of the metaverse ingredients are with us now – think interacting with lots of people and content made by them, in persistent, immersive worlds across many devices, including virtual reality. The more these components intertwine, the closer we get to a fuller version of the metaverse".
Hackl (Alaghband, 2022)	"I believe it's a convergence of our physical and digital lives. It's our digital lifestyles, which we've been living on phones or computers, slowly catching up to our physical lives in some way, so that full convergence. It is enabled by many different technologies, like AR and VR, which are the ones that most people tend to think about. But they're not the only entry points. There's also blockchain, which is a big component, there's 5G, there's edge computing, and many, many other technologies. To me, the metaverse is also about our identity and digital ownership. It's about a new extension of human creativity in some ways".
ITU (2023)	"Metaverse and multiverse refer to virtual universes with close connections to and interactions with the real world, with the support of a set of digital technologies and information and communication technologies (ICTs), including AI, IoT, digital twin and blockchain. A metaverse can be considered as a collective space or a unified platform, while the multiverse (metaverses) has several integrated digital platforms and ecosystems that interact".
McKinsey (2022)	"The metaverse is the emerging 3-D-enabled digital space that uses virtual reality, augmented reality, and other advanced internet and semiconductor technology to allow people to have lifelike personal and business experiences online". "At its most basic, the metaverse will have three features: • a sense of immersion • real-time interactivity • user agency And ultimately, the full vision of the metaverse will include the following: • platforms and devices that work seamlessly with each other • the possibility for thousands of people to interact simultaneously • use cases well beyond gaming"

(Continued)

TABLE 2.1 (Continued)

Definitions of the Metaverse

Source	Definition
Narula (2022)	"These [virtual] worlds will be valuable because they will remake our lives by extending the context of society continue realms, allowing for the transfer of wealth, ideas, identity, and influence – the building blocks of human social relations – between our current reality and the digital ones that we create. The combination of these realities, and the transfer of value between them, will comprise the digital Metaverse ... The digital Metaverse that I envision is one that will create untold social, psychological, and economic value for its users and for the wider world".
Radoff	"*The* metaverse is not 'a' metaverse. It is the next generation of the Internet: a decentralized multiverse, led by a new and abundant generation of creators" (Radoff, 2021a). "The metaverse is the internet evolving into a creative space for anyone who wants to craft experiences" (Radoff, 2021b).
Wired (Ravenscraft, 2023)	"'The metaverse' [as defined by technology companies] can include virtual reality—characterized by persistent virtual worlds that continue to exist even when you're not playing—as well as augmented reality that combines aspects of the digital and physical worlds. However, it doesn't require that those spaces be exclusively accessed via VR or AR. Virtual worlds—such as aspects of Fortnite that can be accessed through PCs, game consoles, and even phones—have started referring to themselves as 'the metaverse'".

FIGURE 2.1

Metaverse definition word cloud (generated at https://www.jasondavies.com/wordcloud/).

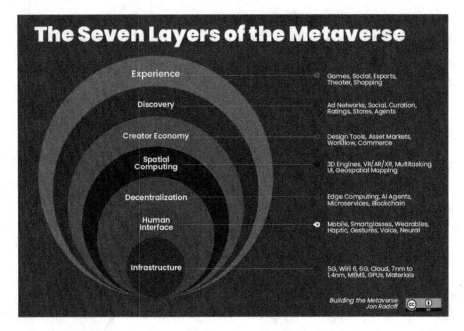

FIGURE 2.2
Jon Radoff's seven layers of the Metaverse model (Radoff, 2021c).

Radoff also has a "Seven Layers of the Metaverse" model (Radoff, 2021c), which breaks the Metaverse ecosystem down as shown in Figure 2.2. Whilst a useful reference, this schematic should not be taken as a technology stack but rather a guide to the value-chain of the metaverse, and the product categories being delivered by the companies enabling the metaverse.

2D versus 3D Web

In reading about the metaverse, the terms "3D Web" or even "3D Internet" are often seen. The term Internet properly refers to the network of computers which are connected through an underlying set of communications protocols with names such as IP, UDP, and TCP. The World Wide Web is just an application that runs over the Internet using a set of protocols in what is called the Application layer, on top of the Internet ones. Web protocols and standards include those such as HTTP (how websites serve content to users and link pages together), HTML (how web content is displayed), Javascript (how web pages are scripted), and WebSockets (how more advanced applications can transfer information between web servers and browsers) (Sahu, 2021).

Metaverse platforms typically transfer information across the Internet either by talking directly to the Internet using Internet protocols (e.g. UDP or

TCP) or by using web protocols such as WebSockets. There is no implication that the Metaverse *replaces* the Internet.

There should also be no implication that the Metaverse will replace the 2D Web, and particularly the mobile web. The 2D model for accessing information, where a user only needs simple hardware and feels safe (and polite) to use it anywhere, is one that will persist well after the Metaverse becomes a common place – and the two should live in harmony and be interconnected. A user should be able to use the 2D Web to access WebXR content and be instantly transported into a DesktopVR or HMD-VR metaversal space (depending on their browser) and to access 2D Web content from inside that metaversal space.

One significant difference that the notion of the "3D Internet" does try and draw out is that while the Web consists of a large number of websites abstractedly linked to each other, the metaverse is more likely to comprise "locations" which have some sort of spatial relationship with each other – by theme or viewpoint or even by time or physical or virtual geography (e.g. Neal Stephenson quoted in Au, 2023). Perhaps, the term "spatial Internet" (Vogelsang, 2021), or better "spatial Web" (Newton, 2021), may be more appropriate. As mentioned in the Introduction, the current in-phrase "spatial computing" (Ball, 2024) strikes us as being too technology centric rather than people centric, although it may be quite applicable to the Apple Vision Pro concept of doing your personal computing in space around you rather than using your head-mounted display XR (HMD-XR) for predominantly social interactions.

Web3 and the Metaverse

Another term which is confusing in the context of the Metaverse is "Web3". This is *not* the Web in 3D but rather a contraction of Web 3.0 – although confusingly, some see Web 3.0 as being about the evolution of the semantic web (Nabben, 2023). Web 1.0 was the original informational World Wide Web, and Web 2.0 is the growth of user-generated content, social media, and a transactional web. Web3 was defined by Gavin Wood (Wood, 2014) and is seen as a "decentralized and democratized internet that puts users in control of their data and online identities" and which creates "a more equitable, secure, and interconnected digital world" (Ray, 2023). It is driven primarily by blockchain technologies and approaches such as decentralised applications (DApps), decentralised finance (DeFi), non-fungible tokens (NFTs), and decentralised autonomous organisations (DAOs) (Buterin, 2013). While Web 2.0 was more about a change in the content of, and how people used, the Web, Web3 is more about the underlying structure of control of the web and Internet. It is also an almost philosophical shift in how people view and structure the Internet – although tensions are reported between the crypto movement and the Web3 label (Gilbert, 2022).

Whilst some may see the Web3 as the "technological infrastructure of the Metaverse" (Momtaz, 2022), it is more appropriate that the metaverse be seen as distinct from Web3 – the latter focused on ownership and control, whilst the former is about the user experience (Kshetri, 2022a). Jarvinen et al. (2023) present a "metaverse-Web3 convergence model" to help businesses better understand which technology and design combinations from both these spaces meet their specific service needs.

As Chapter 1 has already shown, metaverse-like experiences can be built using a variety of Web 2.0 technologies, and whilst a metaverse could, and perhaps should, be built using Web3 technologies or approaches, they are not essential to it – this is further explored in Chapter 4.

A Spectrum of Definitions

Most of the definitions of the metaverse sit on a spectrum, as shown in Figure 2.3, which ranges from the metaverse as a collection of disparate, unconnected, experiences to the metaverse as a singular, all-encompassing Metaverse.

At the left-hand end are definitions which just see "metaverse" as an all-encompassing term for any VR (or even augmented reality [AR] or mixed reality [MR]) experience. At this left hand of the spectrum, "metaverse" could just as easily be replaced with "XR experience".

In the centre of the spectrum, the definitions recognise that "the metaverse" is something more than just an XR experience and that common standards and technologies may be useful, and in particular, it may/must be social, possibly persistent, and possibly granting the user a higher degree of agency. This mid-spectrum definitions reject (or are agnostic about) the idea of one

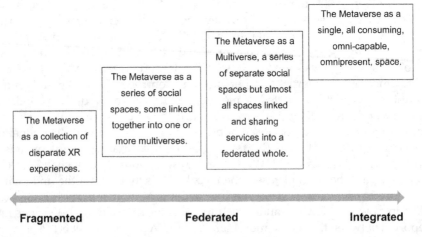

FIGURE 2.3
A spectrum of metaverse definitions.

true Metaverse and instead see a future built around multiple environments, which may have higher or lower levels of integration between them.

At the right of the centre is a more holistic but still federated view, where most worlds are built on the same technologies and may even share common services. This results in one or more multiverses connecting all these other worlds together in the same way that the Hypergrid connects *OpenSim* worlds and the DNS network connects web servers (but doesn't enable identity or asset transfer).

At the right end of the spectrum is the "one Metaverse to rule them all" model – where there is a singular Metaverse, built using a common technology set, and every metaversal space is a part of that Metaverse.

This book largely concerns itself with the right of centre definitions, although worlds and experiences which meet the left of centre ones have certainly helped to build the use cases for metaversal experiences, as will be seen in Chapter 3. Chapter 6 will further explore how the right of centre and right of spectrum definitions might play out.

The Metaverse Roadmap Model

Although it's over 15 years old, the Metaverse Roadmap's model of the Metaverse is worth revisiting (S. G. Lee et al., 2011). The model is shown in Figure 2.4.

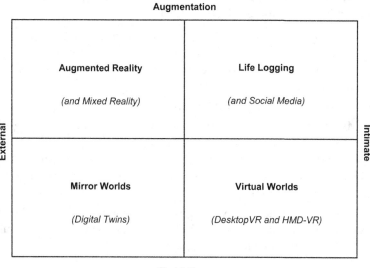

FIGURE 2.4
The Metaverse roadmap model.

It identifies the parts of what was then considered the Metaverse in terms of whether they are about augmenting or simulating reality and about individuals (intimate) or the world at large (external). This results in four different types of experience being defined:

- **Virtual Worlds** – which nowadays incorporate DesktopVR and HMD-VR worlds, and which are about social interaction;
- **Mirror Worlds** – which can today be called digital twins;
- **Augmented Reality** – which now include mixed reality; and
- **Life Logging** – which was a big term in the early 2000s but could now be taken to include the documentation of our lives through X/ Twitter, TikTok, Facebook, and other social media platforms.

Ten Axioms for the Metaverse

Rather than trying to present yet another one-sentence definition of the Metaverse, we present 10 axioms which we believe a true Metaverse should follow. Many metaverse platforms follow some of them, but none yet implements them all to a high degree. The axioms have been arranged roughly from technically focused to human focused to societal focused.

#1 The Metaverse Is a Multi-User, Interactive, Social, Shared and Subjective Experience – Delivered Digitally

This is the motherhood-and-apple-pie statement about the Metaverse:

- It MUST be multi-user. No point in being in the Metaverse on your own;
- It MUST be interactive. The Metaverse isn't a passive experience;
- It MUST be social. This means not only multi-user but also giving you the time and features to enable you to interact with other people and build relationships (short or long duration) with them;
- It MUST be shared. What I see is what you see, where I can go, you can go. It is consensual; and
- It MUST be subjective. We might all see the same things, but the experience for each of us as an individual will be different, coloured by our own interests and life experiences.

And of course, it's primarily digital. How the physical and digital worlds may combine in the metaverse is discussed later.

#2 The Metaverse Is Editable from Within Itself

The Metaverse MUST be editable by its users, within the permissions allowed, WITHIN the Metaverse, so you can change what you see, what things do, and how things work and create original content and all without leaving the Metaverse (just as you don't have to exit the physical world in order to build a house, or to do some DIY in it). Separate editing software is an optional extra.

#3 The Metaverse Is Persistent

The Metaverse MUST be persistent. If somebody changes something, it stays changed until someone changes it again. No refreshing every day or every session. It is also always there, always on, and always available, a persistent feature of your whole life.

#4 The Metaverse Is Open

The Metaverse is not about one company's technology or platform or eco-system, nor (currently) predicated on any particular hardware (such as a VR headset) or technological approach (e.g. blockchain or Web3) and nor should it be only a visual experience.

The Web is more the model to aspire to, where its basic operation is defined by open standards, with multiple companies then able to create the software that runs it, and runs on it, and all those components then work (relatively) seamlessly together so that they are transparent to the user. Whether the code itself actually needs to be open-source is a moot point (it is open standards that are more important), and there is also the crucial question of who runs and owns the equivalent of the DNS that might link the different servers and spaces of the Metaverse together.

Ever since the launch of the Oculus DK1 kickstarted the current generation of head-mounted display (HMD)-based VR, there appears to have been an unwritten assumption that the Metaverse is all about HMD-VR. However, as Chapter 1 has hopefully shown, a lot of the DesktopVR social virtual worlds of the late 1990s and early 2000s were (and in some cases continue to be) far closer in spirit and execution to the idea of the Metaverse than many (and possibly all) of the current crop of HMD VR applications being touted as "the Metaverse".

Perhaps it even goes further than that. To those who experienced them the text-based multi-user dungeons (MUDs) and multi-user object-orientated dungeons (MOOs) of the mid-1990s, whilst lacking the visual element of even the DesktopVR-based social virtual worlds, succeeded in creating a multi-user, interactive, social, editable, shared, subjective, and persistent experience with high user agency, and perhaps have as much right of being considered

at least as proto-metaverses as the graphical social virtual worlds that followed them. This independence of technological implementation extends to
modern trends such as blockchain and NFTs. More positively, it also suggests
that a Metaverse could be experienced by some as a primarily audio experience, and indeed the Metaverse should be designed to provide as much
accessibility as possible.

#5 The Metaverse Is a Superset of Technologies and Experiences and Likely Contains Within It, Multiple, More Constrained Environments

The Metaverse includes MR, DesktopVR, HMD-VR, and similar experiences. Also, within the physical world, we close off spaces as offices, hospitals, training facilities, nature reserves, football stadia, and so on, and
we should expect to be able to do the same in the Metaverse, with such
spaces possibly having a more constrained implementation of the freedom and facilities of the wider Metaverse – and potentially even having
some features not available within the wider community. These spaces
may be "logically" enclosed – such as by the boundary barriers in *Second
Life* which you can see but not move through – or they may be separate
microverses or pocket-metaverses, pinched off from the bigger Metaverse
(similar to rooms in *RecRoom* or *OpenSim* servers in a Hypergrid), but
with a high ability to move assets, identity, and information between
them all.

#6 The Metaverse May Be a Multiverse in Which Case Interoperability and Portability Should Be as Extensive as Possible

This is an extension of #5 to a degree, but the focus here is on the overall
architecture of the Metaverse rather than on pinching off microverses for
specific use cases. The Web is again a reasonable example, with everyone
running their own servers (even if they are increasingly physically being
combined into cloud server farms) but connecting together websites in
a relatively seamless manner. *OpenSim* and its Hypergrid are a more
directly relevant metaverse example, and Mastodon (an alternative to X/
Twitter) is a more general example. But as we know from the web, the portability of identity and other assets between services is a real challenge,
with third-party mediation (your Google or Facebook account) increasingly being the way to manage it – and in the ReadyPlayerMe service
(https://readyplayer.me), some elements of that in terms of avatar management are coming to immersive environments. The Multiverse versus
Single Metaverse tension is one that will take time to play out, and so it
is likely that some form of Multiverse is going to be the model for a while
and will be further discussed later.

#7 You Should Be Able to Live a Complete Life in the Metaverse: Learn, Teach, Earn, Create, Sell, Buy, Trade, Collaborate, Communicate, Explore, Make Friends, Play, Have Fun, Entertain, Be Entertained, Have Relationships, Have New Experiences, and Leave a Legacy

This extends #1 and is expressed in terms of the user experience not the system features – and a good candidate for part of a single sentence definition. There are lot of spaces that might argue that they meet #1 but totally fail here. If the Metaverse is to be a true digital extension of our physical existence, then we should be able to use it do (almost) all the things that we can do in the physical world, plus some new things beside. The Metaverse also needs to support its own native, in world, economy and marketplaces – and ones which are linked seamlessly to the physical world.

We're certainly not advocating that we forsake the physical world, but if we want to use the Multiverse for something that stretches across large parts of our lives, both thematically and temporally, we should be able to do so.

#8 The Metaverse Should Provide the User with as Much Scope for Agency and Action in the Immersive Digital World as in the Physical World, Probably More so, with the Only Limits on Their Action Being (Initially) Those Reflecting the Laws, Ethics, and Morals of the Physical World

In the Metaverse, you should have the agency to do whatever you want, just as you can within the physical world. This is what enables #7. Yes, that may be bounded by skills or knowledge (which can both be learnt), by aptitude or resources, and by what is seen as being moral, ethical, and lawful, but otherwise you just do what you want. Priestley argues that there is a good case that the most successful virtual worlds have been those that "weren't necessarily built for one specific reason or audience - they were mainly agnostic to let the players create their own worlds out of roleplay or some other aspect of imagination or interaction" and whose uses "emerged because the platforms allowed an open-ended structure to their virtual worlds", enabling a "real, emergent creator economy" to develop (Priestley, 2022a). The Metaverse needs to be built from the inside out, not the outside in.

The challenge as to whose laws, ethics, and morals should apply will be discussed in Chapter 5, and the "initially" caveat is a nod to the fact that ultimately the laws, ethics, and morals within the Metaverse may well diverge from the physical world.

#9 Not Everyone in the Metaverse Will Be Human Controlled

This is deliberately not phrased as "not everyone in the Metaverse will be human" as that could be taken to be about avatars and appearance, and as discussed in Chapter 1, proto-Metaverses like *Second Life* and *VRChat* are full of furries, robots, and other non-human avatars. Instead, the emphasis here is on what is controlling the avatars. There are three particular cases of interest:

- Simple "non-AI" driven avatars performing routine tasks in the Metaverse, such as greeters, helpers, personal assistants/stand-ins, non-player characters and so on – just as we already have in many of the proto-Metaverses;
- AI-driven avatars which begin to live their own semi or fully independent lives within the Metaverse. Virtual world spaces like the Metaverse are probably the ideal learning and proving grounds for more developed AIs as they provide a grounded and "realistic" experience for an embodied AI (Burden & Savin-Baden, 2019);
- Digital Amortals, ex-human-driven avatars, where the virtual selves that we might create to double for us in the Metaverse continue to live and work in it well beyond the point where our physical selves have died (Burden, 2020).

Planet B (Broughton & Dromgoole, 2009) is a fun exploration of some of these forms in a fictional proto-Metaverse, and Caprica (Aubuchon & Moore, 2010) is probably the best exploration of the last consideration.

#10 The Boundary between the Physical Universe and Virtual Metaverse Is as Porous as Each User Wants It to Be, Within Moral, Ethical, and Legal Reason

The Metaverse and its users need to find the right balance between the attribution of action to physical individuals, and the protection against doxing and other forms of on-line (or subsequent off-line) abuse. Just as with social media platforms, this will be no easy task. People should be free to create different identities within the Metaverse in order to explore their different selves, but there should be some, protected, form of attribution chain.

This boundary and interface to the physical world also include things like financial exchanges (money earned in the Metaverse should be spendable in the physical world) and cyber and information system (extending your mobile phone and your favourite web and desktop applications into the Metaverse).

Whilst we see the Metaverse as being integrated with the physical world, to the point where you might forget what you did in the physical world and what you did in the virtual world, we think it loses focus and even devalues the term metaverse to apply that to both virtual and physical world. Perhaps a new term is needed, or we just accept that the sum of the Metaverse and the physical world is just life.

---

10 AXIOMS FOR THE METAVERSE

For convenience, here are the 10 axioms brought together.

#1 The Metaverse is a multi-user, interactive, social, shared and subjective experience – delivered digitally.

#2 The Metaverse is editable from within itself.

#3 The Metaverse is persistent.

#4 The Metaverse is Open.

#5 The Metaverse is a superset of technologies and experiences and likely contains within it, multiple, more constrained environments.

#6 The Metaverse may be a Multiverse in which case interoperability and portability should be as extensive as possible.

#7 You should be able to live a complete life in the Metaverse: learn, teach, earn, create, sell, buy, trade, collaborate, communicate, explore, make friends, play, have fun, entertain, be entertained, have relationships, have new experiences, and leave a legacy.

#8 The Metaverse should provide the user with as much scope for agency and action in the immersive digital world as in the physical world, probably more so, with the only limits on their action being (initially) those reflecting the laws, ethics, and morals of the physical world.

 # 9 Not everyone in the Metaverse will be human controlled.

#10 The boundary between the physical universe and virtual Metaverse is as porous as each user wants it to be, within moral, ethical, and legal reason.

Although not really an axiom, a final point to keep in mind is that "virtual" should be contrasted with "physical" not "real". There are plenty of examples which show that the virtual world can evoke real emotions and have real impact on people's lives in the physical world – so the correct dichotomy is virtual versus physical not virtual versus real.

Some similar lists of metaversal traits and rules are provided by Parisi (2021), Forster (2022), and Buchholz et al. (2022), and there is a meta-analysis of Parisi, Ball, and others in Priestley (2022b). Useful taxonomies of metaversal worlds are provided by Merrick and Gu (2011), L. H. Lee et al. (2021), Kshetri (2022b), and Park and Kim (2022)

Assessing Current Platforms

Figure 2.5 provides a very rough assessment of some of the current metaversal platforms against the 10 axioms. *Mozilla Hubs* had a similar shaped profile to Virbela's *Frame*, most other cryptoworlds would have profiles similar to *Decentraland*, and other game-based worlds similar to *Roblox*. Updated graphs, graphs for other worlds, and more detail on the methodology used are on the series website at http://www.themetaverseseries.info/.

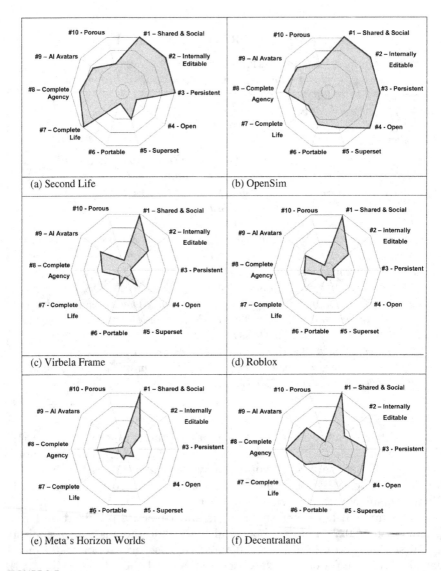

FIGURE 2.5
Assessing current platforms against the 10 axioms: (a) *Second Life*, (b) *OpenSim*, (c) Virbela Frame, (d) Roblox, (e) Meta's Horizon Worlds, and (f) Decentraland.

Comparing (and Deriving) Terms

Having hopefully established a clearer idea of what the Metaverse is, it may be useful to show how some of the terms already discussed relate to this larger scope.

Environment Types

These terms relate to a complete environment space and are largely technology neutral.

- **Synthetic Environment** – the broadest term encompasses any environment that provides a synthetic or artificial sense of reality. Although some people even include manual synthetic systems such as paper wargames in this definition (e.g. Perla, 2011), it is usually taken as referring to *digital* synthetic environments. It can be further refined into:
  - *Immersive/Subjective digital synthetic environments* where the user has a first-person experience (even if from an over-the-shoulder third-person view); and
  - *Objective digital synthetic environments*, such as agent-based modelling environments where the user observes the behaviour of multiple algorithmically driven agents within a space – such as for crowd and traffic modelling – objectively from outside of the simulation.
- **Virtual Reality Environment/Experience** – a more specific term which in more recent usage tends to imply the use of a VR headset but can also be used to refer to mobile and desktop VR experiences as well – and is used in this sense in this book. It includes VR experiences that are single user and with relatively little user agency (including viewing a 360° photo or video) that might be excluded from a "virtual world" definition;
- **Virtual World** – during the 1990s/2000s, "virtual world" (VW) was the dominant term for the worlds that people were exploring such as *Second Life*, *Qwaq*, *OpenWonderland*, and *Forterra*. The key features are that users are represented by an avatar, share the space with other avatars, and can explore and interact with a rich 3D environment – which in some cases might be just one room but in others entire continents. Whilst training- and business-orientated virtual worlds might limit agency and persistence, the more socially orientated spaces had fewer restrictions and more capability;
- **Massively-Multi-player Online Games (MMOs)** – they provide many of the features of a virtual world, but since they are presented as a game, they naturally constrain player choices and agency. Sandbox MOOs, or MMOs with sandbox or creative modes, tend to overlap with social virtual worlds, such as with *Fortnite Creative*, *Roblox*, and *Minecraft*;
- **Multi-User Virtual Environment (MUVE)** – a term commonly used within the learning and education community to describe a virtual world which is focused on education, training, and learning;

- **Social Virtual Worlds (SVW)** – a more specific type of virtual world which emphasises social interaction rather than using the world only for training, education, business, or entertainment, etc. These can range from low agency worlds such as *Fortnite* and *RecRoom* to the proto-metaverses such as *Second Life, OpenSim,* and *Somnium Space,* which are characterised by high user agency and low direction. The most open social virtual worlds have in-world tools to build and script new objects and experiences as user-generated content (UGC). Ideally, the whole virtual world (and the Metaverse) should be built from UGC; and
- **Proto-Metaverse** – a social virtual world which covers most but not all of the 10 axioms above, or covers all of them but to only a moderate degree, and so whilst being close to a Metaverse "ideal" falls (currently) slightly short of it.

Metaverse Terms

The following terms can be useful to describe how metaversal spaces may be created within a larger virtual world or metaverse (but which have restricted access, and possibly reduced functionality or agency), or through the interconnection of multiple smaller metaversal spaces.

- **Microverse** – a metaverse created for a very specific function – such as a training course, project, meeting, group, or entertainment event (Ffiske, 2022). It could be the metaverse equivalent of an Intranet – an area of metaverse type functionality, but which is restricted to access by a single company or organisation, or for a single event or task;
- **Pocket Metaverse** – similar in concept to a Microverse, but with more of an implication of being "pinched out" of a larger metaverse and so sharing the same infrastructure;
- **Multiverse** – a network of metaversal spaces which are interconnected so that users can move (relatively) seamlessly from one to another. Ideally, they can take their identity and assets with them, and spaces may share common technologies and even services. Each space or collection of spaces is hosted by a different entity, but there should be a common discovery and possibly asset and management service and standardised access devices and applications;
- **Federated Multiverse** – a more formal form of the Multiverse, where common approaches are mandated, more services are shared, and interconnectivity is (near) complete;
- **Confederated Multiverse** – a variant of the Federated Multiverse where there is more of a peer-to-peer approach with only the bare minimum of services needing to be centrally provided; and

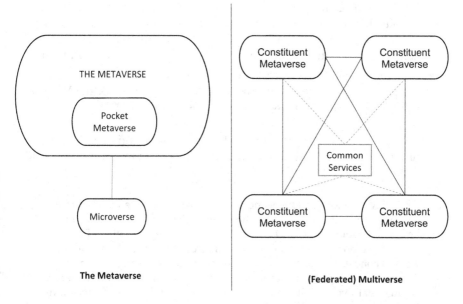

FIGURE 2.6
Metaverse types.

- **Constituent Metaverse** – within the context of a multiverse, a meta-verse which is connected into the larger multiverse and which may implement local rules and likely runs on its own infrastructure. Some also refer to these as satellite metaverses.

The relationships between these are shown in Figure 2.6.

Is Second Life the Metaverse?

As may be apparent from Chapter 1, *Second Life* and its associated open-source and hypergrid-enabled derivative *OpenSim* already provide many of the features that are specified for a Metaverse and can be correctly termed proto-Metaverses. This is borne out by their graphs in Figure 2.5. They may not be the Metaverse, but they are still the closest current experience that there is to it.

Where *Second Life* is not seen as being a metaverse (e.g. Naveen, 2023) this is often because:

- It is claimed not to have an HMD-VR interface – although as Chapter 1 described, it does have viewers (albeit unofficial) who support HMD-VR, and as the discussion above argues, the Metaverse should not be dependent on any one interface mode;

- It doesn't implement blockchain technologies and crypto-currencies, despite having its own 20-year-old digital currency, and, as discussed in Chapter 1, having an in-world economy that is more profitable than either the cryptoworlds or the larger consumer worlds; and
- It is very much only a virtual world, with minimal connectivity to the physical world and no broader intention to rethink the Web or Internet, or indeed how we live our lives (Virgilio, 2022).

However, others see the value in what it has created, and how it has helped to improve the understanding of what any Metaverse might be like. Liddle (2022) notes how:

> Arguably, previous products and games have already demonstrated the concepts and virtual activities that companies like Meta want fans to be excited about: games, 3D creation, virtual gatherings, virtual currencies, and so on. But no other company has done it quite like Linden Lab with Second Life......Second Life is essentially an example of a metaverse with a centralized authority. While Second Life wasn't intended to change real lives, it still demonstrates many of the concepts present in Meta's idea for the metaverse.
>
> **(Liddle, 2022).**

In slightly more colourful language, another article describes *Second Life* as "clunky, squalid, and largely populated by people more comfortable in pixels than in real life. If only Facebook's metaverse platform could be as good" (Lamb, 2022). As The Guardian describes it, in an article entitled *You Call That a Metaverse* when talking about Zuckerberg's grand vision of the metaverse, "those still existing happily on Second Life … may be wondering what all the fuss is about" (Parkin, 2023). However, Priestley argues that one of the biggest issues may be the failure of "Linden Lab's ability to capitalize on the renewed interest in it with Second Life" and that it has also failed "to both improve the platform at the same pace as technology has moved, or done anything in the current cycle to market itself as the place to be" (Priestley, 2022c).

If there were to be a "to-do" list to make *Second Life* and *OpenSim* closer to the Metaverse ideal, it would likely include:

- To open source all the code (as *OpenSim* already has, and Linden Lab has for the Viewer);
- Extend the Hypergrid approach of *OpenSim*, particularly to support full account portability and allow people to host their own servers (as *OpenSim* already does);
- Officially support HMD-VR access, and perhaps even MR access, especially for building;
- Further enhance the graphical look;
- Enhance controls for privacy and to counter abuse;

- Create DesktopVR and HMD-VR user interfaces which are more intuitive to new users; and
- Implement a WebXR viewer so that the worlds can run in a browser.

Second Life and *OpenSim* are already beginning to introduce support for glTF and physically based rendering (PBR), which should improve both the look and interoperability (Pey, 2023).

The challenge, though, may be that the core architecture of *Second Life* is such that supporting some of these changes is impracticable (Gregory, 2023) in which case it's time for either *Second Life 2.0* or *OpenSim 2.0*, or for a new entrant or existing player to take inspiration from *Second Life* and *OpenSim* and to build a platform which has both their legacy features and the suggested improvements, and without adding additional barriers to participation – such as through the use of unstable crypto-currencies.

The Psychological Underpinnings of Virtual Experiences[1]

Through the use of VR technology, the metaverse experience is tightly bound to the psychology of how the brain experiences immersion, presence, agency, embodiment, and flow. It is this relationship which makes metaversal experiences feel more powerful than other conventional digital and media experiences and contributes to why the Metaverse may have a more profound effect on us and our lives than other digital experiences.

Researchers have identified five key features which virtual environments (whether DesktopVR or HMD-VR) deliver in a unique way, and they are shown graphically in Figure 2.7. Understanding how to leverage each of these is key to taking the fullest advantage of what VR and metaverse

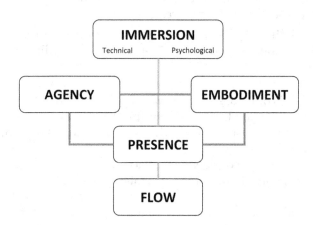

FIGURE 2.7
The psychological drivers of the virtual environment experience.

environments have to offer. Note, though, that VR is a highly individual experience, based on context and our own psychology and physiology. Some of the first researchers in the field even identified imagination as being one of the most important factors (Burdea & Coiffet, 2003). So, be aware that no matter how "good" a VR experience is, maybe not everyone will get the same things from it.

Immersion

Immersion is the sense of being "enveloped by, included in, and interacting with an environment that provides a continuous stream of stimuli and experiences" (Witmer & Singer, 1998). Immersion is increased by having less awareness of your "real" physical environment (so HMD-VR typically delivers more immersion than DesktopVR), natural control over your actions (so fewer menus), and the environment responding to your presence.

Researchers (e.g. Mütterlein, 2018; Rueda et al., 2018) often consider immersion in terms of:

- its technical aspects (e.g. screen resolution and refresh rate); and
- the psychological aspects (e.g. the emotional response and sense of "being there").

Presence

Presence is a step beyond simple immersion, and it is where you feel that you are "interacting directly, not indirectly or remotely, with the environment. You feel that you are part of that environment" (Witmer & Singer, 1998). Slater (2009) splits presence down into:

- the place illusion, the sense of being there generated by the technological immersion and visual realism; and
- the plausibility illusion, the sense that the perceived events are actually happening – and informed by a sense of credibility, agency, and narrative.

True presence is often described as when you have a real feeling of having visited a place when you leave VR – the "place illusion", which is reinforced by the "plausibility illusion" of the virtual experience itself of being "real" (Slater, 2009).

Co-presence is also a consideration; places usually feel more "real" when there are other people (represented as avatars) there, even if computer controlled. Some researchers have even found that training effectiveness was increased when virtual bystanders were present (e.g. Strojny et al., 2020), and platforms like VARK mentioned in Chapter 1 aim to increase the realism of a solo concert-going experience by populating your environment with addition, truly virtual, concert-goers.

Agency

Agency is the extent to which you feel that you are in control of your own actions (Piccione et al., 2019) and can control, or at least influence, the (virtual) world around you (Jicol et al., 2021). If you feel a high sense of agency, then research suggests that your presence, spatial awareness, and co-presence will be higher, which should lead to better performance. Factors that assist in generating agency in VR include:

- Viewing the world from a first-person perspective (Piccione et al., 2019);
- Being able to move freely and explore with minimal constraints (Jicol et al., 2021); and
- Being able to do as you want within the virtual environment (Jicol et al., 2021).

Note, though, that in DesktopVR, contrary to possible expectations, there can be more sense of agency and presence from a third, rather than first, person perspective (Black, 2017).

Embodiment

Embodiment is the degree to which you feel that your avatar is your own representation of yourself. Kilteni et al. (2012) break the sense of embodiment into three components:

- The feeling of being located inside the avatar's body;
- The feeling of being in control of the avatar; and
- The feeling of owning the avatar's body.

Embodiment is damaged when there are glitches in the animation (for instance, hands moving through the body, or elbows at odd angles – challenging proprioception as will be discussed in Chapter 4), and interestingly, there is some debate over whether full body avatars offer more embodiment than partial (e.g. head and hands) avatars (e.g. Lugrin et al., 2018; Y. Pan & Steed, 2019).

One proof of embodiment in VR is that experiments have shown a "persistence of non-verbal norms in online virtual environments" – such as the social distance between avatars (Yee et al., 2007).

There also needs be no match between your own physical appearance and your avatar's, and in fact, VR provides a powerful opportunity to put yourself in someone else's body and to "walk a mile in someone else's shoes" (Wiederhold, 2020).

Flow

Flow is defined as "the state of intense involvement in an activity, an extreme version of immersion, losing self-consciousness, being unaware of fatigue and having a modified sense of time" (Csikszentmihalyi, 1990) and is linked to immersion and presence. Learners, those performing professional activities (e.g. musicians), and even gamers are believed to perform at their best when in a flow state and when the level of challenge of the activity is appropriate to their skill level. In VR, anything that jars with the experience, or where the user consciously has to think about how to use the environment, will immediately drop them out of the flow state and should be avoided.

HMD-VR versus DesktopVR

Whilst much of the recent media attention has been on HMD-VR, researchers are undecided as to whether it provides better outcomes than DesktopVR in all use cases.

A key analysis by Rueda et al. (2018) – see Figure 2.8 – clearly shows the distinction between how users are accessing the virtual environment and the experience which they are having once connected. This idea that

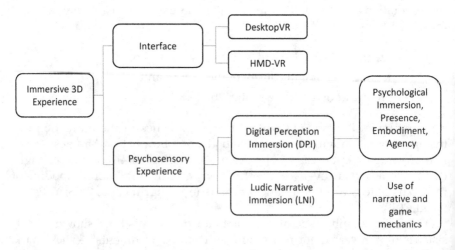

FIGURE 2.8
Analysis of the virtual reality experience (adapted from Rueda et al., 2018).

the user experience is distinct from the technology is reinforced by the user-system-experience (USE) model (Cowley et al., 2006), where the user experience is the result of the mental and physical state of the user and their interaction with the technical components of the system – including the authored experience. This is reminiscent of the earlier distinctions between technical and psychological immersion, and between the place illusion and the presence illusion. The fact that Rueda applies equal prominence to the narrative and ludic (game) elements in creating the experience as to the more perceptual elements is also notable.

In comparing HMD-VR with DesktopVR and other media, it has often been found that greater immersion (i.e. HMD-VR) does not necessarily relate to higher performance, seeming to be very task and user dependent (e.g. Chen, 2019; Pallavicini et al., 2019; Srivastava et al., 2019). What seems to correlate better with performance is presence (Grassini et al., 2020) – which seems to be as achievable with DesktopVR as with HMD-VR. Issues with cumbersome VR controls and safe movement can detract from that sense of presence, so good human-machine interface (HMI) design is essential. Users are also likely to be able to spend longer in DesktopVR sessions than they can in HMD-VR – partly due to the reduced incidence of cybersickness (CS), which is further discussed below.

Problems of VR

Quite apart from the efficacy debate, there are several key areas where VR experiences might cause problems to users, and any metaverse needs to be designed and used with these in mind. These are in addition to some of the broader issues of social virtual worlds and metaverses discussed in Chapter 5.

Cybersickness (CS)

A key issue in the use of VR is that of CS, prevalent in HMD-VR but not typically in DesktopVR. One review (although based on pre-2019 headsets) found that "60–95% of participants experience some level of CS during exposure to a virtual environment, whereas 6–12.9% of the participants prematurely end their exposure" (Caserman et al., 2021). There are indications that continuing improvements in resolution, refresh rates, and latency may be reducing the incidence of CS. Having a DesktopVR alternative to any HMD-VR experience would though still seem a sensible option, particularly since DesktopVR can also be experienced on mobile and tablet devices, and so can be more location (and time) independent.

Ethics

HMD-VR can be a very visceral experience, and users can feel more intimidated than in DesktopVR spaces as it's not so easy to just look away. Designers need to think about the situations they put users in and what choices they give them in order to ensure that any experience is being ethically (and morally) delivered – since VR can give users a "first-person experience of what it is like to perform certain immoral actions" (Brey, 1999). Another concern is that VR can lead to the creation of false memories and even to unintended behaviour change back in the real world (Pan & Hamilton, 2018), and Heller (2020) has even argued that "we should examine immersive media through a human rights-oriented lens".

Gender and Bias

Linked to the issue of ethics, it is very easy to make a gender-biased or misrepresentative VR experience. First-person experiences in particular need to consider whether they need male and female options, and whether that has any implications on the rest of the experience design (Stanney et al., 2020). Racial and other biases offer a further challenge, avoiding the stereotyping of non-player characters (NPCs) (Kim & Wei, 2011; Moreno & Flowerday, 2006). There can also be issues with HMD-VR equipment design that can make them less usable for female users (Stanney et al., 2020), although it should be noted that there is some evidence that females may feel more presence and can perform better in VR than males (Grassini & Laumann, 2020).

Privacy and Surveillance

HMD-VR allows an unprecedented level of user tracking. One concern is that tracking data could not only allow a user to be finger-printed by interaction behaviour (Pham, 2018), but also physical and emotional triggers identified (Heller, 2020). There is also the linked phenomenon known as "anonymous intimacy" where a user may reveal more in a conversation with an NPC in a virtual environment than they would do to a person in real life (Pan & Hamilton, 2018).

Health and Safety

Since HMD-VR users have minimal awareness of their physical environment (although in-built safety features are improving), users need to ensure that they are in a safe space, and potentially watched by someone else to keep them safe. A key consideration is how long an HMD-VR session can last, and some research has suggested a maximum of 55–70 minutes, depending on the quality of the experience design (Kourtesis et al., 2019) – however, time within a DesktopVR experience seems unlimited.

Summary

This chapter has considered some of the different definitions of the "metaverse" and presented 10 axioms that have guided the analysis of the Metaverse within this book. It has looked at the different types of virtual experience that are usually associated with the metaverse concept, and introduced the ideas of proto-metaverses, microverses, and the multiverse. The chapter has considered how *Second Life* and *OpenSim* can be seen as arguably the best examples of a proto-metaverse – and how they could be further improved. Finally, the chapter has considered the psychological underpinnings of the VR experience which are at the heart of most metaverse concepts, and which make them so compelling, and identified some of the challenges inherent within VR use. Chapter 3 will look at the different ways in which these virtual world spaces and XR technologies have been used across a wide range of different sectors and use cases in order to demonstrate that the Metaverse is not just a good idea, but that it can bring proven benefit.

Note

1 Note: Some parts of this section are derived from Evidence Based Models for VR Training co-written by Maggi and David with Victoria Mason-Robbie and produced by Daden Limited for the UK Ministry of Defence and made available under a CC BY 4.0 Licence.

References

Alaghband, M. (Host). (2022). *What is the metaverse—And what does it mean for business?* [Podcast]. McKinsey. https://www.mckinsey.com/capabilities/mckinsey-digital/our-insights/what-is-the-metaverse-and-what-does-it-mean-for-business

Au, W. J. (2023). *Making a metaverse that matters: From Snow Crash & Second Life to a virtual world worth fighting for.* John Wiley & Sons.

Aubuchon, R., & Moore, R. D. (Creators). (2010). *Caprica* [TV series]. Syfy.

Ball, M. (2022). *The Metaverse: And how it will revolutionize everything.* Liveright Publishing.

Ball, M. (2024). *On spatial computing, metaverse, the terms left behind and ideas renewed.* Mathew Ball. https://www.matthewball.vc/all/metaversespatialandmore

Black, D. (2017). Why can I see my avatar? Embodied visual engagement in the third-person video game. *Games and Culture, 12*(2), 179–199.

Brey, P. (1999). The ethics of representation and action in virtual reality. *Ethics and Information Technology, 1*(1), 5–14.

Broughton, M., Dromgoole, J., Hoyle, S., & Robinson, J. (Creators), & Dromgoole, J. (Producer). (2009). *Planet B* [Radio series]. BBC

Buchholz, F., Oppermann, L., & Prinz, W. (2022). There's more than one metaverse. *i-com*, *21*(3), 313–324.

Burdea, G., & Coiffet, P. (2003). *Virtual reality technology*. Wiley.

Burden, D. J. H. (2020). Building a digital immortal. In M. Savin-Baden & V. Mason-Robbie (Eds.), *Digital afterlife (pp. 143–160)*. CRC.

Burden, D. J. H., & Savin-Baden, M. (2019). *Virtual humans: Today and tomorrow*. CRC.

Buterin, V. (2013, September 19). Bootstrapping a decentralized autonomous corporation: Part I. *Bitcoin Magazine*. https://bitcoinmagazine.com/technical/bootstrapping-a-decentralized-autonomous-corporation-part-i-1379644274

Caserman, P., Garcia-Agundez, A., Gámez Zerban, A., & Göbel, S. (2021). Cybersickness in current-generation virtual reality head-mounted displays: Systematic review and outlook. *Virtual Reality*, *25*, 1153–1170.

Chen, M. F. (2019). *Understanding flow and immersion in virtual reality: An exploratory pilot study*. Ohio State University. https://www.researchgate.net/publication/347766448_Understanding_Flow_and_Immersion_in_Virtual_Reality_An_exploratory_pilot_study

Cowley, B., Charles, D., Black, M., & Hickey, R. (2006, June). User-system-experience model for user centered design in computer games. *International conference on adaptive hypermedia and adaptive web-based systems* (pp. 419–424). Springer.

Csikszentmihalyi, M. (1990). *Flow: The psychology of optimal experience*. Harper & Row.

Ffiske, T. (2022). *The Metaverse: A professional guide*. Amazon.

Forster, A. [@AntoniaRForster]. (2022, March 2). *"I don't believe anyone is a "Metaverse expert""* [Tweet]. X/Twitter. https://twitter.com/AntoniaRForster/status/1498987122124070916

Gilbert, S. (2022). *Crypto, web3, and the Metaverse*. Bennett Institute for Public Policy, Cambridge, Policy Brief. https://www.bennettinstitute.cam.ac.uk/wp-content/uploads/2022/03/Policy-brief-Crypto-web3-and-the-metaverse.pdf

Grassini, S., & Laumann, K. (2020). Are modern head-mounted displays sexist? A systematic review on gender differences in HMD-mediated virtual reality. *Frontiers in Psychology*, *11*, 1604.

Grassini, S., Laumann, K., & Rasmussen Skogstad, M. (2020). The use of virtual reality alone does not promote training performance (but sense of presence does). *Frontiers in Psychology*, *11*, 1743.

Gregory, S. (2023). *Second Life: A glimpse into virtual worlds, but not quite the Metaverse*. ASCILITE Technology Enhanced Learning Blog. https://blog.ascilite.org/second-life-a-glimpse-into-virtual-worlds-but-not-quite-the-metaverse/

Greig, E. (n.d.). *Ed on the Metaverse*. Deloitte. https://www2.deloitte.com/uk/en/pages/consulting/articles/what-is-the-metaverse.html

Heller, B. (2020). *Reimagining reality: Human rights and immersive technology*. Carr Center for Human Rights Policy, Harvard Kennedy School, Harvard University.

ITU. (2023). *Exploring the metaverse: Opportunities and challenges*. International Telecommunications Union. https://www.itu.int/dms_pub/itu-t/opb/fg/T-FG-MV-2023-PDF-E.pdf

Jarvinen, A., Baloiu, A., & Williams, V. (2023). *The Metaverse meets Web3: The state of convergence in the UK*. Digital Catapult. https://www.digicatapult.org.uk/wp-content/uploads/2023/07/The-metaverse-meets-Web3-report-July-2023.pdf

Jicol, C., Wan, C. H., Doling, B., Illingworth, C. H., Yoon, J., Headey, C., Lutteroth, C., Proulx, M., Petrini, K., & O'Neill, E. (2021, May). Effects of emotion and agency on presence in virtual reality. *Proceedings of the 2021 CHI conference on human factors in computing systems* (pp. 1–13). Association for Computing Machinery.

Kilteni, K., Groten, R., & Slater, M. (2012). The sense of embodiment in virtual reality. *Presence: Teleoperators and Virtual Environments, 21*(4), 373–387.

Kim, Y., & Wei, Q. (2011). The impact of learner attributes and learner choice in an agent-based environment. *Computers & Education, 56*(2), 505–514.

Kourtesis, P., Collina, S., Doumas, L. A., & MacPherson, S. E. (2019). Validation of the virtual reality neuroscience questionnaire: Maximum duration of immersive virtual reality sessions without the presence of pertinent adverse symptomatology. *Frontiers in Human Neuroscience, 13*, 417.

Kshetri, N. (2022a). Policy, ethical, social, and environmental considerations of Web3 and the metaverse. *IT Professional, 24*(3), 4–8.

Kshetri, N. (2022b). A typology of metaverses. *Computer, 55*(12), 150–155.

Lamb, H. (2022). *What can the Metaverse learn from Second Life?* IET. https://eandt.theiet.org/content/articles/2022/04/what-can-the-metaverse-learn-from-second-life/

Lee, L. H., Braud, T., Zhou, P., Wang, L., Xu, D., Lin, Z., Kumar, A., Bermejo, C., & Hui, P. (2021). *All one needs to know about metaverse: A complete survey on technological singularity, virtual ecosystem, and research agenda.* arXiv preprint arXiv:2110.05352.

Lee, S. G., Trimi, S., Byun, W. K., & Kang, M. (2011). Innovation and imitation effects in Metaverse service adoption. *Service Business, 5*, 155–172.

Liddle, J. (2022). *Second Life beat 'Metaverse' projects to the punch.* Game Rant. https://gamerant.com/second-life-sansar-metaverse-design-philosophy-history/

Lugrin, J. L., Ertl, M., Krop, P., Klüpfel, R., Stierstorfer, S., Weisz, B., Rück, M., Schmitt, J., Schmidt, N., & Latoschik, M. E. (2018). Any "body" there? Avatar visibility effects in a virtual reality game. *2018 IEEE conference on virtual reality and 3D user interfaces (VR)* (pp. 17–24). IEEE.

McKinsey. (2022). *What is the Metaverse?* McKinsey & Company. https://www.mckinsey.com/featured-insights/mckinsey-explainers/what-is-the-metaverse

Merrick, K. E., & Gu, N. (2011). Case studies using multiuser virtual worlds as an innovative platform for collaborative design. *Journal of Information Technology in Construction (ITcon), 16*(12), 165–188.

Momtaz, P. P. (2022). Some very simple economics of web3 and the metaverse. *FinTech, 1*(3), 225–234.

Moreno, R., & Flowerday, T. (2006). Students' choice of animated pedagogical agents in science learning: A test of the similarity-attraction hypothesis on gender and ethnicity. *Contemporary Educational Psychology, 31*(2), 186–207.

Mütterlein, J. (2018). *The three pillars of virtual reality? Investigating the roles of immersion, presence, and interactivity.* Proceedings of the 51st Hawaii International Conference on System Sciences, Big Island, Hawaii.

Nabben, K. (2023). Web3 as 'self-infrastructuring': The challenge is how. *Big Data & Society, 10*(1), 20539517231159002.

Narula, H. (2022). *Virtual society: The metaverse and the new frontiers of human experience.* Currency.

Naveen, C. (2023). *The Metaverse vs. Second Life: Exploring the differences.* LinkedIn. https://www.linkedin.com/pulse/metaverse-vs-second-life-exploring-differences-naveen-c/

Newton, E. (2021). *What is the spatial web and how will businesses use it?* Milestone. https://blog.milestoneinternet.com/web-design-promotion/what-is-the-spatial-web-how-will-businesses-use-it/.

Pallavicini, F., Pepe, A., & Minissi, M. E. (2019). Gaming in virtual reality: What changes in terms of usability, emotional response and sense of presence compared to non-immersive video games? *Simulation & Gaming, 50*(2), 136–159.

Pan, X., & Hamilton, A. F. D. C. (2018). Why and how to use virtual reality to study human social interaction: The challenges of exploring a new research landscape. *British Journal of Psychology, 109*(3), 395–417.

Pan, Y., & Steed, A. (2019). How foot tracking matters: The impact of an animated self-avatar on interaction, embodiment and presence in shared virtual environments. *Frontiers in Robotics and AI, 6*, 104.

Parisi, T. (2021). *The seven rules of the Metaverse.* Medium. https://medium.com/meta-verses/the-seven-rules-of-the-metaverse-7d4e06fa864c

Parkin, S. (2023, June 10). You call that a metaverse. *The Guardian.*

Park, S. M., & Kim, Y. G. (2022). A metaverse: Taxonomy, components, applications, and open challenges. *IEEE Access, 10*, 4209–4251.

Perla, P. (2011). *Peter Perla's art of wargaming.* History of Wargaming Project.

Pey, I. (2023). *A simple introduction to PBR materials, reflection probes & glTF in second life.* Inara Pey: Living in a Modemworld. https://modemworld.me/2023/11/28/a-simple-introduction-to-pbr-materials-reflection-probes-gltf-in-second-life/

Pham, D. M. (2018). Human identification using neural network-based classification of periodic behaviors in virtual reality. *2018 IEEE conference on virtual reality and 3D user interfaces (VR)* (pp. 657–658). IEEE.

Piccione, J., Collett, J., & De Foe, A. (2019). Virtual skills training: The role of presence and agency. *Heliyon, 5*(11), e02583.

Priestley, T. (2022a). *The Metaverse doesn't need your use case to work.* Medium. https://medium.com/@theo/the-metaverse-doesnt-need-your-use-case-to-work-22751eb2cd47

Priestley, T. (2022b). *The metaverse is already broken (and how to fix it—Chapter one).* Medium. https://medium.com/@theo/the-metaverse-is-already-broken-and-how-to-fix-it-chapter-one-170722ba1f7c

Priestley, T. (2022c). *Second Life is trading its future in for nostalgia.* Medium. https://medium.com/@theo/second-life-is-trading-its-future-in-for-nostalgia-d8b4313b0b4d

Radoff, J. (2021a). *What is the metaverse?* Medium. https://medium.com/building-the-metaverse/what-is-the-metaverse-a170108458e8

Radoff, J. (2021b). *Metaverse definition.* Medium. https://medium.com/building-the-metaverse/metaverse-definition-51e6b1c5baf3

Radoff, J. (2021c). *The metaverse value-chain.* Medium. https://medium.com/building-the-metaverse/the-metaverse-value-chain-afcf9e09e3a7

Ravenscraft, E. (2023). *What is the metaverse, exactly?* Wired. https://www.wired.com/story/what-is-the-metaverse/

Ray, P. P. (2023). Web3: A comprehensive review on background, technologies, applications, zero-trust architectures, challenges and future directions. *Internet of Things and Cyber-Physical Systems, 3*, 213–248. https://www.sciencedirect.com/science/article/pii/

Rueda, C., Godínes, J. C. V., & Rudman, P. D. (2018). Categorizing the educational affordances of 3 dimensional immersive digital environments. *Journal of Information Technology Education: Innovations in Practice, 17*(1), 83–112.

Sahu, S. (2021). *WebSocket: An in-depth beginner's guide.* Medium. https://javascript. plainenglish.io/websocket-an-in-depth-beginners-guide-96f617c4c7a5

Slater, M. (2009). Place illusion and plausibility can lead to realistic behaviour in immersive virtual environments. *Philosophical Transactions of the Royal Society of London, 364*(1535), 3549–3557.

Srivastava, P., Rimzhim, A., Vijay, P., Singh, S., & Chandra, S. (2019). Desktop VR is better than non-ambulatory HMD VR for spatial learning. *Frontiers in Robotics and AI, 6,* 50.

Stanney, K., Fidopiastis, C., & Foster, L. (2020). Virtual reality is sexist: But it does not have to be. *Frontiers in Robotics and AI, 7,* 4.

Strojny, P. M., Dużmańska-Misiarczyk, N., Lipp, N., & Strojny, A. (2020). Moderators of social facilitation effect in virtual reality: Co-presence and realism of virtual agents. *Frontiers in Psychology, 11,* 1252.

Virgilio, D. (2022). *What comparisons between second life and the metaverse miss.* Slate. https://slate.com/technology/2022/02/second-life-metaverse-facebook-comparisons.html

Vogelsang, B. (2021). *Developers: Creating a new reality with spatial computing.* Qualcomm. https://www.qualcomm.com/news/onq/2021/05/creating-new-reality-spatial-computing

Wiederhold, B. K. (2020). Embodiment empowers empathy in virtual reality. *Cyberpsychology, Behavior, and Social Networking, 23*(11), 725–726.

Witmer, B. G., & Singer, M. J. (1998). Measuring presence in virtual environments: A presence questionnaire. *Presence, 7*(3), 225–240.

Wood, G. (2014). *ÐApps: What Web 3.0 looks like.* Gavin Wood. https://gavwood.com/dappsweb3.html

Yee, N., Bailenson, J. N., Urbanek, M., Chang, F., & Merget, D. (2007). The unbearable likeness of being digital: The persistence of nonverbal social norms in online virtual environments. *CyberPsychology & Behavior, 10*(1), 115–121.

3

The Uses and Benefits of the Metaverse

Introduction

In looking at the benefits which the Metaverse can offer – to individuals, organisations, and society – and why it is that the Metaverse matters, there are two main questions:

- What are the benefits of applications based on metaverse technologies?
- Why would a single Metaverse or Multiverse be of more use that just a set of separate applications?

The structure of this chapter follows this segmentation. First, it looks at the foundational benefits (particularly from collaboration and consumer-to-consumer [C2C] uses) of metaverse technologies and then examines the benefits and use cases which have emerged across multiple sectors, from business-to-consumer (B2C) to Business to Business (B2B) applications. Second, it considers why delivering these benefits through a more integrated metaverse may be preferable to delivering them through discrete worlds and applications. Chapter 5 will further explore the issue of why the Metaverse as a more holistic entity matters, how it can contribute to a broader human and societal context, and some of the challenges that the Metaverse presents. Hopefully, together, these two chapters will go some way to answering the question of what the problems are that the Metaverse is trying to solve.

Figure 3.1 provides a graphical overview of the first part of the chapter.

Note: Other books in the Metaverse Series will explore more of these use cases in greater detail. Check out the website at www.themeta-verseseries.info for a current list of planned and published books. Synopses of some of the planned books are included in this book at the relevant place.

DOI: 10.1201/9781003395461-4

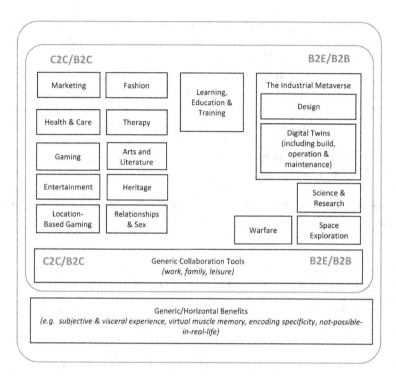

FIGURE 3.1
Metaversal use cases.

Foundational Benefits and Collaboration

The Generic Benefits of VR/MR/AR

In assessing the benefits of metaverse technologies across almost all use cases, it is important to compare the benefits to both the physical world alternatives *and* to the non-metaversal digital alternatives. For instance, whilst metaverse applications can save cost, time, and carbon from reduced travel, such benefits also apply to the more traditional two-dimensional (2D) alternatives – such as Zoom calls. The solely metaversal benefits typically come from where they bring the benefits of the physical world to digital interactions and the benefits of the digital world to physical interactions, including:

- Being immersed within the experience, as discussed in Chapter 2, which can improve understanding and recall (e.g. Haber et al., 2023). S. A. Smith (2019) has a wide-ranging review of the relationship between virtual reality (VR) and episodic memory;
- The changed group dynamics within a virtual space – which can encourage more inclusive participation (Nesson & Nesson, 2008);

- The ability to operate at a human scale in an environment which emphasizes the social nature of the interactions and enhances serendipitous discovery (Webber, 2013); and
- The ability to do and experience things which would be positively uneconomic, dangerous, or unethical in the physical world, or even simply just "not possible in real life" (NPIRL) – from creating (and destroying) mock-ups of buildings in minutes and practicing dangerous medical procedures to holding meetings on a virtual Mars or learning from inside the atomic structure of crystals (e.g. Maksimenko et al., 2021).

A cross-comparison of the physical, digital, and metaversal is summarised in Table 3.1.

TABLE 3.1

Comparing Metaversal Benefits to Physical and Digital Alternatives

	To ... Physical	Digital	Metaversal
Compare ... Physical		• Environmental immersion • Tactile/haptic feedback • Subjective, visceral experience • Encoding specificity	• Gold standard environment, immersion, risk and emotion • More complex, chaotic environments
Digital	• *Saves time* • *Saves cost* • *Saves carbon* • *Remote activities* • *Anytime/anyplace/ anywhere usage* • *Exact repetition* • *Detailed metrics* • *Easy AI integration*		• Simpler technologies • Simpler authoring • Natural video • Natural facial expressions
Metaversal	• *Saves time* • *Saves cost* • *Saves carbon* • *Remote activities* • *Anytime/anyplace/ anywhere usage (nearly)* • *Exact repetition* • *Detailed metrics* • *Easy AI integration* • Impossible, impractical, uneconomic activities (not possible in real life – NPIRL)	• Subjective, visceral experience • Virtual muscle memory • Encoding specificity • Broader range of cues from a richer environment • More natural team working/collaboration • More realistic (and unprompted) choices • Broader inter-personal communications	

Note: Italics show benefits shared by traditional 2D digital and metaversal solutions.

Collaboration in VR

Collaboration is perhaps the low-hanging fruit when it comes to the use of the Metaverse and can apply to almost everything from users just hanging out with friends or keeping in touch with family to pursuing hobbies and undertaking education to business meetings, conferences, and training.

The basic requirement is simply to have a space where users can meet and communicate. Whilst the marketing for these worlds often showcases sleek modern boardrooms and collaboration spaces modelled after their real-world counterparts, there is no reason why the meeting space shouldn't reflect the topic under discussion (meeting in a building under construction, on a factory floor, or in a showcase of the client's products), or somewhere that reflects the nature and level of interaction and creativity required (a fire-pit, a sandy beach, a pub, a cinema room, an orbital space-station, etc.).

Table 3.2 details collaboration tools which are already present in one or more virtual worlds, and the ideal collaborative metaverse would probably have them all.

TABLE 3.2

Generic Collaboration Features for the Metaverse

Spatial voice chat	So you know who is talking to your left or right, or so you can gather into smaller groups away from the main chat.
Ad-hoc "rings of silence"	So that no one else can hear what you are saying to those nearest to you even if you are close to other users.
Text chat	To support parallel discussions and provision of extra information, either to the whole group or selected participants.
Webcam feeds	So people can see the physical you. At various times, these have been rendered on avatar's stomachs, floating above the avatar's shoulder, fixed on a wall in the world or placed on the user interface rather than in-world.
Emoticons	2D and 3D emoticons to support non-verbal communications.
Desktop sharing	So you can share presentations and documents as though on a Zoom call.
Dial-in users	So people can call in from audio telephones or from a video conferencing system like Zoom.
In-World Web browser	So you can collaboratively access web content, including videos and services such as Google Docs so you can even work on documents collaboratively and synchronously with non-virtual world participants.
Virtual white boards and sticky notes	Of course, there's no reason to constrain either drawing or note placement to walls or boards when you can just draw or place objects anywhere in the 3D space.
2D drag and drop	Drag and drop of images, PDFs, audio and video files and other media types from your desktop into the virtual world.

(Continued)

TABLE 3.2 (Continued)

Generic Collaboration Features for the Metaverse

3D drag and drop	Drag and drop 3D objects (animated and unanimated) from 3D design and CAD tools or libraries – and then the ability to annotate them with virtual sticky notes.
In-world building (and even scripting)	For creative exploration and illustration of ideas as they occur.
Custom voting tools	Custom devices to assist in voting and thematic grouping of participants – e.g. the Opinionator (Cunningham & Harrison, 2010).
Data visualisation tools	Rendering data in 3D rather than just 2D, and, where relevant, text and code visualisation (e.g. Balogh & Beszedes, 2013).
Session recording	Audio, video, and text capture of the session.
3D session capture	3D capture of the session for replay – so you can watch yourself in the meeting later!

There is a significant body of literature around the design, use, and effectiveness of these types of tools in virtual worlds, often under the banner of collaborative virtual environments (CVEs), including:

- The role of play and sociability in CVEs (Brown & Bell, 2006);
- Using colour and space design to both help anchor participants expectations from the physical world and provide space to encourage non-physical world activities such as creating objects on demand (Uribe Larach & Cabra, 2010);
- Exploring the use of Media Synchronicity Theory that showed that CVEs aided "convergence processes in teams working on a decision making task, leading to increased shared understanding between team members" and hence an increase in the performance of decision-making teams (Schouten et al., 2010);
- Developing a "theoretical model of effective team collaboration in 3D virtual environments" focused around information processing, communication support, and shared understanding (Van der Land et al., 2011); and
- Using virtual environments to support collaborative meetings in healthcare quality improvement, highlighting the potential challenges to those with weaker information technology (IT) skills (Taylor et al., 2020).

An entire Special Issue of the *Journal of the Association for Information Systems* was on Team Collaboration in Virtual Worlds, including papers on *A Longitudinal Field Study of Virtual World Use for Team Collaboration* and on a *Structured Approach for Designing Collaboration Experiences for Virtual Worlds* (Boughzala et al., 2012).

Some of the current (2023) platforms focused on the generic collaboration use case include *Arthur* (2020, https://www.arthur.digital/), *Glue* (2020, https://glue.work/), and *MeetInVR* (2019, https://www.meetinvr.com/), but it is a volatile space.

Collaboration in AR/MR

There has also been significant research on the use of augmented reality/ mixed reality (AR/MR) for collaboration on physical tasks (e.g. Ladwig & Geiger, 2019). Wang et al. (2021) provide a useful analysis of over 215 papers, covering a range of sectors including manufacturing, telemedicine, architecture, and tele-education. They identify five main ways of sharing non-verbal cues between the field and remote workers:

- Virtual replicas or physical proxy (VRP);
- AR annotations or a cursor pointer (ARACP);
- Avatar position and movement;
- Gesture; and
- Gaze.

Current issues with MR are field of view (as discussed in Chapter 1) and illumination limitations – even when participants are co-located (Alizadehsalehi et al., 2020) – although video pass-through approaches seem to have largely solved these issues. The already realisable vision – as seen in Meta's promotional videos for the Metaverse (Meta, 2021), and proven in MR applications such as Arkio and Wooorld – is where the participants are in different physical locations but through the MR headsets can appear in the physical locations of the other participants.

The main argument for MR (as against VR) collaboration is that the user maintains local situational awareness – which may be vital in some use cases – and can respond to both virtual and physical world prompts and events – and indeed MR may even be able to enhance situational awareness (Wallmyr et al., 2019). Another argument is that users get (at least in the co-located model) to interact with the physical people and so they can better detect non-verbal cues – assuming that the MR headset doesn't mask most of the users' faces making facial expression hard to see. This is compounded by the narrow field of view which makes it hard to look at both participants and any virtual information at the same time (although again video pass-through largely solves this, and the Apple Vision Pro even puts your "eyes" on the front of the headset!).

As people begin to experiment with this newer generation of MR devices, there is a significant opportunity to enhance remote collaboration. Whether the *Avatar* style holographic command centre will be better met by MR or simply moving everyone into a VR space will be interesting to see – and of course both routes may be valid depending on the use case.

Having considered the generic benefits of metaversal spaces, the chapter now examines the more sector-specific use cases. Since learning, training, and education overlap between B2C, B2E, and C2C, they will be considered first, before moving on to specific B2C and B2B use cases.

Learning, Education, and Training

At the most trivial level, a metaverse which supports collaboration can also support education. Much of the early history of education in virtual worlds was in subverting game worlds which did not explicitly support education (e.g. *World of Warcraft*) to use them for teaching and learning (e.g. Wiklund & Ekenberg, 2009).

At the heart of using the Metaverse for learning is that it supports a wide range of related pedagogical approaches such as Kolb's Learning Cycle (Kolb, 2014), constructivism (Loke, 2015), experiential learning (Dewey, 1986), cognitive load theory (P. Chandler & Sweller, 1991), situated cognition/encoding specificity (Greeno et al., 1993), and problem-based learning (Savin-Baden, 2007).

The key affordances of immersive 3D environments have been identified as being able to let the user experience what is being taught, to learn in context, to be able to relate to knowledge spatially, to be engaged with the learning, and to collaborate in the learning (Dalgarno & Lee, 2010). Teaching and learning in the Metaverse enable tutors and students to leverage those affordances in order to develop better learning, a deeper understanding, and better recall. The psychological underpinnings of VR, and particularly the relationship between technical immersion and psychological immersion, were discussed in Chapter 2. That headset-mounted VR displays (HMD-VR) and DesktopVR should be user choices and not designer choices is a vital considerations. A key design decision in VR learning is getting the right balance and approach to the fidelity of the environment, task, and interactions and ensuring that they match to the needs of the learning (Stone, 2008). Beck et al. (2021) of the Immersive Learning Research Network provide a useful Immersive Learning Knowledge Tree, a conceptual framework for mapping knowledge and tools within XR learning.

Many of the broader benefits of the Metaverse for learning beyond "better learning" are captured by the generic metaversal benefits. Particularly relevant elements are that of being able to put the user in the environment that is the focus of the learning – no matter how dangerous, costly, or plain impractical that would be in the physical world, and to change the group dynamics so as to give quieter students more chance to participate and encourage group learning and group co-creation in ways that would be hard to replicate in physical or more traditional digital learning spaces.

Metaverse learning can be applied at all levels from K12/primary education through to tertiary education, onboarding, and into vocational and work training and continuing professional development, covering both hard and soft skills. Some recent studies of learning and training using metaverse technologies and platforms include:

- Mining educational implications of Minecraft – (Baek et al., 2020);
- A systematic review on the use of Roblox in learning (Han et al., 2023);
- A review on virtual reality skill training applications – covering first responder training, medical training, military training, and workforce training (Xie et al., 2021); and
- An examination of the challenges of using VR for chemical, biological, radioactive, and nuclear (CBRN) training (Regal et al., 2023).

For a survey of *Second Life*-era use cases, the material produced at the time by John Kirriemuir recording the global use of *Second Life* and *OpenSim* for education, principally the Virtual World Watch, is still an excellent resource (Kirriemuir, 2009).

Engage (https://engagevr.io/), with its so-far unique ability to record and play back a session and watch yourself within it, is probably the most visible of the current metaverse platforms that are focused on education and training. Amongst other companies active in the space (particularly for enterprise training) are Luminous Group (https://www.luminousxr.com/), Immerse (https://immerse.io/), Strivr (https://www.strivr.com/), TrainBeyond (https://www.trainbeyond.com/), Acadicus (https://acadicus.com/), and ClassVR (https://www.classvr.com/).

However, a lot of work is still taking place in custom builds and proprietary platforms built with Unity and Unreal, rather than on shared public or semi-public platforms, and as a result both hiding activity levels and reducing the ability to share learning and training experiences and assets between organisations.

It should be noted that using game-based technologies for learning *is not* the same as gamification, which is more about generating intrinsic motivation (Hamari et al., 2014) – although you can use gamification processes within metaverse learning applications.

Business to Consumer Use Cases

Marketing

Marketing is always an early adopter of new technology, and as described in Chapter 1, marketing was one of the big uses of *Second Life* back in the early 2000s. This has continued with the current crop of metaverse type environments, such as the marketing campaigns by Walmart (Blackwood, 2023) and Nike (Sutcliffe, 2022) in *Roblox* and by Marvel and the NFL in *Fortnite* (Goodman, 2023). However, Microsoft and Mojang have so far restricted corporate marketing on *Minecraft* (Grubb, 2016).

Marketing activities are largely brand-awareness campaigns – so the tens and hundreds of millions of active users on platforms like *Roblox* and *Fortnite* are hard to ignore. While there is already an established system for billboard-type adverts in video games (Dixie, 2023), the marketing approaches to virtual worlds do tend to take a different tack as there is no way of guaranteeing "eyes-on" a particular billboard (unlike, for example, in a racing game), and so instead marketing is more experiential focused, often in dedicated spaces, rather than an act of passive viewing (A. Lee, 2023).

The use of AR for marketing has been as more of a sales-support tool – as in the Ikea example already quoted. Using AR or MR, a company can put its own products in a potential customer's house before they buy, or put a product anywhere that people are gathering without the need (and cost and security) of physically moving the product there.

An oft-talked-about use case is that of creating virtual adverts outside of shops, but the persistent AR/MR devices that consumers would need to be wearing for it to be effective – such as the failed Google Glass or Ray-Ban Meta Smart Glasses – are not yet commonplace and have seen some social resistance and privacy concerns (de Ruyter et al., 2020). However, some creative opportunities for using AR/MR for one-off events – such as seen at Dubai's Shopping Festival – do exist (ARKx, 2022).

Fashion

Metaverses are social virtual worlds, and as such the appearance of a user's avatar can be a key consideration. Many of the social virtual worlds already support vibrant fashion communities, and many physical world brands such as Nike, Prada, and Tommy Hilfiger have experimented with making their products available to virtual users (L. Smith, 2022). The term "phygital" has been coined to identify products which link both the virtual and physical worlds (Moravcikova & Kliestikova, 2017). Today, when you buy some products (e.g. a book or a map) you can get both the physical and digital copies – and it may not be too long before the same happens when you buy a new top or shoes. Or, perhaps, we'll buy virtual clothes for impact, look and variability, and physical clothes for permanence and sustainability (Cannone, 2021).

This is one area where a lack of standards is potentially hampering the market, since virtual clothes do not tend to be portable from one world to another – a jacket bought in *Fortnite* won't be usable in *Roblox* (Prem, 2023). External intermediation services, such as ReadyPlayerMe (https://ready-player.me/), where the avatar and clothing are managed by a third party and then supported by individual virtual worlds, are one way forward – but perhaps not the most ideal solution. The virtual fashion market (including marketing and virtual goods) has been predicted to be worth $55 billion by 2030 (Deloitte, 2022).

The use of virtual worlds as a learning ground for physical fashion designers and retailers should also not be overlooked. A number of fashion schools have used virtual worlds to give their students the opportunity to design new items, show them in a virtual runway show, and then sell them in virtual shops to real people (e.g. Uhomoibhi & Ross, 2013[1]).

The other significant element of virtual fashion is the concept of "virtual try-on", typically using AR technologies to see how cosmetics and clothes would look on you. Offerings in this area have already been explored by companies such as MAC and L'Oreal (Cannone, 2021), Prada, Levi's, and Ray-Ban (Lavoye et al., 2023), and applications such as TINT (https://www.banuba.com/tint-makeup-virtual-try-on) and Google's "Try On".

Health and Care

There have been a number of studies which show that exercise in virtual worlds can actually make a difference to physical health and mental well-being (e.g. Appel et al., 2020; Costa et al., 2019; Wagener et al., 2021). The medical community were also early adopters of VR for surgery training (Paro et al., 2022), and of virtual worlds for a variety of medical training scenarios including paramedic training (e.g. Conradi, 2009[2]) and nursing training (Plotzky et al., 2021). VR has even been used to provide pain relief during surgery (Freitas & Spadoni, 2019). There have also been studies on the use of VR to support cognitive training (Bauer & Andringa, 2020), physiotherapy (Heiyanthuduwa et al., 2020), and entertainment (Lai et al., 2019) within the care of the elderly. There are useful systematic reviews of VR in healthcare by Kononowicz et al. (2019) and Barteit et al. (2021).

Health and care is probably a good example where the distinctions between environment, interaction, and task fidelity apply. Surgery is typically about fine manipulation, and so the technical demands on a VR system are very high; ideally the surgical tools need a haptic response, and with modern keyhole surgery, the surgeon can use the real tools but have them instrumented into the virtual environment. In contrast, other medical and care tasks – such as the correct procedures to follow for a post-partum haemorrhage or a home visit – are more about process, and so make lesser demands of the simulation.

In the medical sector, there is also extensive use of mannequins for training, which have themselves become more instrumented and even integrated with virtual environments – so that the student can interact with a patient in VR and then with an AR/MR-augmented mannequin of the same patient (e.g. Schild et al., 2022). As with much virtual world activity, medical simulations have tended to be driven by individual and independent initiatives, but there have been attempts to create consolidated virtual hospitals or medical centres where a range of medical simulations can be shared across a wider institutional base – something which a Metaverse would make far more achievable. There have also been attempts to use standards such as the Medbiquitous Virtual Patient (Ellaway et al., 2008) or Artificial Intelligence Markup Language (Danforth et al., 2009) to allow medical exercises to be defined in relatively platform neutral ways to encourage portability.

As well as educating medical staff, virtual environments can be used to educate patients – letting them walk through a hospital visit or medical procedure to better understand what is going to happen to them to relieve anxiety or make more informed choices (Mahajan et al., 2021). There have also been projects to use virtual environments to help with life-style choices – for instance, diet or smoking (McGuirt et al., 2020) – enabling people to walk around inside their virtual body after the impact of several decades of smoking, or to see the changes in their look and abilities after years of a poor diet.

Considering care in a different setting, there have also been numerous studies looking at the use of VR within prisons in areas such as education (McLauchlan & Farley, 2022), improving behaviour management (Farley, 2018), and re-entry back into society (Teng & Gordon, 2021).

Therapy

Whilst the "Proetus Effect" (Yee & Bailenson, 2007) has shown that users with idealized avatars will tend to live up to this idealized self and have a greater sense of self-worth in the virtual world, there is also evidence that virtual experiences can help maintain that improved self-worth in the physical world (e.g. C. J. Falconer et al., 2016). VR has also been used in areas such as Virtual Reality Exposure Therapy (VRET) to help treat combat-related posttraumatic stress disorder (PTSD) (Mozgai et al., 2020), social anxiety (although with uncertain results), addiction, autism, and attention-deficit hyperactivity disorder (ADHD) (Emmelkamp et al., 2020).

Therapists can use virtual worlds as safe shared spaces to meet with clients, adapting the environment to the client's needs, and introducing imagery, audio, video, and even objects as required to support a session (Sampaio et al., 2021). There is even the potential to consider how the therapist could be supported by an automated avatar so that the client could access support at any time of the day or night (e.g. Ren, 2020).

Entertainment

The use of virtual worlds to support passive entertainment experiences such as music concerts and sporting events also has a long history. IBM used *Second Life* to present Wimbledon in 2008 (Cremorne, 2008), and as mentioned, Suzanne Vega performed in *Second Life* as far back as 2006. Alongside the use of generic platforms such as *Fortnite* by performers such as Ariana Grande and Travis Scott and sporting brands such as NFL, there are also a number of platforms that are seeking to make concerts or sports their main business model. Examples include the refocussed *Sansar* (2014, https://www.sansar.com/), *Vark* (2018, https://vark.co.jp/), and *AmazeVR* (2022, https://www.amazevr.com/). *AmazeVR* produced a stand-alone VR performance by Megan Thee Stallion called *Enter Thee Hottieverse* (sic) in 2022 (Skarredghost, 2022). In the AR space, Immersal (https://immersal.com/) is focussed on apps to enhance the stadium experience for sports games.

One problem that these companies have is that having more than a few hundred avatars in one place, all interacting with each other, is still a huge computing and network challenge, and this is discussed in more detail in Chapter 4. So, whilst the idea of using the Metaverse for huge crowds to attend big music and sporting events appears in much of the publicity of the Metaverse, the technical challenges of achieving it in a way that mirrors the physical experience are non-trivial, and perhaps a reason why performers should be looking for more metaverse-native ways of expressing their art.

Gaming

Many of the platforms with metaversal elements are those which have been developed primarily to support games – whether it's *Roblox, Fortnite,* or *Minecraft*. A first-person shooter played solo does not feel very metaverse-like, but as soon as that game becomes multi-player, and especially if there's a pause or an opportunity to sit down, have a chat, and go off-script the game feels more social and more metaverse-like. As a result, there is a very blurred area between games which are purely games and those which are meta-versal experiences. One of the big benefits of taking a metaverse approach to designing gaming platforms is that it encourages the creation of user-generated games and content – as with *Fortnite, Roblox,* and *Rec Room* – further strengthening the platform with minimal investment from platform owners and building user engagement. It may be that at some point in the future, all games are just areas within a more generic Metaverse – just as all physical games are within the physical universe.

Tabletop Gaming

One other form of gaming that should be mentioned is that of tabletop gaming – whether it's for *Ticket to Ride, Dungeons and Dragons,* or *Risk*. There are already a number of platforms which exist to enable such gaming to happen remotely, including:

- *Vassal* (2002, https://vassalengine.org/) – a relatively early and straightforward 2D implementation of games, wargames focused, but for which anyone can create or port games;

- *Roll20* (2012, https://roll20.net/) – 2D again, and optimized for role-playing games, but usable by other types – again users can create their own game, but official modules for commercial games are also available. Roll20 reported 10 million registered users in 2022 (Meehan, 2022); and
- *Tabletop Simulator* (2015, https://www.tabletopsimulator.com/), which gives users a fully realized 3D table with 3D playing pieces, but since it doesn't actually implement the rules of a game (as largely with both of the above), users can use the space and pieces however they want. Tabletop Simulator also has around 10 million registered users and around 875,000 active users (Playtracker, 2023).

What stops most of these spaces from being metaversal is that the user is typically only present through their agency in the game – their ability to move pieces and roll the dice. At most, they might also be present as an audio stream or a webcam stream, but they aren't present as avatars or able to just walk around the table and do something else. As the ability to script becomes more common within metaverse platforms, there is no reason why the players shouldn't sit around their gaming table in a generic metaverse platform as avatars. As a result, here may be again less need for a dedicated platform – and there have already been developments in this area – such as *TableTop Craft* in *Minecraft* and *VRC Dominion* in *VRChat*. What this combination of worlds brings is not so much in enhancing the game play but in enabling participants to move more smoothly (and routinely) between game play and other metaversal activities, and as will be discussed below, it is this integrative aspect of the Metaverse which promises to help lift it beyond a series of bespoke metaverse technology experiences.

Mention should also be made of AR and MR in the tabletop gaming context, such as the system being developed by Tilt Five (https://www.tiltfive.com/) and the possibilities in the new breed of XR headsets. They may enable the flexibility of a digital gaming space to be brought into the physical world by projecting shared visuals onto a physically empty table.

Location-based VR Gaming

A final area to consider in terms of the Metaverse and entertainment is location-based VR gaming. This is the modern equivalent of the laser-tag centre, where players don VR headsets, hold instrumented weapons, and then explore a large space populated with virtual enemies or monsters, or both (Williams, 2023). The trick is that the space itself is effectively neutral in colour and context – just a set of walls, stairs, tables, chairs, and other objects – and the VR headset then produces the graphics to provide the context of the game. But the VR graphics are aligned to the physical world, and if you walk into a virtual wall, you'll feel a real wall, and if you encounter some virtual stairs, you'll have to physically walk down them.

In some ways, this is the closest experience that currently exists to the *Star Trek* holodeck experience. A significant amount of investment has been going into this industry, with one of the (self-declared) more cautious forecasts seeing the market growing from around $2 billion in 2018 to nearly $9 billion by 2028 (Mordor, 2023). Whether they count as part of a metaverse is moot – they are certainly using metaverse technology and are highly social in nature – but they are fundamentally stand-alone experiences with no persistence and minimal opportunity to subvert. However, in a more complete Metaverse, such spaces could be co-opted to support a wider range of both entertainment and serious (e.g. training) activities and so just become a different user interface for the Metaverse.

Arts and Literature

The most visible use of metaverse technologies by artists has been in virtual installations and art galleries, such as a virtual Tate Gallery in *Minecraft* (Styles, 2016) and the use of HMD-VR to access virtual Art Galleries and explore famous works of art (ARTDEX, n.d.). However, whilst being able to walk into a painting and experience it from inside can offer people a unique perspective on the art, the real opportunities come in creating art that is only possible using metaverse technologies and in metaversal spaces. Hagerty (2012) explores some of the more philosophical perspectives on art within virtual spaces, and interesting examples of XR-native performances include:

- Shakespeare's *Hamlet* in *Grand Theft Auto Online* (Vincent, 2021);
- The Royal Shakespeare Company's performance of *A Midsummer Night's Dream* which had the audience at home controlling fairy sprites which were visible to the performers, along with the virtual set, in their HMDs (https://audienceofthefuture.live/dream/);
- Immersive theatre company Punchdrunk's *#BelieveYourEyes* production for Samsung, a ghost story mixing VR video and interaction with a physical performer (https://www.punchdrunk.com/project/believe-your-eyes/);
- The Opera Beyond project by the Finnish National Opera and Ballet (https://operabeyond.com/); and
- The short-form immersive musical, an "immersical", being developed at the University of York (Lock & Stewart-David, 2022).

Another aspect is how the Metaverse can help art historians and academics to better understand the art of the past. A notable project in the early days of *Second Life* was Theatron, which recreated theatres and performance spaces of the past and let researchers then use them to try and put on the plays of the time and so get a better understanding of the interaction between play and play-house (Childs, 2008).

History and Heritage

One of the much-touted abilities of virtual environments is their ability to drop you into a life-like representation of the past. Museums and historic locations such as Angkor Wat (Chandler & Clulow, 2019) and Avebury Ring (Falconer et al., 2020)[3] have been built using VR to help researchers and visitors better understand the past, or help educate the community that lives amongst a site (Forte et al., 2010). Heritage Immortalised (https://www.facebook.com/hereimmc/) has run competitions in Minecraft to build both UNESCO World Heritage Sites and Intangible Cultural Heritage representations. AR has also been used in site-specific ways to overlay now missing buildings on the modern landscape, or to better examine objects which would otherwise be in glass cases (Luna et al., 2019). There has been a tension as to the extent to which museums (and galleries) should use VR to enable remote access to their collections (Ocausse, 2016).

In a Metaverse, one would ideally like every museum to have its collection (and not just what fits on public display) accessible by XR, and ideally not only as gallery artefacts but shown in context. The Metaverse should also allow institutions to collaborate, so that, for instance, a virtual iron age village can be filled with the best artefacts from across Europe's museums and presented in whatever language, and to whatever educational level, the user desires. The virtual locations need not be passive but could be filled with human or artificial intelligence (AI)-controlled avatars to provide the "living history" experience, explaining the cultural, artistic, or scientific significance. Visitors could even be invited to role-play within the environment themselves. Making such resources available on demand would also enable educators to better integrate them into all levels of the curriculum, so the "museum trip" doesn't (just) become a once-a-year thing but is something that can be brought into every relevant lesson. There are of course issues of scalability here, and students should absolutely still have the chance to see and potentially handle the physical objects and walk the physical sites.

Another important aspect is the use of metaverse technologies to help professionals explore and understand the past. The use of photogrammetry and light detection and ranging (LIDAR) to capture accurate 3D models of objects or terrains is well developed. Enabling researchers to experience this information in a subjective as well as an objective way inside a virtual environment – and one into which they can readily invite fellow researchers from across the globe (and in which they may have available all of the collaboration tools mentioned earlier) – is already helping archaeologists to collaboratively interpret the artefacts that they are finding (De Bonis et al., 2022).

Relationships and Sex

As already described, virtual worlds give people the opportunity to play with their identities, and sex and pornography have been significant elements in the development of virtual worlds. This section will look at the more organized uses of metaverse technologies in support of relationships and sex, and Chapter 5 will return to the issue of the metaverse and identity.

The dating application market was worth nearly $5bn in 2022, mostly from Tinder owner's Match group (Curry, 2023), and Tinder has around 75 million monthly active users (Iqbal, 2023). Several companies, such as Flirtual (https://flirtu.al/) and Nevermet (https://www.nevermet.io/), have looked at how VR can be used to provide a "virtual first date" experience – providing something potentially as engaging as a video call or real-world meeting, but without the same level of risk (emotional and physical). Virtual dating apps can also provide a more "organic" way of introducing people (Sharabi, 2022).

In considering the use of VR for pornography, HMD-VR headsets can be used to privately view either ordinary video or stereoscopic video (see Chapter 5), the latter giving a greater sense of immersion and a more visceral reaction to what is being viewed (Simon & Greitemeyer, 2019). Moving beyond video, individual users are already exploring avatar sex, and so it should be no surprise that businesses are also investigating this as a new business model. One of the first was the Red Light Centre, a virtual world focused on human-controlled avatar-based sexual encounters (Schultz, 2019). Another approach is the use of computer-controlled avatars in applications such as Virt-a-Mate, and there seems to be a growth in applications that include the virtual "girlfriend experience" (Milrod & Monto, 2012) and story-path choices, merging narrative and pornographic genres (Joho, 2021).

Evans (2023) reviewed 23 articles on VR pornography, including the role of VR as an "empathy machine", and developments such as teledildonics and their implications for fidelity. Pornographic VR has also been used therapeutically to help with sperm donors and cancer victims (Rosenkjær et al., 2022).

Alongside pornography are the serious issues concerning the exploitation of sex workers and the objectification and self-objectification of women. Cijntje and van Gisbergen (2023) studied the impact of VR pornography (VRP) on relationship fidelity and betrayal, considering the differences between passively watching VRP and engaging in interactive VRP, and where avatars resemble real partners. Fox et al. (2013) studied how women's self-perception and attitudes changed viewing sexualized or non-sexualized avatars in a virtual world, especially when the avatars had the participant's face. Nesbitt (n.d.) notes that with the emergence of VR "society begins to encounter new questions of cybersex work. Is regulation needed to neutralize dangerous sectors of virtual reality cybersex work?".

Business to Business Use Cases

The Industrial Metaverse

The "industrial metaverse" has been defined as "a subset of the metaverse focused on production, maintenance and collaboration between experts in the field of industry", with digital twins (see below) as perhaps its most important part (Bellalouna & Puljiz, 2023). The purpose of the industrial metaverse is "to speed up processes like repairs/maintenance, starting new manufacturing lines, remote monitoring/troubleshooting, remote control, and new user/manager training through simulation" (J. Lee & Kundu, 2022). As such, it draws on many of the collaborative tools described at the beginning of this chapter, as well as the training and education opportunities, and adds the digital twin concept. A 2023 "Metaverse at Work" survey by Nokia and EY (and hence interested parties) looked at businesses in the automotive, manufacturing, logistics, and utilities sectors. The survey found that organisations were seeing benefits in "capital expenditure (capex) reduction, sustainability and safety improvement", although "enterprises saw the highest potential in the use of extended reality (XR) for training to onboard and upskill the workforce, while three out of the four industries surveyed chose the use of virtual research and development to enhance product design and processes" (O'Halloran, 2023). Some see that the industrial metaverse might eclipse the consumer one (Lawton, 2022).

Design

The use of 3D tools to support product and built environment design dates back to at least the 1960s (Tornincasa & Di Monaco, 2010). One of the main downsides of the high-gloss renders that are typical of modern design outputs is that they are typically not rendered in real time, but, like computer-generated imagery (CGI) movies, are rendered (often overnight) and then made into video (Ratcliffe & Simons, 2017). At the other end of the spectrum, the tools that support the actual machining of a part, or the construction of a building, take a very low-level, database-like approach to the problem, traditionally using wire-frame graphics although this is now being supplemented by real-time renders (Johansson et al., 2015). The Building Information Modelling (BIM) standard (https://www.bsig-roup.com/en-GB/iso-19650-BIM/) is a way of trying to manage the flow of information between the design, build, and maintain sections of the product lifecycle (Razali et al., 2019). BIM information can be used to support both VR and MR visualisations of a new building (Y. Huang, 2020; Wen & Gheisari, 2020).

However, these two approaches typically leave out the user, whereas the virtual world offers an ideal opportunity to embed participation in the

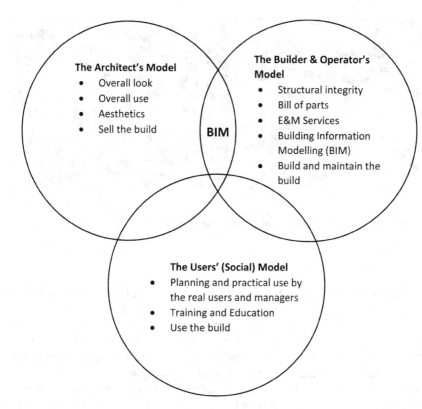

FIGURE 3.2
The three-ring design model.

design workflow (Hudson-Smith, 2022). What is needed instead is a three-ring approach (as shown in Figure 3.2) where the user also has access to a model optimized to their needs and can find out what it is like to actually use the product or building (Burden, 2020).

Virtual worlds are ideally suited to this approach as they allow multiple people to explore an item or location at the same time, sharing notes and approaching the product on their own terms – rather than that of the designer or builder (Anderson et al., 2014). Examples of such approaches include City4.0/Curiocity – which was created using Unity (Hunter et al., 2022), Tirol Town in Brazil – which was created in *Minecraft* (de Andrade et al., 2020) and the Virtual Library of Birmingham (see Figure 3.3) – which was created in *Second Life* (Hand, 2011)[4]. These models need not just be passive representations. Users can be given design choices to try out, and the environment can contain 3D post-it notes to allow users to annotate (and comment and vote up/down) particular issues or can try and navigate a building or use a device when impaired by some disability.

FIGURE 3.3
Comparing virtual and physical builds of the Library of Birmingham.

Digital Twins

The Digital Twin concept dates back to 2002 and Florida Institute of Technology's Center for Advanced Manufacturing (Grieves, 2003; Mihai et al., 2022). At its core is the idea that an organisation maintains a digital copy of a real piece of equipment (or even place or team), feeds that model with all of the data about the physical instance, and so can perform continual "what-ifs" in terms of how the physical system may respond over time either in terms of chronic issues such as maintenance failures or acute issues such as sudden changes in the operating conditions. The target system could be anything from the engine on a ship – or the ship as a whole – to an entire factory and all its production lines, or even a whole city. Both Dubai and Shanghai have announced their intention to build digital twins of themselves (Gazit, 2024), and London, New York, Tokyo, Seoul, Santa Monica, and Singapore all have some form of digital twin city underway (Ibrahim, 2022) – although what actually ends up being actually built, beyond a visual representation, is moot. Juárez-Juárez et al. (2021) provide a typology of digital twins and a good overview of the technologies and approaches potentially involved, including data modelling, data management, communications, and multi-agent systems.

Whilst the Digital Twin need only be realized in numbers and code, there is a natural inclination to present it at least through a 2D diagrammatic interface, or even as a 3D model. Where the overlap with the Metaverse really starts to happen is when managers and maintainers can walk around that model, getting a subjective as well as an objective view as to what is happening. They can use their virtual tablet computers, heads-up displays (HUDs), or AR displays to examine both the physical and digital versions of performance (Eyre & Freeman, 2018) or to experience the Digital Twin data as a Fused Twin in the same space in the physical world as the Physical Twin (Grübel et al., 2022). The primary benefit is that the operator is able to have a holistic perspective on the whole of the system in a way that is more immediate, accessible, context-aware, memorable, and potentially insightful than a spreadsheet full of numbers or a 2D graphic.

Science and Research

Whilst much of the scientific use of virtual worlds is covered by the collaboration features discussed earlier, or leverages some of the other use cases already described, there are a number of more science and research specific applications for metaverse technologies and virtual worlds. One of the most obvious is the ability to subjectively experience things at a micro or macro scale – be it examining bonds in a molecule (e.g. Seritan et al., 2021) or the interaction and evolution of galaxies (e.g. Jarrett et al., 2021).

The use of virtual worlds to display any data in an immersive, interactive visualisation is another significant area of potential use – a disciple referred to as Immersive Visual Analytics (Cybulski et al., 2014; Thomas & Cook, 2005). Examples include the Immersive Analytics Toolkit (Cordeil & Dwyer, 2019), or David's own work with Datascape (Burden, 2021) – as shown in Figure 3.4. Such visualisations operate on an egocentric principle (all the information is relative to viewer), rather than on an allocentric basis (where all the information is relative to an arbitrary origin) (Klatzky et al., 1998). Since people interact with the physical world on a primarily egocentric basis, it may be that they can better explore, interpret, and remember data when it is presented in

FIGURE 3.4
Viewing cybersecurity data within VR using Datascape.

an egocentric way. With the right scripting tools, any virtual world or meta-verse environment could support such collaborative 3D data visualisations.

Related to this is the idea of "data gardens" (Driver, 2009), which may be better described as information gardens – a place where you can walk around and learn about a topic, augment it with your own comments and research and meet other people to discuss it – a cross between a poster session, a peer-reviewed journal, a wiki, and a museum. In many ways, these are an extension of the "memory palace" model for improving memory (Vindenes et al., 2018) but in a shared and virtually realized environment. Such a space implements the egocentric model, so you remember information partly because of its spa-tial location and the journey you took to find it (and there could be many routes, each with its own theme). Augment that model with automated ava-tars who can not only guide you through the information but also share other people's interpretation of that information, and you have a new potential model for the collection, sharing, communication, and development of scien-tific knowledge. Working at the "coal face" of scientific research could almost literally be extending that garden out into a new territory.

THE METAVERSE: A CRITICAL INTRODUCTION'S INFORMATION GARDEN

A basic information garden has been produced in VR to support this book. Each chapter has its own area with information and links related to the book's content. And since it's a social environment, you may even meet other readers – or even the authors! You can access it through the series website at http://themetaverseseries.info/.

Warfare and the Military

Much of the early work around HMD-VR, and on simulation more broadly, grew out of a need for safer and less costly ways to train military personnel. The military were also early adopters of CAD technology to help to design new systems. Whilst much of this activity has been on closed systems (such as *Virtual Battle Systems* (VBS) mentioned in Chapter 1), the arrival of social virtual worlds encouraged more grass-roots activity to look at how virtual worlds could be used to support military activities from training (Maxwell, 2012) to understanding anti-submarine warfare (Aguiar & Monte, 2011). Many of these were brought together through the US Government's Federal Virtual World Consortium (Harris, 2010).

The military also has a keen interest in digital twins, both in how they can help in the management of military systems and in the understanding and planning of operations in (typically urban) locations across the globe. An early example of a simple digital twin was the 3D model built of Osama

Bin Laden's compound before it was attacked by the US Special Forces (R. E. Smith & Vogt, 2014). More recently, the US Army (and no doubt others) have been examining the use of VR for planning and the use of helmet integrated MR headsets to improve the situational awareness of their soldiers (Shear, 2023) and pilots (Webster, 2021).

However, the Snowden/NSA documents mentioned earlier (NSA, 2008) also highlighted that the opposition may be using virtual worlds too, and that what is sometimes referred to as grey zone warfare (Brands, 2016) may already be happening in social virtual worlds, just as it already is on more traditional social media platforms (Matisek, 2017). The ultimate expression of this may be of war in the Metaverse – carried out both through "in-world" activities and by cyberattacks aimed at the platform code and infrastructure. Militaries hence need to be aware of the challenges of the Metaverse as well as its opportunities.

The Exploration of Space

VR is already being used to enable students to explore the worlds of the solar system (W. Huang et al., 2021) and by scientists and engineers to plan and support real space missions, such as in NASA's Mars XR Operations Support System (XOSS) environment (https://www.buendea.com/xoss). AR and VR have also been used in the International Space Station for tasks ranging from robotic and experiment control to exercising (Guzman, 2021). For many of a certain age, watching the 1969 Moon landings on a grainy black and white TV set was a life-defining moment. But what might the first crewed Mars landing be like? Any landing site will have been well surveyed beforehand and equipment pre-positioned, and as a result, the team will already have a detailed 3D model and simulation and a whole section of virtual Mars to practice and plan with. This has already been started with XOSS, and with the Mars rovers, where NASA teams can use VR to stand next to the rover on Mars to plan its next move (Samuelson, 2018), and the UAE is using the Metaverse to plan its own Mars settlement (Hasan, 2023). The US Space Force even calls its vision of how to use XR technologies to support space operations the "SpaceVerse" (Kauchak, 2023).

Come the first human landing on Mars, there is no reason why a version of that virtual Mars shouldn't be made publicly available so that anyone can stand on virtual Mars and watch the first astronauts step foot on the planet – both in live video and as avatars in front of them. In a private version of that same environment, the support team can be doing the same thing – and the astronauts can have MR displays in their headsets so that they can see the support team as though they were stood on Mars with them and work collaboratively as a physical-virtual team to explore Mars. Of course, there is the minor issue of the 3-21-minute time delay on transmissions between the two planets, so it may be that both teams are actually interacting with automated avatars, digital twins of the physical humans, who are being continually updated as plans and activities unfold.

An Integrated Metaverse

Having looked at a wide range of proven uses for metaverse technologies, it is important to consider what it is that some form of integrated Metaverse offers that implementing each of these use cases piecemeal on a variety of different metaversal systems probably won't deliver. The focus in this section is on the more technical aspects of this argument, whereas Chapter 5 considers the more social aspects. Whilst Au (2023) sees the words "the metaverse" as becoming a term akin to "social media", with no necessary underlying shared technology or integration, this section argues that some level of integration should be the objective, and one that should be based on open standards.

Reducing Costs and Increasing Re-Use

By sharing technologies and approaches, the development time and costs for the infrastructure that supports the different metaverse experiences can be expected to be reduced due to high re-use, just as with the Web. Web server costs are typically a negligible part of any Web application unless being scaled for high usage. The Metaverse needs to be the same – setting up the core infrastructure for a new experience (whether local servers or cloud hosted) should be a simple, quick, and cheap task so as to democratize the access to creating new experiences.

Likewise, the time and cost to then develop those experiences on the Metaverse can be expected to be lower if they are all using the same core toolset and approaches. A citizen-developer only needs to learn once and can then apply that knowledge to any experience, whether related to work, play, hobbies, or family. Tools and objects developed in one experience can easily be re-used in a different experience, saving further time and cost.

Consistency of Access and Experience

Whilst on mobile phones, users are used to the "there's an app for that" model of a separate app for each application (even if many just encapsulate a URL for a web browser) on PCs "everything through the web" seems increasingly to be the dominant model (expect possibly for computer games, which is itself significant). The challenges of delivering virtual worlds over the past couple of decades have meant that the desktop application has been almost the only way to go, but that is now changing with WebXR. For most metaverse applications, it seems reasonable to predict that in the next five to ten years, they could be readily delivered through a browser-based model, so accessing different experiences becomes no different from clicking on Favourites in your web browser – and indeed it could (and probably should) be the same browser. And whether delivered through downloadable applications or web URLs, there needs to be an adequate set of discovery tools, both curated and non-curated, to help users find the metaversal experiences that they need when they want them – such as the idea of a Lively style "immersive" tab on a Google search mentioned in Chapter 1.

In addition to that consistency of access, there is also the issue of the consistency of experience. In the early days of the Web, there was a high level of consistency in the way that web pages and sites worked, driven in part by the usability work of people like Nielsen and Loranger (2006). A shared technical underpinning of the Metaverse should make it easier to encourage consistency in the user interface across applications, even if just in the basics such as the use of iconography, terms, navigation commands, and understanding how links between worlds will work (akin to the underlined hyperlink on the web). This is not to say that every experience needs to look and work in the same way – and indeed the Web has moved a long way from the Nielsen-era recommendations as it has become more "app" like – but certainly in the early stages, when new users are just beginning to get used to metaversal experiences, providing them with some consistency of experience should significantly help with growing adoption.

Continuity of Experience and Synergistic Opportunities

By providing a consistency of experience, and particularly by providing links between experiences, users will not need to switch mindset or risk losing a chain of thoughts as they go from one experience to another. Changes in work-life models are resulting in a greater blurring between physical work and personal and hobby experiences (Kossek, 2016). Shouldn't the Metaverse also enable this, allowing users to blur their use of the Metaverse across all of their interests? Of course, many will want to maintain separate identities for work, family, and hobbies, and the Metaverse must actively support this – particularly in terms of avatar look and in-world naming. Ideally, this shared use of metaverse environments across work, family, and play should also encourage people to identify and act on synergies between the different experiences, resulting in even greater creativity and innovation. The wide variety of different platforms used for all the examples given in this chapter is testament to the fragmented nature of the current metaverse experience - with duplication no doubt being common and synergistic possibilities missed.

Continual Evolution

Returning to Nielsen, a website of 1996 looks nothing like a website (or web app) of 2023. The Web has enabled sites to evolve to meet the changing and evolving needs and expectations of users by continually updating some of its key components, bringing in such features as Cascading Style

Sheets, WebSockets, and WebGL, augmented by ever-changing development approaches such as Ruby on Rails, React, and node.js. Any Metaverse can be expected to evolve too. In the segmented, standalone metaverse model, each new development is likely to arise on one platform, which others may or may not be able to copy, and the proprietary model limits development to just the system's owner. Whilst the innovation in multiple systems may be faster (each has fewer stakeholders, and there are less legacy and scalability issues), the dissemination of that innovation is likely to be much reduced.

Avoiding Redundancy and Perpetuating Experiences

Linked to the issue of continual evolution is that of redundancy and the danger of creating orphan worlds. A web page of 1996 should be just as displayable and usable in a modern browser as it was when it was created. However, the computer gaming world, in particular, is littered with games which can just no longer run on today's computers or gaming platforms (Guttenbrunner et al., 2010). Loss of experiences also comes from cessation of platform operation, or just changes in business models – many *Second Life* projects of the 2000s are no longer available as the owners could not afford or justify the monthly payments on the sim, and unlike on *OpenSim*, there was no way of creating an off-line archive of the build. By adopting a common, foundational approach to the technology of the Metaverse, the longevity of an application should no longer be limited by the availability of (or changes to) its original platform. It should be possible to readily move the experience between Metaverse service providers and ultimately to create an off-line archive which can be returned to life at any point.

Community

It is not just a technical argument as to why the Metaverse should be, at minimum, a series of connected worlds, but also a social one. Whilst some aspects of this topic will be considered in more detail in Chapter 5, the key issue of communities is best addressed here. Some have expressed the view that the Metaverse is principally about communities – and that the interconnectedness of metaverse worlds is of less importance than the interconnectedness of communities (e.g. Au, 2023). As long as each community can find a home, it does not matter how connected each world in the Metaverse is to another. An argument against that is that each person is likely to be a member of multiple communities – family, locale, work, hobby, interests, etc. If each community is running on a different platform, then that is an instant barrier in moving between them, sharing experiences and in joining new communities.

This is something that already hampers users where communities may be spread across *WhatsApp*, *Facebook*, *LinkedIn*, *Discord*, *TikTok*, *Telegram*, and countless other services. The Metaverse is a chance to try and do this right – having enough common foundation to ease access between services but also enabling partitioning of identity when required and providing the tools to enable maximal expression in each community.

As has been mentioned earlier, a key aspect of the social virtual world experience is that it does come back down to a (relatively small) group of people gathered around a campfire, chatting. The anonymity and lack of presence that comes with current social spaces – where even the most niche interest can attract hundreds or thousands of users – often mitigates against rich and engaged dialogue and relationships. Using the Metaverse as a primary means of supporting communities and their discourses could change this.

The Challenges to an Integrated Metaverse

A principal challenge to an integrated Metaverse or Multiverse is that of agreement between the developers and the choice, implementation, and adherence to standards. The metaverse industry hasn't yet achieved a set of standards beyond relatively low-level technical ones such as WebXR, despite their being cross-industry standards work since at least the 2000s. The several "standards" initiatives currently underway (which is of course part of the problem!) will be discussed in Chapter 4. Even if agreement can be reached on the key elements, they will still need to be adopted by platform developers and big business as well as by enthusiasts if they are to make any real difference. Tied into this is the debate of open versus proprietary standards, which again is covered later.

Agreement takes time, and so do changes to any agreement, so the integrated Metaverse may evolve more slowly than multiple disconnected, non-standard metaverses. There is also the risk that standardisation stifles creativity. Any standards need to allow developers to push the envelope as has happened on the Web, trying out new approaches, possibly in a private fork of the code on a private system or whilst maintaining adherence to the core standards and providing backward compatibility for users whose "metaverse browser" does not support their new features. Those new features that stand the test of time can be incorporated back into the standards.

Chapter 5 will consider further challenges, particularly those related to privacy, surveillance, and control, all of which could be made more acute by an interconnected Metaverse.

Summary

This chapter has shown the wide range of use cases that already exist for metaverse technologies, many of which have been explored and exploited for personal and business benefit for well over a decade. These show how beneficial metaverse technologies can be, and as each sector makes more use of the metaverse, their importance is only set to grow. The chapter has also argued how implementing these applications in, at minimum, some form of linked metaverse where common standards and approaches are shared across platforms, and links made between platforms and experiences, may offer a better overall solution than a series of isolated virtual world, VR, or "metaverse" experiences.

Creating a Metaverse which unifies the approach to creating and accessing virtual world experiences, just as the World Wide Web did for on-line content, probably offers the best chance to create a Metaverse which is not only democratic – enabling people to create and use whatever content they want – but also one which will also grow and survive. However, there are potential challenges of such an approach – to be examined in Chapter 5, and some of the possible consequences which will be explored in Chapter 6.

The next chapter will look in more detail at the technologies that underpin the Metaverse and continue to build the argument for some form of integrated, open-standards-based metaverse.

Notes

1 David's company built this project for Southampton Solent University.
2 Both Maggi and David were involved in this project.
3 Both Maggi and David were involved in this project.
4 This was a project that David and Daden Limited led.

References

Aguiar, S., & Monte, P. (2011). Virtual worlds for C2 design, analysis, and experimentation. *Proceedings of the 16th International Command & Control Research & Technology Symposium.* https://apps.dtic.mil/sti/pdfs/ADA547157.pdf

Alizadehsalehi, S., Hadavi, A., & Huang, J. C. (2020). From BIM to extended reality in AEC industry. *Automation in Construction, 116,* 103254.

Anderson, A., Dossick, C. S., Azari, R., Taylor, J. E., Hartmann, T., & Mahalingham, A. (2014, May). Exploring BIMs as avatars: Using 3D virtual worlds to improve collaboration with models. *Construction research congress 2014: Construction in a global network* (pp. 179–188). American Society of Civil Engineers.

Appel, L., Appel, E., Bogler, O., Wiseman, M., Cohen, L., Ein, N., Abrams, H. B., & Campos, J. L. (2020). Older adults with cognitive and/or physical impairments can benefit from immersive virtual reality experiences: A feasibility study. *Frontiers in Medicine, 6,* 329.

ARKx. (2022, July 24). Dubai Shopping Festival 2022—Augmented metaverse. *Medium.* https://medium.com/@arkx/dubai-shopping-festival-2022-augmented-metaverse-263fdf06ac96

ARTDEX. (n.d.). *The complete guide on virtual art.* ARTDX. https://www.artdex.com/the-complete-guide-on-virtual-art

Au, W. J. (2023). *Making a metaverse that matters: From Snow Crash & Second Life to a virtual world worth fighting for.* John Wiley & Sons.

Baek, Y., Min, E., & Yun, S. (2020). Mining educational implications of Minecraft. *Computers in the Schools, 37*(1), 1–16.

Balogh, G., & Beszedes, A. (2013). CodeMetrpolis—A Minecraft based collaboration tool for developers. *2013 First IEEE working conference on software visualization (VISSOFT)* (pp. 1–4). IEEE.

Barteit, S., Lanfermann, L., Bärnighausen, T., Neuhann, F., & Beiersmann, C. (2021). Augmented, mixed, and virtual reality-based head-mounted devices for medical education: Systematic review. *JMIR Serious Games, 9*(3), e29080.

Bauer, A. C. M., & Andringa, G. (2020). The potential of immersive virtual reality for cognitive training in elderly. *Gerontology, 66*(6), 614–623.

Beck, D., Morgado, L., Lee, M., Gütl, C., Dengel, A., Wang, M., Warren, S., & Richter, J. (2021). Towards an immersive learning knowledge tree-a conceptual framework for mapping knowledge and tools in the field. *2021 7th International conference of the immersive learning research network (iLRN)* (pp. 1–8). IEEE.

Bellalouna, F., & Puljiz, D. (2023). Use case for the application of the industrial metaverse approach for engineering design review. *Procedia CIRP, 119,* 638–643.

Blackwood, G. (2023). Roblox and Meta Verch: A case study of Walmart's Roblox games. *M/C Journal, 26*(3). https://doi.org/10.5204/mcj.2958

Boughzala, I., de Vreede, G. J., & Limayem, M. (2012). Team collaboration in virtual worlds: Editorial to the special issue. *Journal of the Association for Information Systems, 13*(10), 6.

Brands, H. (2016). *Paradoxes of the gray zone* (SSRN scholarly paper No. 2737593). https://doi.org/10.2139/ssrn.2737593

Brown, B., & Bell, M. (2006). Play and sociability in there: Some lessons from online games for collaborative virtual environments. *Avatars at work and play: Collaboration and interaction in shared virtual environments* (pp. 227–245). Springer Netherlands.

Burden, D. J. H. (2021). *Immersive visual analytics: A white paper.* Daden Limited. https://www.daden.co.uk/_files/ugd/0c2908_0369a471a71d4e8291f6d4730daf129d.pdf

Burden, D. J. H. (2020). Using 3D visualisation technology to improve design and visitor orientation. In R. Parry, R. Page, R., & A. Moseley (Eds.), *Museum thresholds: The design and media of arrival* (pp.124–152). Routledge.

Cannone, G. (2021). *Latest digital fashion trends: Insights into virtual clothing.* Fashion Technology Accelerator. https://www.ftaccelerator.it/blog/digital-fashion-virtual-clothing/

Chandler, T., & Clulow, A. (2019). *Building a virtual city for the classroom: Angkor.* Not Even Past: Features.

Chandler, P., & Sweller, J. (1991). Cognitive load theory and the format of instruction. *Cognition and Instruction, 8*(4), 293–332.

Childs, M. (2008). Using a mediated environments reference model to evaluate learners' experiences of Second Life. *Proceedings of the sixth international conference on networked learning* (pp. 38–45). University of Lancaster/SEERC.

Cijntje, E., & van Gisbergen, M. S. (2022, April). Arousing real or real threat? How realism in avatars affects the perception of virtual reality pornography and relationships for heterosexual women. *International XR Conference* (pp. 319–331). Springer International Publishing.

Conradi, E., Kavia, S., Burden, D., Rice, A., Woodham, L., Beaumont, C., Savin-Baden, M., & Poulton, T. (2009). Virtual patients in a virtual world: Training paramedic students for practice. *Medical Teacher, 31*(8), 713–720.

Cordeil, M., & Dwyer, T. (2019). Introduction to IATK: An immersive visual analytics toolkit. *Proceedings of the 2019 ACM international conference on interactive surfaces and spaces* (pp. 431–435). Association for Computing Machinery.

Costa, M. T. S., Vieira, L. P., de Oliveira Barbosa, E., Oliveira, L. M., Maillot, P., Vaghetti, C. A. O., Carta, M. G., Machado, S., Gatic-Rojas, V., & Monteiro-Junior, R. S. (2019). Virtual reality-based exercise with exergames as medicine in different contexts: A short review. *Clinical Practice and Epidemiology in Mental Health: CP & EMH, 15*, 15–20.

Cremorne, L. (2008). Wimbledon in Second Life. *The Metaverse Journal.* http://meta-versejournal.com/2008/06/18/wimbledon-in-second-life/

Cunningham, C. A., & Harrison, K. (2010). The affordances of Second Life for PreK-12 education. In J. Braman & G. Vincenti (Eds.), *Teaching through multi-user virtual environments: Applying dynamic elements to the modern classroom* (pp. 120–138). IGI Global.

Curry, D. (2023). *Dating app revenue and usage statistics (2023).* Business of Apps. https://www.businessofapps.com/data/dating-app-market/

Cybulski, J., Keller, S., & Saundage, D. (2014). *Metaphors in interactive visual analytics. Proceedings of the 7th international symposium on visual information communication and interaction* (pp. 212–215). Association for Computing Machinery.

Dalgarno, B., & Lee, M. J. (2010). What are the learning affordances of 3-D virtual environments? *British Journal of Educational Technology, 41*(1), 10–32.

Danforth, D. R., Procter, M., Chen, R., Johnson, M., & Heller, R. (2009). Development of virtual patient simulations for medical education. *Journal for Virtual Worlds Research, 2*(2) 4–11.

de Andrade, B., Poplin, A., & Sousa de Sena, Í. (2020). Minecraft as a tool for engaging children in urban planning: A case study in Tirol Town, Brazil. *ISPRS International Journal of Geo-Information, 9*(3), 170.

De Bonis, M., Nguyen, H., & Bourdot, P. (2022, October). A literature review of user studies in extended reality applications for archaeology. *2022 IEEE international symposium on mixed and augmented reality (ISMAR)* (pp. 92–101). IEEE.

de Ruyter, K., Heller, J., Hilken, T., Chylinski, M., Keeling, D. I., & Mahr, D. (2020). Seeing with the customer's eye: Exploring the challenges and opportunities of AR advertising. *Journal of Advertising, 49*(2), 109–124.

Deloitte. (2022). *Try this on for size: Metaverse fashion may be $55B industry by 2030.* Deloitte. https://action.deloitte.com/insight/1514/try-this-on-for-size

Dewey, J. (1986). Experience and education. *The educational forum* (Vol. 50, No. 3, pp. 241–252). Taylor & Francis Group.

Dixie, A. (2023). *Programmatic advertising: It's in the game.* MediaWrites. https://medi-awrites.law/programmatic-advertising-its-in-the-game/

Driver, E. (2009). *ThinkBalm Data Garden is live!* ThinkBalm. https://thinkbalm.com/thinkbalm-data-garden-is-live/

Ellaway, R., Poulton, T., Fors, U., McGee, J. B., & Albright, S. (2008). Building a virtual patient commons. *Medical Teacher, 30*(2), 170–174.

Emmelkamp, P. M., Meyerbröker, K., & Morina, N. (2020). Virtual reality therapy in social anxiety disorder. *Current Psychiatry Reports, 22*, 1–9.

Evans, L. (2023). Virtual reality pornography: A review of health-related opportunities and challenges. *Current Sexual Health Reports, 15,* 26–35. https://doi.org/10.1007/s11930-022-00352-9

Eyre, J., & Freeman, C. (2018). Immersive applications of industrial digital twins. The Industrial Track of EuroVR 2018. *Proceedings of the 15th annual EuroVR conference* (pp. 11–13). VTT Technical Research Centre of Finland.

Falconer, C. J., Rovira, A., King, J. A., Gilbert, P., Antley, A., Fearon, P., Ralph, N., Slater, M., & Brewin, C. R. (2016). Embodying self-compassion within virtual reality and its effects on patients with depression. *BJPsych Open, 2*(1), 74–80.

Falconer, L., Burden, D., Cleal, R., Hoyte, R., Phelps, P., Slawson, N., Snashall, N., & Welham, K. (2020). Virtual avebury: Exploring sense of place in a virtual archaeology simulation. *Virtual Archaeology Review, 11*(23), 50–62.

Farley, H. S. (2018). Using 3D worlds in prison: Driving, learning and escape. *Journal for Virtual Worlds Research, 11*(1)1–11.

Forte, M., Lercari, N., Galeazzi, F., & Borra, D. (2010). *Metaverse communities and archaeology: The case of Teramo.* 3rd International conference dedicated on digital heritage, Limassol, Cyprus.

Fox, J., Bailenson, J. N., & Tricase, L. (2013). The embodiment of sexualized virtual selves: The Proteus effect and experiences of self-objectification via avatars. *Computers in Human Behavior, 29*(3), 930–938.

Freitas, D. M. D. O., & Spadoni, V. S. (2019). Is virtual reality useful for pain management in patients who undergo medical procedures? *Einstein (Sao Paulo), 17.* https://doi.org/10.31744/einstein_journal/2019MD4837

Gazit, E. (2024). *Between Dubai and Shanghai: The Metaverse's future in the AI era (part 1).* MetaYeda. https://metayeda.substack.com/p/dubai-and-shanghai-metaverse-ai-odyssey

Goodman, K. (2023). *How Fortnite weaves brands into the game & makes billions.* Weird Marketing Tales. https://weirdmarketingtales.com/fortnite-integrates-brands-makes-billions/

Greeno, J. G., Smith, D. R., & Moore, J. L. (1993). Transfer of situated learning. In D. K. Detterman & R. J. Sternberg (Eds.), *Transfer on trial: Intelligence, cognition, and instruction* (pp. 99–167). Ablex Publishing.

Grieves, M. (2003). *Digital twin: Mitigating unpredictable, undesirable emergent behavior in complex systems.* Florida Institute of Technology Center for Advanced Manufacturing and Innovative Design (CAMID). https://polytechnic.purdue.edu/sites/default/files/files/Fall16-%20Grieves%20-%20Digital%20Twin%20Mitigating%20Uppredicatable%20systems.pdf

Grubb, J. (2016). *Microsoft bans corporations from using Minecraft as a marketing tool.* VentureBeat. https://venturebeat.com/games/microsoft-bans-corporations-from-using-minecraft-as-a-marketing-tool/

Grübel, J., Thrash, T., Aguilar, L., Gath-Morad, M., Chatain, J., Sumner, R. W., Hölscher, C., & Schinazi, V. R. (2022). The hitchhiker's guide to fused twins: A review of access to digital twins in situ in smart cities. *Remote Sensing, 14*(13), 3095.

Guttenbrunner, M., Becker, C., & Rauber, A. (2010). *Keeping the game alive: Evaluating strategies for the preservation of console video games. The International Journal of Digital Curation, 5*(1). https://doi.org/10.2218/ijdc.v5i1.144

Guzman, A. (2021). *Nine ways we use AR and VR on the international space station.* NASA. https://www.nasa.gov/mission_pages/station/research/news/nine-ways-we-use-ar-vr-on-iss

Haber, J., Xu, H., & Priya, K. (2023). Harnessing virtual reality for management training: A longitudinal study. *Organization Management Journal, 20*(3), 93–106.

Hagerty, P. (2012). The metaverse pioneers and the colonization of OpenSimulator. *Metaverse Creativity (New Title: Virtual Creativity), 2*(1), 97–114.

Hamari, J., Koivisto, J., & Sarsa, H. (2014, January). Does gamification work? A literature review of empirical studies on gamification. *2014 47th Hawaii international conference on system sciences* (pp. 3025–3034). IEEE.

Hand, R. (2011). *Virtual Library of Birmingham opens its doors for public exploration.* VizWorld. https://vizworld.com/2011/07/virtual-library-birmingham-opens-doors-public-exploration/

Han, J., Liu, G., & Gao, Y. (2023). Learners in the Metaverse: A systematic review on the use of Roblox in learning. *Education Sciences, 13*(3), 296.

Harris, C. (2010). *Government consortium to investigate virtual world best practices.* Government Technology. https://www.govtech.com/dc/articles/government-consortium-to-investigate-virtual-world.html

Hasan, S. (2023). *UAE's 2117 Mars settlement plan is to be built in the Metaverse.* Wired. https://wired.me/technology/uaes-2117-mars-settlement-plan-is-to-be-built-in-the-metaverse/

Heiyanthuduwa, T. A., Amarapala, K. N. U., Gunathilaka, K. V. B., Ravindu, K. S., Wickramarathne, J., & Kasthurirathna, D. (2020). VirtualPT: Virtual reality based home care physiotherapy rehabilitation for elderly. In *2020 2nd international conference on advancements in computing (ICAC)* (Vol. 1, pp. 311–316). IEEE.

Huang, Y. (2020). Evaluating mixed reality technology for architectural design and construction layout. *Journal of Civil Engineering and Construction Technology, 11*(1), 1–12.

Huang, W., Roscoe, R. D., Johnson-Glenberg, M. C., & Craig, S. D. (2021). Motivation, engagement, and performance across multiple virtual reality sessions and levels of immersion. *Journal of Computer Assisted Learning, 37*(3), 745–758.

Hudson-Smith, A. (2022). Incoming metaverses: Digital mirrors for urban planning. *Urban Planning, 7*(2), 343–354.

Hunter, M. G., Soro, A., Brown, R. A., Harman, J., & Yigitcanlar, T. (2022). Augmenting community engagement in City 4.0: Considerations for digital agency in urban public space. *Sustainability, 14*(16), 9803.

Ibrahim, D. (2022). *8 Metaverse cities to keep a close eye on in 2023.* The Metaverse Insider. https://metaverseinsider.tech/2022/12/16/metaverse-cities/

Iqbal, M. (2023). *Tinder revenue and usage statistics (2023).* Business of Apps. https://www.businessofapps.com/data/tinder-statistics/

Jarrett, T. H., Comrie, A., Marchetti, L., Sivitilli, A., Macfarlane, S., Vitello, F., Becciani, U., Taylor, A. R., van der Hulst, J. M., Serra, P., Katz, N., & Cluver, M. E. (2021). Exploring and interrogating astrophysical data in virtual reality. *Astronomy and Computing, 37*, 100502.

Johansson, M., Roupé, M., & Bosch-Sijtsema, P. (2015). Real-time visualization of building information models (BIM). *Automation in Construction, 54*, 69–82.

Joho, J. (2021). *The best virtual reality porn games, and how to play adult VR.* Mashable. https://mashable.com/article/best-vr-porn-games

Juárez-Juárez, M. G., Botti, V., & Giret Boggino, A. S. (2021). Digital twins: Review and challenges. *Journal of Computing and Information Science in Engineering, 21*(3), 1–23. https://doi.org/10.1115/1.4050244

Kauchak, M. (2023). *Bringing 'SpaceVerse' to reality.* Halldale Group. https://www.halldale.com/articles/21010-mst-bringing-spaceverse-to-reality

Kirriemuir, J. (2009). *Portfolio*. Silversprite. https://www.silversprite.com/?page_id=285

Klatzky, R. L., Loomis, J. M., Beall, A. C., Chance, S. S., & Golledge, R. G. (1998). Spatial updating of self-position and orientation during real, imagined, and virtual locomotion. *Psychological Science, 9*(4), 293–298.

Kolb, D. A. (2014). *Experiential learning: Experience as the source of learning and development*. FT Press.

Kononowicz, A. A., Woodham, L. A., Edelbring, S., Stathakarou, N., Davies, D., Saxena, N., Car, L. T., Carlstedt-Duke, J., Car, J., & Zary, N. (2019). Virtual patient simulations in health professions education: Systematic review and meta-analysis by the digital health education collaboration. *Journal of Medical Internet Research, 21*(7), e14676.

Kossek, E. E. (2016). Managing work-life boundaries in the digital age. *Organizational Dynamics, 45*, 258–270.

Ladwig, P., & Geiger, C. (2019). A literature review on collaboration in mixed reality. *Smart industry & smart education: Proceedings of the 15th international conference on remote engineering and virtual instrumentation 15* (pp. 591–600). Springer International Publishing.

Lai, X., Lei, X., Chen, X., & Rau, P. L. P. (2019). Can virtual reality satisfy entertainment needs of the elderly? The application of a VR headset in elderly care. *Cross-cultural design. Culture and society: 11th International conference, CCD 2019*, held as part of *the 21st HCI international conference, HCII 2019*, Orlando, FL, USA, July 26–31, 2019, proceedings, part II (pp. 159–172). Springer International Publishing.

Lavoye, V., Sipilä, J., Mero, J., & Tarkiainen, A. (2023). The emperor's new clothes: Self-explorative engagement in virtual try-on service experiences positively impacts brand outcomes. *Journal of Services Marketing, 37*(10), 1–21.

Lawton, G. (2022). *Why the industrial metaverse will eclipse the consumer one*. VentureBeat. https://venturebeat.com/virtual/why-the-industrial-metaverse-will-eclipse-the-consumer-one/

Lee, A. (2023). *In the in-game advertising world, tension is mounting between intrinsic ads and immersive brand experiences*. DIGIDAY. https://digiday.com/marketing/in-the-in-game-advertising-world-tension-is-mounting-between-intrinsic-ads-and-immersive-brand-experiences/

Lee, J., & Kundu, P. (2022). Integrated cyber-physical systems and industrial metaverse for remote manufacturing. *Manufacturing Letters, 34*, 12–15.

Lock, D., & Stewart-David, M. (2022). *The Making of an Immersical®*. The Writing Platform. https://thewritingplatform.com/2022/05/the-making-of-an-immersical/

Loke, S. (2015). How do virtual world experiences bring about learning? A critical review of theories. *Australasian Journal of Educational Technology, 31*(1), 112–122.

Luna, U., Rivero, P., & Vicent, N. (2019). Augmented reality in heritage apps: Current trends in Europe. *Applied Sciences, 9*(13), 2756.

Mahajan, U. V., Sunshine, K. S., Herring, E. Z., Labak, C. M., Wright, J. M., & Smith, G. (2021). Virtual reality in presurgical patient education: A scoping review and recommended trial design guidelines. *The American Journal of Surgery, 222*(4), 704–705.

Maksimenko, N., Okolzina, A., Vlasova, A., Tracey, C., & Kurushkin, M. (2021). Introducing atomic structure to first-year undergraduate chemistry students with an immersive virtual reality experience. *Journal of Chemical Education, 98*(6), 2104–2108. https://doi.org/10.1021/acs.jchemed.0c01441

Matisek, J. W. (2017). Shades of gray deterrence: Issues of fighting in the gray zone. *Journal of Strategic Security*, *10*(3), 1–26.

Maxwell, D. (2012). *Military grid hits performance goals*. Hypergrid Business. https://www.hypergridbusiness.com/2012/11/military-grid-hits-performance-goals/

McGuirt, J. T., Cooke, N. K., Burgermaster, M., Enahora, B., Huebner, G., Meng, Y., Tripicchio, G., Dyson, O., Stage, V. C., & Wong, S. S. (2020). Extended reality technologies in nutrition education and behavior: Comprehensive scoping review and future directions. *Nutrients*, *12*(9), 2899.

McLauchlan, J., & Farley, H. (2022). A fast track to knowledge: Using virtual reality for learning in prisons. In *Histories and philosophies of carceral education: Aims, contradictions, promises and problems* (pp. 229–251). Springer International Publishing.

Meehan, A. (2022). *Roll20's userbase has doubled since 2020, more than 10 million people join online RPG platform*. Dicebreaker. https://www.dicebreaker.com/companies/roll20/news/roll20-userbase-doubles

Meta. (2021, October 28). *The Metaverse and how we'll build it together—Connect 2021* [Meta]. YouTube. https://www.youtube.com/watch?v=Uvufun6xer8&ab_channel=Meta

Mihai, S., Yaqoob, M., Hung, D. V., Davis, W., Towakel, P., Raza, M., Karamanoglu, M., Barn, B., Shetve, D., Prasad, R. V., Venkataraman, H., Trestian, R., &Nguyen, H. X. (2022). *Digital twins: A survey on enabling technologies, challenges, trends and future prospects*. IEEE Communications Surveys & Tutorials. https://eprints.mdx.ac.uk/36014/1/DT_Survey_Final_Accepted.pdf

Milrod, C., & Monto, M. A. (2012). The hobbyist and the girlfriend experience: Behaviors and preferences of male customers of internet sexual service providers. *Deviant Behavior*, *33*(10), 792–810.

Moravcikova, D., & Kliestikova, J. (2017). Brand building with using phygital marketing communication. *Journal of Economics, Business and Management*, *5*(3), 148–153.

Mordor. (2023). *Location based VR market size & share analysis—Growth trends & forecasts (2023–2028)*. Mordor Intelligence. https://www.mordorintelligence.com/industry-reports/location-based-virtual-reality-vr-market

Mozgai, S., Hartholt, A., Leeds, A., & Rizzo, A. S. (2020). *Iterative participatory design for VRET domain transfer: From combat exposure to military sexual trauma. Extended abstracts of the 2020 CHI conference on human factors in computing systems*, Honolulu, HI, USA.

Nesbitt, D. (n.d.) *Monitoring cyberspace: The internet's love affair with sex*. https://www.academia.edu/download/58017701/Monitoring_Cyberspace_-_The_Internets_Love_Affair_with_Sex.pdf

Nesson, R., & Nesson, C. (2008). The case for education in virtual worlds. *Space and Culture*, *11*(3), 273–284.

Nielsen, J., & Loranger, H. (2006). *Prioritizing web usability*. Pearson Education.

NSA. (2008). *Exploiting terrorist use of games & virtual environments*. NSA. https://www.theguardian.com/world/interactive/2013/dec/09/nsa-files-games-virtual-environments-paper-pdf

O'Halloran, J. (2023). *Enterprise and industrial metaverses exceeding expectations*. Computer Weekly. https://www.computerweekly.com/news/366541564/Enterprise-and-industrial-metaverses-exceeding-expectations

Ocausse. (2016). *Why VR could mean the end of Art museums*. Harvard University. https://d3.harvard.edu/platform-rctom/submission/why-vr-could-mean-the-end-of-art-museums/

Paro, M. R., Hersh, D. S., & Bulsara, K. R. (2022). History of virtual reality and augmented reality in neurosurgical training. *World Neurosurgery, 167*, 37–43.

PlayTracker. (2023). *Tabletop simulator on steam*. PlayTracker. https://playtracker.net/insight/game/4468

Plotzky, C., Lindwedel, U., Sorber, M., Loessl, B., König, P., Kunze, C., Kugler, C., & Meng, M. (2021). Virtual reality simulations in nurse education: A systematic mapping review. *Nurse Education Today, 101*, 104868.

Prem, A.-L. (2023). *Future trends: What's next for digital fashion and beyond in 2023.* Metaverse Fashion Council. https://metaversefashioncouncil.org/news/future-trends-whats-next-for-digital-fashion-in-2023-and-beyond

Ratcliffe, J., & Simons, A. (2017). How can 3D game engines create photo-realistic interactive architectural visualizations? *E-learning and games: 11th International conference, edutainment 2017* (pp. 164–172). Springer International Publishing.

Razali, M. F., Haron, N. A., Hassim, S., Alias, A. H., Harun, A. N., & Abubakar, A. S. (2019, November). A review: Application of Building Information Modelling (BIM) over building life cycles. *IOP conference series: Earth and environmental science* (Vol. 357, No. 1, p. 012028). IOP Publishing.

Regal, G., Pretolesi, D., Schrom-Feiertag, H., Puthenkalam, J., Migliorini, M., De Maio, E., Scarrone, F., Nadalin, M., Guarneri, M., Xerri, G. P., Di Giovanni, D., Tessari, P., Genna, F., D'Angelo, A., & Murtinger, M. (2023). Challenges in virtual reality training for CBRN events. *Multimodal Technologies and Interaction, 7*(9), 88.

Ren, X. (2020). Artificial intelligence and depression: How AI powered chatbots in virtual reality games may reduce anxiety and depression levels. *Journal of Artificial Intelligence Practice, 3*(1), 48–58.

Rosenkjær, D., Pacey, A., Montgomerie, R., & Skytte, A. B. (2022). Effects of virtual reality erotica on ejaculate quality of sperm donors: A balanced and randomized controlled cross-over within-subjects trial. *Reproductive Biology and Endocrinology, 20*(1), 1–8.

Rueda, C. J. Á., Godínes, J. C. V., & Rudman, P. D. (2018). Categorizing the educational affordances of 3 dimensional immersive digital environments. *Journal of Information Technology Education. Innovations in Practice, 17*, 83–112.

Sampaio, M., Navarro Haro, M. V., De Sousa, B., Vieira Melo, W., & Hoffman, H. G. (2021). Therapists make the switch to telepsychology to safely continue treating their patients during the COVID-19 pandemic. Virtual reality telepsychology may be next. *Frontiers in Virtual Reality, 1*, 576421.

Samuelson, A. (2018). *Mars virtual reality software wins NASA Award*. NASA. https://mars.nasa.gov/news/8374/mars-virtual-reality-software-wins-nasa-award/

Savin-Baden, M. (2007). *A practical guide to problem-based learning online*. Routledge.

Schild, J., Carbonell, G., Tarrach, A., & Ebeling, M. (2022, August). ViTAWiN-Interprofessional medical mixed reality training for paramedics and emergency nurses. *2022 IEEE 10th international conference on serious games and applications for health (SeGAH)* (pp. 1–8). IEEE.

Schouten, A. P., van den Hooff, B., & Feldberg, F. (2010). Real decisions in virtual worlds: Team collaboration and decision making in 3D virtual worlds. *Proceedings of the international conference on information systems (ICIS) 2010*. https://aisel.aisnet.org/icis2010_submissions/18

Schultz, R. (2019). *Utherverse and the red light center: A brief introduction*. RyanSchultz.com. https://ryanschultz.com/2018/05/26/utherverse-and-the-red-light-center-a-brief-introduction/

Seritan, S., Wang, Y., Ford, J. E., Valentini, A., Gold, T., & Martínez, T. J. (2021). InteraChem: Virtual reality visualizer for reactive interactive molecular dynamics. *Journal of Chemical Education*, 98(11), 3486–3492.

Sharabi, L. (2022). *Inside the Datingverse: Your guide to virtual reality dating.* Psychology Today. https://www.psychologytoday.com/gb/blog/dating-in-the-digital-age/202210/inside-the-datingverse-your-guide-virtual-reality-dating

Shear, F. (2023). *IVAS' campaign of learning ensures development, production and fielding remain on track.* US Army. https://www.army.mil/article/264773/ivas_campaign_of_learning_ensures_development_production_and_fielding_remain_on_track

Simon, S. C., & Greitemeyer, T. (2019). The impact of immersion on the perception of pornography: A virtual reality study. *Computers in Human Behavior*, 93, 141–148.

Skarredghost. (2022). *AmazeVR "Hottieverse" concert review.* The Ghost Howls. https://skarredghost.com/2022/12/04/amazevr-hottieverse-review/

Smith, L. (2022). *Digital fashion has a new look.* FWD. https://www.wix.com/studio/blog/digital-fashion.2021

Smith, S. A. (2019). Virtual reality in episodic memory research: A review. *Psychonomic Bulletin & Review*, 26, 1213–1237.

Smith, R. E., & Vogt, B. D. (2014). *A proposed 2025 ground systems, systems engineering process* (ADA608885). Defense Acquisition University.

Stone, R. (2008). *Human factors guidelines for interactive 3D and games-based training systems design.* Human Factors Integration Defence Technology Centre Publication. Ministry of Defence. https://www.semanticscholar.org/paper/Human-Factors-Guidelines-for-Interactive-3-D-and-Stone/2042c99a1956314ddb0b4e13045c9215fafbeb08

Styles, E. B. (2016). Tate worlds: Art and artifacts reimagined in Minecraft. *Advances in Archaeological Practice*, 4(3), 410–414.

Sutcliffe, C. (2022). *21m People have now visited Nike's Roblox store. Here's how to do metaverse commerce right.* The Drum. https://www.thedrum.com/news/2022/09/22/21m-people-have-now-visited-nike-s-roblox-store-here-s-how-do-metaverse-commerce

Taylor, M. J., Shikaislami, C., McNicholas, C., Taylor, D., Reed, J., & Vlaev, I. (2020). Using virtual worlds as a platform for collaborative meetings in healthcare: A feasibility study. *BMC Health Services Research*, 20(1), 1–10.

Teng, M. Q., & Gordon, E. (2021). Therapeutic virtual reality in prison: Participatory design with incarcerated women. *New Media & Society*, 23(8), 2210–2229.

Thomas, J. J., & Cook, K. A. (Eds.). (2005). *Illuminating the path: The research and development agenda for visual analytics.* IEEE Computer Society.

Tornincasa, S., & Di Monaco, F. (2010, September). The future and the evolution of CAD. *Proceedings of the 14th international research/expert conference: Trends in the development of machinery and associated technology* (Vol. 1, No. 1, pp. 11–18). University of Zenica.

Uhomoibhi, J., & Ross, M. (2013). E-learning development trends in computer and engineering education. *International Journal of Engineering Pedagogy*, 3(2), 26–29.

Uribe Larach, D., & Cabra, J. F. (2010). Creative problem solving in Second Life: An action research study. *Creativity and Innovation Management*, 19(2), 167–179.

Van der Land, S., Schouten, A., & Feldberg, F. (2011). Modeling the metaverse: A theoretical model of effective team collaboration in 3D virtual environments. *Journal of Virtual Worlds Research*, 4(3) 1–16.

Vincent, J. (2021). *Performing Hamlet in GTA Online is simply the best theater experience lockdown can offer.* The Verge. https://www.theverge.com/tldr/2021/6/17/22538361/hamlet-gta-online-rustic-mascara-lobby

Vindenes, J., de Gortari, A. O., & Wasson, B. (2018). Mnemosyne: adapting the method of loci to immersive virtual reality. *Augmented reality, virtual reality, and computer graphics: 5th international conference, AVR 2018, Otranto, Italy, June 24–27, 2018, proceedings part I* (pp. 205–213). Springer International Publishing.

Wagener, N., Duong, T. D., Schöning, J., Rogers, Y., & Niess, J. (2021). The role of mobile and virtual reality applications to support well-being: An expert view and systematic app review. *Human-computer interaction—INTERACT 2021: 18th IFIP TC 13 international conference, Bari, Italy, August 30–September 3, 2021, proceedings, part IV* (pp. 262–283). Springer International Publishing.

Wallmyr, M., Sitompul, T. A., Holstein, T., & Lindell, R. (2019). Evaluating mixed reality notifications to support excavator operator awareness. *Human-computer interaction—INTERACT 2019: 17th IFIP TC 13 international conference, Paphos, Cyprus, September 2–6, 2019, proceedings, part I 17* (pp. 743–762). Springer International Publishing.

Wang, P., Bai, X., Billinghurst, M., Zhang, S., Zhang, X., Wang, S., Weiping, H., Yan, Y., & Ji, H. (2021). AR/MR remote collaboration on physical tasks: A review. *Robotics and Computer-Integrated Manufacturing, 72,* 102071.

Webber, S. (2013). Blended information behaviour in Second Life. *Journal of Information Science, 39*(1), 85–100.

Webster, E. (2021). *An inside look at F-35 pilot helmet fittings.* US Air Force. https://www.af.mil/News/Article-Display/Article/2719003/an-inside-look-at-f-35-pilot-helmet-fittings/

Wen, J., & Gheisari, M. (2020). Using virtual reality to facilitate communication in the AEC domain: A systematic review. *Construction Innovation, 20*(3), 509–542.

Wiklund, M., & Ekenberg, L. (2009). Going to school in world of Warcraft: Observations from a trial programme using of-the-shelf computer games as learning tools in secondary education. *Designs for Learning, 2*(1), 36–55.

Williams, K. (2023). *Virtual Arena: London's latest VR attractions.* Mixed. https://mixed-news.com/en/virtual-arena-londons-latest-vr-attractions/

Xie, B., Liu, H., Alghofaili, R., Zhang, Y., Jiang, Y., Lobo, F. D., Li, C., Li, W., Huang, H., Akdere, M., Mousas, C., & Yu, L. F. (2021). A review on virtual reality skill training applications. *Frontiers in Virtual Reality, 2,* 645153.

Yee, N., & Bailenson, J. (2007). The Proteus effect: The effect of transformed self-representation on behavior. *Human Communication Research, 33*(3), 271–290.

4

Technologies of the Metaverse

Introduction

This chapter provides a high-level description of the technologies which underpin the Metaverse. As discussed in Chapter 2, the "metaverse" and "virtual reality" (VR) are often seen as synonymous, and most of the technologies that underlie the Metaverse are also found in virtual worlds, massively-multi-player online role-playing games (MMORPGs), video games in general, and in three-dimensional (3D) collaboration and training software. At a technical level, a metaverse is just a distinct way of combining these elements.

The technologies are broken down here into eight broad areas, as shown in Figure 4.1:

- **3D environments**, including objects, physics, rendering, senses, and scenes;

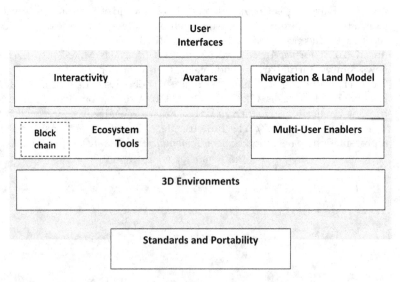

FIGURE 4.1
The key technology areas of the Metaverse.

DOI: 10.1201/9781003395461-5

- **Multi-user enablers**, including game servers, sharding, etc.;
- **Navigation and land model**;
- **Avatars**, including avatar appearance (and animation), avatar interaction, and virtual agents;
- **Interactivity**, including voice, text chat, tools, building, scripting, and interfacing;
- **Ecosystem tools**, including market/economy, rights and permissions, user management;
- **Standards and portability**; and
- **User interfaces**.

In addition, this chapter will also consider the role of artificial intelligence (AI) and blockchain technology, including cryptocurrency and non-fungible tokens (NFTs).

Not explicitly considered here are some of the back-end elements needed to make almost any software application, such as access control, databases, security management, etc.

3D Environments

The 3D environment is what the user sees (and possibly hears or even feels) on their screen or XR device. It can be split into six different elements, as shown in Figure 4.2:

- Objects (including avatars);
- Physics;
- Lighting and rendering;
- Audio;
- Other human sense triggers;
- Non-human sense phenomena; and
- Scenes.

Objects

3D virtual environments are conventionally made of 3D digital objects placed within a space defined by a set of x,y,z co-ordinates. Those 3D objects could be as simple as a cube or as complex as a bunch of flowers and as small as a louse or as big as a city. Each object typically comprises three elements:

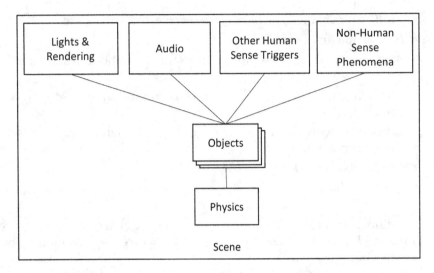

FIGURE 4.2
The components of the 3D environment.

- **Geometry** – the shape of the object, typically defined by lines (also called edges) and vertices (also called points), which are often used to make up triangles (tris) or other polygons (polys), a collection of which then fit together to form the desired shape. When an object is displayed purely in terms of its geometry, it is called a wire-frame;
- **Texture** – how an object looks in terms of colour and pattern. This is often defined by having a two-dimensional (2D) image (in JPG, PNG, or other formats) either "pasted" onto each surface of the object, or having the faces of the object "wrapped" by a complex arrangement of textures in something called a UV map; and
- **Material** – how an object reflects light, giving a surface a sense of depth and what people would conventionally call "texture" (i.e. does it look smooth or rough, made of fur or cloth, etc.), defined by what is often called a "bump" or "normal" map.

Figure 4.3 shows a simple wooden cabin in terms of its wireframe, plain texture, image texture, and material.

The more complex an object in terms of geometry, textures, and materials, the more memory it takes to store, the more bandwidth to transmit, and the more processing power to render and display. As a result, virtual environments designed for lower power devices (such as mobiles) have tended to use blockier, more cartoony, objects and a simple, primary colour palette – but improvements in mobile phone processors are increasingly closing the gap in the difference in usable detail between smartphones and desktop computers.

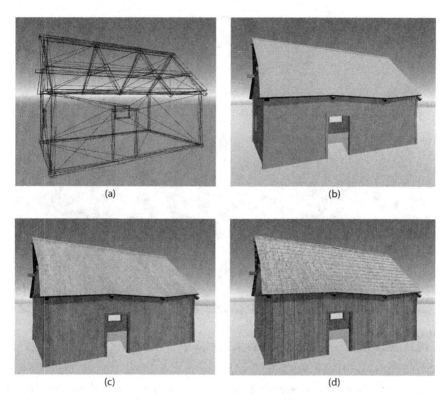

FIGURE 4.3

A wooden shack shown in (a) wireframe, (b) plain texture, (c) image texture, and (d) material including bump-maps.

Most 3D objects are created using dedicated 3D graphics applications such as Blender (https://www.blender.org/), Z-Brush (https://www.maxon.net/en/zbrush), and 3D Studio Max (https://www.autodesk.co.uk/products/3ds-max/). These applications generate objects as digital files in formats such as Wavefront OBJ (.obj), Autodesk Filmbox (.fbx), and more recently Graphics Library Transmission Format glTF (.gltf), which can then be imported into a virtual space. The composition of the objects within the 3D space is typically achieved using a game engine such as Unity3D (https://unity.com/) or Epic Game's Unreal (https://www.unrealengine.com/).

However, this model of using external applications to build 3D objects and then compose them into a scene does not really meet the axioms defined earlier about being able to create and edit from within the Metaverse. In a true Metaverse, the user should be able to build and create objects from within the world, just as they would do in the physical world. *Second Life*, *OpenSim*, and *Somnium Space* are the main virtual worlds that fully embrace in-world building – rather than just object placement. In the earlier versions of *Second Life* (from 2003 to 2011), in-world building was all there

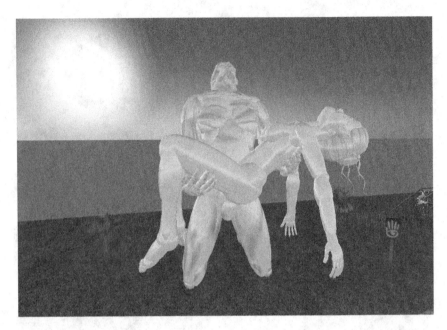

FIGURE 4.4
A *Second Life* sculpture by SL artist Starax created using "prim-torture".

was, assembling and distorting simple Platonic solid "primitives" (usually shortened to "prims") such as cubes, cones, and cylinders in a process called prim-torture into quite incredible structures, devices, and artworks (see Figure 4.4). *Second Life* introduced mesh (i.e. 3D model imports) in 2011 and is starting to support glTF, and users can now freely choose between the two approaches.

Physics

If the virtual world is going to act anything like the physical world, it needs physics – if a user lets go of something, it should drop, and if they throw something, it should arc. Of course, this is a virtual world, so users might want to be able to selectively switch physics off or change values, so they can experience being on a moon or another planet or even in weightlessness. Another key element is how objects react when they touch or bump into each other: should they just pass through and ignore the other object, should they bounce off like billiard balls (so-called hard-body physics), or should they deform slightly as they touch and repel (so-called soft-body physics).

Physics in virtual worlds are typically implemented by "physics engines" from specialist providers such as Havoc (https://www.havok.com/) and the open-source Bullet Physics (https://github.com/bulletphysics/bullet3/), which are then plugged into the virtual world or game engine in use. The physics settings are typically well hidden from the user, but some worlds might allow the value of gravity, or even its direction, to be altered.

Lighting and Rendering

Just creating a 3D object and placing it within a 3D space is not enough to make the object appear to the user. Two other things are required – lights and a lighting model – the end result being the "rendering" of the object within the 3D space. Lights come in different forms such as point, spot, or ambient. They can be defined in terms of colour, intensity, and how quickly the light dims with distance. The lighting model defines how the light incident on an object will illuminate and even reflect off the object, dependent on its material and texture.

Another key element of a scene are the shadows caused by objects blocking any light source. A quick way to improve the realism of any scene is to pay more attention to the shadows. Lighting models take a lot of calculation, and so many computer games do all the calculations beforehand and "bake" them into the textures of the objects, but this is not a route available to an editable metaverse as objects can be continually moved, deleted, or added. This is one reason why traditionally social virtual worlds looked inferior graphically to games, but modern graphics cards enable far more lighting calculations to be done in real time.

Reflections are a real challenge. Mirrors were traditionally created in virtual environments by placing an invisible in-world camera in front of the mirror object and then rendering its output onto the mirror's surface. Reflections from surfaces like shiny metal or water are nowadays achieved through software called shaders which are small bits of code that run on a computer's graphics card which enhance the look of a scene in a wide variety of ways (Vivo & Lowe, 2015).

More advanced approaches to lighting require far more processing power and are only slowly becoming available for real-time rendering. Most of these are physically based rendering (PBR) approaches which base their behaviour broadly on the actual physics of how light works (3DAce, 2021). A specific example, and more accurate than simpler PBR approaches, is ray-tracing. Here, rays are cast into the scene to calculate all the possible reflections, obscurations, and colour changes between the light sources and the virtual eye (Glassner, 1989). An even more advanced approach is light field imaging technology which captures information that is not typically processed by the eye but that allows greater manipulation of the view of a scene (Ihrke et al., 2016, and could promise headset-free VR (Kara et al., 2023).

Virtual worlds have adopted a range of styles in terms of their overall look, from the highly cartoon form of *Virbela*, through the stylish but obviously artificial look of *Second Life* and *Fortnite* to the more "realistic" look of more modern environments such as *EngageVR* and *Rumii*. Just as an "uncanny valley" exists for avatars (see below), so to it seems that many users would rather have a good-looking "artificial" environment than a badly realized "realistic" environment, and there are also issues with having an environment that is so glossy that it detracts from any collaboration or training task that is meant to be attending, as well as adding unnecessarily to the cost of a system (Scerbo & Dawson, 2007).

Audio

Virtual worlds are often viewed as being purely visual spaces, but even for sighted users, adding audio significantly increases the immersion of virtual spaces – even just the background noise of an office, traffic, wind, or birdsong (e.g. Lindquist et al., 2020). However, virtual worlds should also be accessible to non-sighted users and partially sighted users. Ironically, the original text-based multi-user dungeons (MUDs) and multi-user object-orientated dungeons (MOOs) were probably more accessible as they could be used with simple screen readers, and there is still interest in the concept of audio games and even combining them with augmented reality (AR) (Moustakas et al., 2019). Moving toward a more semantic metaverse (see below) would considerably aid the creation of audio and other sense interfaces for virtual spaces.

Other Human Sense Triggers

What of the other senses? A metaversal space should be able to generate the cues for touch, smell, and potentially even taste. As with sight and sound, the elements to enable them within the virtual space are just code and data – although, just as a world needs an illumination model as well as lights, it would also need a diffusion model as well as smells (for instance) to create a realistic environment. Research is ongoing on smell generators for use with computer games and potentially virtual world applications (e.g. Makin, 2023), with some early systems reaching commercialisation (Milevo, 2020). Taste simulation is likewise the subject of some interesting research (e.g. Aoyama, 2020; Kerruish, 2019).

In addition to the five common senses, the body also relies on at least two more senses, proprioception (the sense of where the parts of one's body are) and interoception (the sense of what is happening in your body). Whilst the former tends to impact navigation, positioning, and manipulation (e.g. Valori et al., 2020), the latter may have applications from VR therapy (Riva et al., 2021) to pain management (Felnhofer et al., 2023) and may also have a relationship with cybersickness (Heeter et al., 2020).

Non-Human Sense Phenomena

Whilst humans only have five primary senses, is there any reason why a virtual world should be limited to modelling only those? Additional phenomena such as temperature, infra-red, ultrasound, or electro-magnetism could be used either directly by scripted objects (e.g. ultrasound or electro-magnetism detection in animal avatars) or for conversion into visual or audio senses for human-controlled avatars. Interestingly, it is the military which is particularly interested in so-called hyper-spectral modelling in order to better represent issues such as camouflage, thermal signatures (BISim, 2023), radar, and electronic warfare (Wihl et al., 2010).

Scenes

The scene is all that is around the user in VR (which could be as small as a room or potentially as large as a world) and is typically represented as a hierarchy, as shown in Figure 4.5. This is often referred to as the scene graph and is similar to the document object model, which defines a web page. The scene graph tells the rendering system what to render and where.

The scene might be composed using a drag-and-drop editor such as Unity or Unreal, or it might be written in code such as WebGL – which can also be generated by Unity and Unreal. This code can also define the interactivity of the scene, as with a Javascript application embedded in a web page. In fact, it was the three.js Javascript library (https://github.com/mrdoob/three.js) that made WebGL, creating 3D scenes within ordinary 2D web pages, usable to a wider range of developers. The babylon.js library (https://www.babylonjs.com/) further extended what could be done in 3D on the web with a library that included physics, animation, and fluid modelling, and a dedicated web-based editor/game engine, but at the cost

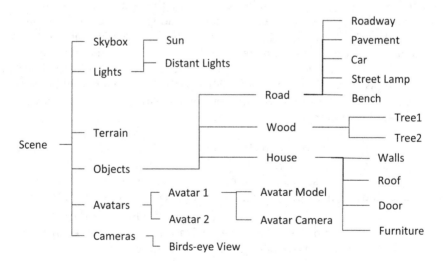

FIGURE 4.5
A prototypical scene graph for a virtual world.

of higher complexity (Jamil, 2023). An alternative development, A-Frame (https://aframe.io/), provided a higher level abstraction on top of three.js delivering an almost hypertext markup language (HTML)style authoring environment for 3D graphics and experiences. WebXR extended WebGL by enabling it to detect whether it was running in DesktopVR or headset-mounted VR displays (HMD-VR) and to render the scene, and take user inputs, accordingly.

Scaling the scene graph from a small single-user scene to a large, multi-user virtual world is a significant challenge. One solution being implemented is the Open Universal Scene Description (OpenUSD) (Lebaredian & Kass, 2022; Peters & Weatherbed, 2023), as used in NVIDIA's Omniverse offering, and based on original work by Pixar. In addition to supporting the standard elements of a scene graph, OpenUSD also supports relationships and inheritance, interoperability with the glTF model standard, support for the WGS84 geospatial referencing schema (enabling the accurate positioning of physical world items), and the capability to scale to large scenes. OpenUSD and its tools are open source and are promoted by the Alliance for OpenUSD (https://aousd.org/), and Unreal, Unity, and Apple are all supporting it.

The Semantic Metaverse

One potential limitation of USD is that it does not enforce any naming or type standards, and so objects can be called anything – a chair might be just "object27354", rather than "chair2" or even "leather armchair". To enable virtual world environments to be accessed by the widest possible range of devices (and by AIs), there is a strong case for adopting a semantic approach to virtual worlds (Burden, 2011; Ibáñez-Martinez & Delgado-Mata, 2006). In a semantic metaverse, everything is defined in semantic terms – what it is and what it can do – independent of how it is rendered. Every element is tied to an ontological type (Messaoud et al., 2015) so that any system will know that "object27354" is a chair, and perhaps even what kind of chair. This provides a number of benefits:

- If a user interface system is unable to render the object given and object model provided in the scene, it can substitute a suitable one which is better suited to its medium (e.g. AR or mixed reality [MR]), its bandwidth, its processing power, or even its user or use case;
- For visually impaired users, an enhanced user interface (UI) can add a suitable audio description, help with navigation, and even highlight the most important objects;
- Any AI accessing the virtual world doesn't have to try and understand the 3D model to work out what the object is, it can just read its ontological type and any associated metadata;

- Portability of scene definitions and interoperability between virtual worlds operating to different formats and standards is enhanced (Soto & Allongue, 1997);

- The world can actually be defined by its creator more rapidly using semantic terms (e.g. Kleinermann et al., 2005); and

- Any relationships between objects can be extracted into the semantic graph containing the objects and do not need to be explicitly coded into every virtual world.

Game Servers

Most of technologies described in this chapter are used by single-user computer games and multi-user virtual worlds alike. What sets the latter apart is the technology to allow multiple users to be in the same virtual space at the same time, and ideally to interact with each other.

At the heart of most multi-user systems are game servers (also called reflection servers or multi-user servers) (Gallagher, 2022). Examples of game servers include *Photon Engine* (https://www.photonengine.com/), *Nakama* (https://heroiclabs.com/nakama/), and *PlayFab* (https://azure.microsoft.com/en-gb/products/playfab), or those built into the *Unreal* and *Unity* platforms.

When a user first logs into a shared space, they are sent the details of where everything (and everybody) is in that space (this may be as a full set of live data or a base set of data plus recent changes). For performance reasons, this may be limited to what is within a certain distance of the user. As avatars move and objects are moved, created, or deleted, the relevant user's software sends a message about the change to the game server, the server updates the state of the world, and then sends update messages to every user present in that space, and their own software then reflects the changes in their local copy. In addition to this centralised approach, it is also possible to take a peer-to-peer approach – where each user's device communicates directly with other users' devices, but the co-ordination and scaling can then be more challenging (Novotny et al., 2020).

The game server is highly optimized for passing very small messages (e.g. object A has moved to location X,Y,Z) to large numbers of people. However, it is not just the performance of the game server that is crucial to giving the user a smooth experience. There are also the network lags across the Internet as messages are sent from the user to the game server and then on to every user, and then to the ability of each user's own computer to manage the updates. Conventional approaches tend to result in a limit of significantly less than 100 people within any one space.

Trying to get large number of avatars in one virtual space is a challenge. Even the 4000 avatars demonstrated in experiments by Improbable

(Improbable, 2021) are well short of the 90,000 people in Wembley Stadium for a big football match. There are currently several approaches to trying to handle this issue, and which can be applied singly or in combination:

- Sharding – every group of ~50–100 avatars is on their own instance of the location. Users in one instance can see and interact with other users in the same instance but don't see and can't interact with users in other instances – although the rest of the crowd may be generic avatars just sketched in. Exceptions can be made for key avatars (such as the performers at a concert) so that they are seen by all users, whichever instance they are on. This sharding approach is widely used by massively multi-player online games (MMOs), and it has also been used for big virtual world events. In some ways, the result may be little different from a real event, where you can directly inter- act with the people in the block of seating you are in, but you only have a sense of the presence of the rest of the crowd (Waldo, 2008);

- Varying levels of fidelity, so people close to you are shown in full resolution, but in decreasing resolution as they get further from you, till they are just a blob in the distance;

- Minimising the interactions between you and other attendees – even to the extent of being able to pass through them;

- Making key objects multi-user – for instance, the ball and players in a game, but other objects (e.g. popcorn boxes) are just handled locally; and

- Massively optimising the game server to distribute updates in the most effective way – such as the systems being developed by Improbable and RP1 (Takahashi, 2021).

The Metaverse needs to be able to cope, in some way, with the full range of human experiences, from a small group sat around a campfire – and indeed for millions of those campfire groups to exist – to allowing 70,000 avatars to attend a virtual Burning Man festival, or for several million to march in protest, or perhaps even tens of millions to gather for homage or prayer.

Navigation and Land Model

If the user is presented with a virtual space, then how do they move around it? Within a specific location, they will probably walk, or even fly, but what about the larger scale? The early virtual worlds such as *Second Life* and *ActiveWorlds* worked on a "single map" model, possibly inspired by the globe-girdling Street in *Snow Crash*. The same model is seen in some cyrptoworlds such as *Decentraland* and *Somnium Space*. In all these, you buy land to build on, and from your land you can see neighbours' land and you can walk (or fly) freely between them, permissions allowing, with the option to teleport (TP) longer distances. You get the feeling of being in a single, shared, persistent virtual world. *Decentraland* talks about a "transversable world" and the importance of "discovery by adjacency", and these are useful concepts to bear in mind (Ordano et al., n.d.).

Many of the HMD-VR-orientated worlds such as *Frames, Horizon Worlds,* and *VRChat* work on more of a "room" model, where you have your own space or spaces (which could be room or potentially planet sized) and you can do what you want in that space, including opening it up to other people, but there is no sense of having any neighbours or any spatial relationships, and you can only TP between rooms. The sense of a shared experience is only when you are in a space with other people; it's not pervasive or persistent.

Some platforms blur or blend the models. For instance, *OpenSim* lets you build your own "world", sublet space on that in a geographic, land parcel, style to other users but then connect your world (and their sublet spaces) to other worlds and spaces anywhere on the Hypergrid. *OpenSim*'s parcel and Hypergrid model seems highly appropriate to any ultimate metaverse, giving the best of both (virtual) worlds.

Avatars

Users are represented within virtual spaces as avatars. Whilst some people prefer avatars that look like themselves, others prefer avatars that are completely different in style, gender, or species, or even to represent themselves as robots, ghosts, or toasters.

This section will not go into the detail of all the technologies and approaches that are used to build realistic looking avatars – for that, the reader is referred to the authors' earlier book *Virtual Humans: Today and Tomorrow* (Burden & Savin-Baden, 2019). Instead, this section will look at some of the key issues and choices concerning avatars in the Metaverse.

Avatar Appearance

The appearance of an avatar includes body shape (and size), skin colour, face shape and colour (including lips, nose, cheeks, eyes), hair (style and colour), and clothes. The user should expect to be able to change their avatar's appearance as often as they want, probably having different avatars (or at least outfits) for different events and roles. A human or even humanoid look should not be mandated. There is a lot of existing research around how people choose their avatar within a virtual world. Motivations for choice include virtual exploration, social navigation, contextual adaptation, and identity representation, with users to some extent portraying their actual selves and reflecting their own aesthetic views in developing a stable avatar that they can relate to over significant periods of time (Lin & Wang, 2014).

In addition to personal choice, the other key issue around avatar appearance is how "well" the technology of the virtual world renders the avatar. Some worlds have very cartoony avatars, whilst others strive for "photo-realistic" avatars. However, the uncanny valley effect (Mori, 1970) means that many people prefer a good, slightly cartoony avatar better than a "photo-realistic" avatar that just doesn't quite pull the photo-realism off.

Some worlds let the user take a webcam photo of their head and then try and wrap that around the head of the avatar (as *Spatial* used to do), whilst others (e.g. *Virtend*) just paste the webcam photo onto a blocky meeples-like body. A slightly different, and perhaps better, approach is that taken by ReadyPlayerMe (https://readyplayer.me/). A webcam takes a head and shoulders photo, but rather than then try and convert this directly into a (probably terrible looking) "photo-realistic" avatar, it uses it to drive the parameters of the configurator, so the result is an obviously artificial-looking avatar, but one that (a) looks pretty good and (b) looks something like you. Figure 4.6c shows David's ReadyPlayerMe avatar created using the process and being used in *Mozilla Hubs*, alongside his avatar in other virtual worlds. Apple's Vision Pro lets the user use the headset to create a 3D scan of their head for use as an avatar.

The same issues as with the real-time rendering of objects have traditionally kept virtual world avatars inferior to those of the latest computer-generated imagery (CGI) film or triple-A game, but hardware improvements and the rising interest in the Metaverse from the fashion industry may help to change that.

The authors have had enough serious business meetings with Daleks, ghosts, and talking parrots in virtual worlds to know that someone's avatar doesn't need to look like them, and in fact, the research suggests that the freedom of avatar choice helps with freedom of expression and being able to express your true personality, as well as being able to indulge in role-playing when you want to (Neustaedter & Fedorovskaya, 2009).

Avatar Animation

Avatar animation takes place at three broad levels:

- the large-scale movements of limbs and body as an avatar walks, flies, swims, or dances (locomotion animation);
- the smaller movements as it points, gesticulates, or throws up its hands in horror (animation-in-place); and
- the animation of the face to express emotion and to synchronise with any audio speech being produced.

Whole body avatars with whole body animation were the norm in *Second Life*, *Active Worlds*, and other virtual worlds around 2000–2010. It's notable

FIGURE 4.6
David's avatar in different virtual worlds. (a) *Second Life*, (b) VirBela, (c) ReadyPlayerMe/Hubs, and (d) EngageVR.

how many HMD-VR-orientated worlds use a head, shoulders/chest and hands approach for avatars – with no arms or legs! This seems to be to avoid the loss of immersion that occurs when the inverse kinematics (which is estimating body position) makes an avatar's elbows and knees bend in weird ways (Parger et al., 2018). Some platforms, such as *EngageVR*, Frame and *Decentraland*, are following the full-body avatar route, and they may soon be coming to

Meta's *Horizon World* (Truly, 2023), so hopefully the de-limbed and disembodied avatars will only be a passing phase.

Whilst locomotion animations are triggered automatically as the avatar moves, animation in-place (including dance moves) and expressions were (and generally still are) triggered manually by the user in DesktopVR (e.g. by function keys), or automatically from keywords in chat (e.g. typing "No" would also result in a shake of the head). It is also notable that having "idling" animations that just move an avatar a bit, shifting weight from foot to foot, or fidgeting with the hands, really enhances the realism of a scene.

With the arrival of HMD-VR, and now hand-tracking, a lot of these animations-in-place are no longer required as they are created by the natural movements of the user – but such gestures still need to be made available to DesktopVR users; otherwise, it can be very obvious just from arm positions who is on HMD-VR and who is on DesktopVR.

One of the last challenges is real-time facial animation, both when talking and smiling or frowning, etc. – which can significantly enhance the realism of social interactions. Initial approaches involved using a webcam to detect facial expression and have it animate an avatar's face (e.g. Apostolakis & Daras, 2015). The latest generation of headsets (e.g. Oculus Quest Pro, Apple Vision Pro) has small back-facing cameras to detect facial expression and eye movement and to pass these on to the avatar (Lang, 2022).

There are though some interesting issues of privacy and deception. For instance, your expressions could be better (i.e. automatically) detected and brought to the attention of the person you are speaking to and may belie the veracity of what you are saying. Alternatively, you might run software to mute, accentuate, or invert the expression feed your headset is sending out into the world.

Avatar Interaction

In early DesktopVR worlds, text-chat tended to dominate, but now voice is the norm, and it is typically spatial audio – so sounds are localized in space and come from the direction of the speaker and at a volume consistent with their distance. However, text-chat has its advantages – it masks a user's physical nature if their avatar is divergent from it (see the earlier discussion on the introduction of voice to *Second Life* in Chapter 1), it provides a useful backchannel during collaborative sessions, and it creates a more equitable discussion space (Nesson & Nesson, 2008). Against this voice is really the only option in HMD-VR at the moment – although decent virtual keyboards might address this. But human interaction isn't just about voice – it's about expressions and gesture and other forms of body language as well. Easy access to 2D and 3D emoticons, as well as to gestures and expressions, is one way of capturing the non-verbal elements of communication. The potential for haptics to enable other modes of avatar interaction will be considered below.

Virtual Agents

All these characteristics also apply to virtual agents embodied as non-player characters (NPCs). Such NPCs may be acting as game characters, or as guides, receptionists, shop assistants, personal assistants, training partners, coaches, tutors, or even as embodied versions of physical world applications or as virtual versions of ourselves when we're not around. A key question is where does the "brain" of that virtual agent lie? As discussed in *Virtual Humans* (Burden & Savin-Baden, 2019), it probably shouldn't lie in the virtual world. It needs to be written in industry-standard code, running on a generic server somewhere on the Internet, and then using an application programming interface (API) to receive information from the virtual world, and to send commands to its avatar (or avatars) within the world (or worlds). And ideally, that avatar needs to be able to do everything that a human-controlled avatar can do.

In 2017, David helped run an experiment with such a chatbot programme controlling an avatar in *Second Life* in a covert Turing Test. Of the users who interacted with the agent, 78% thought it was human operated (Gilbert & Forney, 2015). Virtual worlds really level the playing field when it comes to telling chatbots from humans (Burden et al., 2016). Certainly, at the time of the experiment, people's working assumption was that an avatar was probably human driven, so the agent just had to make sure it didn't give away the fact that it was a computer, rather than having to try to convince the user that it was human.

Virtual worlds can act as useful virtual laboratories for working with theories of embedded and grounded cognition as they represent messy and complex worlds in a way that the traditional "block world" research spaces don't and save researchers from all the hassle of building physical robots to experiment within the physical world. Lucy, the protagonist agent in Fable Studio's *Wolves in the Walls* (Billington, 2018), is one of the best implementations so far of a virtual agent within a VR space in terms of her ability to address you personally and directly wherever you are in the room and to really draw you into her story.

Interactivity

This section considers how the user interacts with the environment itself. At its most basic, it's about touching/clicking on objects and buttons, or with head-mounted display XR (HMD-XR) and hand-tracking reaching out and touching and manipulating something, but this should come as no surprise as that is fundamentally how humans interact with the physical world.

Tools

Most virtual worlds provide a selection of generic tools to support collaboration as described in Chapter 3, including virtual whiteboards and post-it notes, screen-share, and 3D drawing tools. If, as it should, the world also has building, editing, scripting, and marketplace tools, then users should be able to create any tools they want, no matter how niche, and make them available – for free or at a cost, to other users. The range of tools should not be something that is limited by the platform owners.

Just as the physical world has seen smartphones and tablets supplant what used to be multiple separate tools, so too might virtual tablets and virtual smartphones make other functionality available in a familiar form factor, and especially in-world and cross-world apps (such as note taking, messaging, video recording, etc.). At some point, there might even be the ability to have all of a physical tablet's capabilities, apps, and data echoed onto their virtual version (something which Apple's Vision Pro is beginning to do), and the ability for the user to script custom applications for their virtual tablet.

Building

Being able to create or build (and not just place) objects inside of the Metaverse is essential; otherwise, it is just somebody else's VR application. The import of objects should, though, also be supported so that more powerful external build tools (like Blender, etc.) can also be used. Many of the current crop of virtual worlds (e.g. *ChatVR, Fortnite, Decentraland, Roblox*) require users to use Unity, Unreal, or a custom external editor in order build a space and any objects they want in it. *Second Life/OpenSim* is probably still the best example of how to do proper in-world building, although it is also a feature of *Minecraft* and *Somnium Space*.

Scripting

Whilst many worlds allow for object placement, and even modification, very few allow for in-world scripting. This is likely primarily due to performance management and security issues – a bad script can wreak havoc with a space or be used for deliberately malign purposes against users, their accounts, or the platform itself (Muttik, 2008). As an example, back in 2007, David set up an artificial life script on his sim in *Second Life* – it got out of control and replicated itself all over the place and crashed the entire sim!

If users are going to be able to create interactive objects and tools in the same way that they might create gadgets or apps in the real world, then the Metaverse must support scripting, preferably based on an easy and commonly used language such as Javascript. For simpler tasks, a drag-and-drop or visual block programming language (like Scratch) might be useful. Meta's *Horizon Worlds* is using both drag-and-drop and visual block programming to reasonable effect (MetaQuest, n.d.), whilst Ova's *StellarX* (2022, https://www.stellarx.ai/) has a very slick drag-and-drop system for graphically flow-charting interactions. *Hiberworld* (2018, https://hiberworld.com/) has a similar, if less fully featured, scripting interface. *Frame* started to support scripts in early 2024, but, as mentioned earlier, it uses the Wonderland scripting language and so has a steep learning curve for even the most basic interactions.

FIGURE 4.7
Plotting real-time air traffic control data in a virtual world.

Whilst Linden Scripting Language (LSL), as used in *Second Life* and *OpenSim*, may not be as familiar as Javascript, it still provides an easy-to-use yet powerful in-world scripting capability not yet equalled in other worlds.

Scripts should also allow code to be written that can bring in data from the rest of the Internet, and by extension the physical world. For instance, physical geotemporal data (e.g. weather, earthquakes, or air traffic information – see Figure 4.7) can be plotted on a virtual map or globe, or states or commands can be passed to control actions in the virtual world in one direction – e.g. a physical light switch turning on a virtual light, or in the other direction, the movements of an avatar can create a soundscape in the physical world.

Although they are trivial examples, they show how the virtual and physical can (and should) be part of the same larger multiverse. If users want as much agency in the virtual world as they have in the physical world, they'll need to be able to access the same information and systems as they do every day. These interfaces also let developers build the core of any big applications out on the Internet using industry standard tools and just treat the virtual world as the user interface. Developers need to build for the single multiverse, covering the virtual, digital, *and* physical worlds.

Voice Control

One of the downsides of HMD-VR is that virtual keyboard interaction is currently quite problematic – which can make detailed building and scripting tasks and even simple text-chat or note taking, difficult. Hopefully, virtual worlds will increasingly see support for voice control for their interfaces, both through explicit commands and some sort of in-world or in-headset personal assistant. Recent developments around using generative adversarial networks (GANs), ChatGPT, and similar technologies for not only text and

2D imagery but also 3D modelling begin to give a hint of the future power of voice control, where a user could stand in an empty holodeck style space and just say something like "give me a beach with a blue ocean, dancing dolphins, some coconut palms and a large daiquiri", and it all just appears (Chow, 2023). *GOXR* (https://www.xrspace.io/us/goxr) already has NPC avatars that users can talk to verbally, and *Hiberworld* (https://hiberworld.com/) has some primitive AI scene rendering from a simple text description, so merging the two capabilities cannot be far off.

Ecosystem Tools

Not everything required to run a Metaverse is immediately visible to the user, and it is many of the features that are described in this section that begin to separate a social virtual world or metaverse-type space away from more generic multi-user VR applications. Radoff's eco-system model in Figure 2.2 is also a useful guide to the different range of tools required and highlights the need for discovery tools which will exist partly outside of the metaverse and of any one ecosystem.

User Management

Like any social application, there will be a need for a user management layer. This controls not only application and world access but also:

- Profile information, including:
  - Areas of interest;
  - Links (if desired) to profiles on other social networking sites;
- Friend links, and the ability to find, add, and remove friends;
- Group links, and the ability to find, join, leave, create, message, and remove groups;
- Money and transaction information and control; and
- Security management.

Rights and Permissions

If users are going to buy, make, or sell things in the Metaverse, then there needs to be some way to protect intellectual property (IP) and restrict permissions. A common model is for objects, scripts, and places to have an assigned owner (which could be an individual or a group), and then a set of permissions to allow other individuals or groups, or anyone, to access/use, copy, modify, sell, or delete the entity. Things get more complex when artefacts start to be built up from multiple entities. This may be an area where block-chain could actually help, and this is discussed further below.

Market/Economy

If the virtual world creator doesn't provide what a user needs, then why not get it from another user? Worlds such as *Second Life, Minecraft,* and *Roblox* have active in-world marketplaces based around user-generated content.

Some form of virtual currency is almost certainly needed in the Metaverse, and that currency should be freely exchangeable with real-world currencies. Some of the work on studying *Second Life*'s virtual economy was discussed in Chapter 1. Many of the current crop of virtual worlds (the cryptoworlds) are using cryptocurrencies such as Bitcoin or Ethereum as their base, but these have potential issues with both their environmental credentials (see Chapter 5) and are subject to hacking, speculation, and profiteering. Again, the role of cryptocurrencies is dealt with in more detail below.

Standards and Portability

Everything so far described is work that one development company could build into their own world – but the real challenge is how a user can take their avatar, money, objects, and even scripts and move between different virtual worlds or metaverses.

As discussed in Chapter 2, it's probably unrealistic to think that there will only ever be one metaverse, so if the future is the Multiverse, then the issue of portability needs to be addressed. Of course, portability is something which barely exists even on the World Wide Web (all those multiple accounts, different profiles, etc.), so it's no surprise that it doesn't exist in virtual worlds yet. Even object "standards" such as .obj and .fbx mentioned above, which should enable that an object can be moved seamlessly between platforms, frequently fail.

There are some positive signs. The new 3D object standard glTF is prov-ing to be far more portable than earlier standards and has been adopted as an International Standard, ISO/IEC 12113:2022 (https://www.iso.org/standard/83990.html). Even though the Metaverse Roadmap (MVR) (Smart et al., 2007), established as a cross industry body in 2007, fell by the wayside, multiple new groups are taking up the challenge to establish standards for the metaverse:

- The Metaverse Standards Forum (https://metaverse-standards.org/) aims "to foster interoperability standards for an Open Metaverse" and seems to have the largest membership, including most of the industry key players, and an active set of "domain groups";

- The Open Metaverse Foundation (https://www.openmv.org/) is "home to an open, vendor-neutral community dedicated to creating open standards and software to support the open, global, scalable Metaverse", with one of its main projects being O3DE, an open-source game engine in the same space as Unity and Unreal, although it says that it is also working on developing open standards for object portability;

- The Open Metaverse Alliance (OMA3) (https://www.oma3.org/) is a "collaboration of Web3 metaverse platform creators" whose goal is to "ensure virtual land, digital assets, ideas, and services are highly interoperable between platforms and transparent to all communities". As such, it is closely wedded to the Web3 and blockchain approaches;

- The Open Metaverse Interoperability Group (OMIG) (https://omigroup.org/) describes itself as "an open source community of industry professionals, independent creators, and passionate enthusiasts building interoperable technology together, in the open", and aims to bridge "virtual worlds across interfaces and technologies by designing and promoting protocols for identity, social graphs, inventory, and more";

- W3C (who run the World Wide Web standards) maintains a Metaverse Interoperability Community Group (https://www.w3.org/community/metaverse-interop/) and is also a member of the Metaverse Standards Forum;

- The International Telecommunications Union (ITU) has its own Focus Group on the Metaverse (FG-MV) (https://www.itu.int/en/ITU-T/focusgroups/mv/Pages/default.aspx) looking at "pre-standardisation" work, analysing "the technical requirements of the metaverse to identify fundamental enabling technologies in areas from multimedia and network optimization to digital currencies, Internet of Things, digital twins, and environmental sustainability" and examining the role of international standards (ITU, 2023); and

- The Alliance for OpenUSD (https://aousd.org/) promotes OpenUSD as described above.

User Interfaces

User interfaces have been deliberately left to last as whether the user is accessing the Metaverse from their smartphone, laptop, desktop, or HMD should be immaterial to the Metaverse itself.

DesktopVR

This is the umbrella term for accessing a 3D environment through a single 2D screen as found on conventional desktops, laptops, and smartphones. It may not have the same technical level of immersion as HMD-VR, but as explained in Chapter 2, technical immersion is just one part of the whole immersion/presence/embodiment/agency calculus, and as long as the rest of the experience is well designed the user will still get most of the benefits of the environment. Compared to HMD-VR, Desktop VR is also cheaper and a lot more convenient, and users are almost immune to cybersickness.

For both DesktopVR and HMD-VR, access via the browser using WebXR as described in Chapter 1 is a preferable way to deliver worlds to users – removing the need for downloads. It should also be noted that VR experiences typically take *less* bandwidth across the Internet and wireless connections to operate than video conferencing calls (A. G. Campbell et al., 2020).

HMD-VR

Ever since Palmer Luckey released Oculus DK1 in 2013, the media focus has been on the HMD-VR experience. With each generation of headsets screen resolutions, dynamic ranges, fields of view, and battery life have tended to increase, latency and weight have decreased, and the whole HMD-VR experience has become more comfortable and natural. As of 2023, the latest headsets, such as the Meta Quest3, Varjo XR-3, and Apple Vision Pro, now feature forward-facing colour cameras to support mixed reality, and some even have back-facing cameras to detect eye-movement and expression. OpenXR (https://www.khronos.org/openxr/) is emerging as an open-source standard for how HMD-VR devices operate.

DesktopVR or HMD-VR

The choice between a DesktopVR experience and an HMD-VR is one that the user should be able to make on a per-session basis, and it should not be dictated by the application. There are so many use cases where HMD-VR is not feasible (on the train, in a cafe, on the sofa half-watching TV, etc.), and Chapter 2 has already presented some of the research comparing DesktopVR and HMD-VR.

A key issue is that HMD-VR still doesn't have significant market penetration. The install base for HMD-VR is currently estimated (to the end of 2022) at around 50 million units, with Meta Quest 2 accounting for around 46% of sales in 2022 (S. Campbell, 2023). Assuming all these headsets are in use, that puts global penetration at only 0.6%, as against around 55% for the mobile internet (GSMA, 2023). A 2021 report looking only at Minority World[1] countries estimated that household penetration for HMD-VR was around 2.4% (Jijiashvili, 2021). Estimates of HMD-VR growth rates are not spectacular with one analyst downgrading their forecast in 2023 and predicting HMD-VR sales to grow from around 10 million per year in 2023 to around 18 million in 2025 (Erl, 2023). As a result, a twin-track strategy supporting both DesktopVR and HMD-VR has to be the logical choice, with any metaversal space being able to support both classes of interface.

Mobile

The mobile is effectively just as specific case of DesktopVR. Modern smartphones have the processing power, screen resolution, and even screen size to render all but the most complex virtual environments without too much difficulty. There are, however, a few mobile specific issues worth considering:

- The bandwidth of the wireless connection may be too limited to support all the change updates from the game server. As such, a metaverse might support different levels of details (LODs) so that objects are shown more simply if bandwidth or viewing device is limited.
- A user might want to attend a meeting in the Metaverse, or conduct some activity in the Metaverse, but not have the focus or bandwidth to support a fully immersive session. The user should be able to join the meeting as just a webcam view on a screen or robot, and/or be able to access the Metaverse in a top-down 2D map mode.

CAVEs

Cave automatic virtual environments (CAVEs) are VR delivered by a walk-in environment where typically three walls (but potentially up to all six sides) are full screen displays and whose view may change as the user walks around inside the space (Muhanna, 2015). The downside is that they are costly, tend to be single installations within institutions (so have to be booked), and take time and money to maintain (Havig et al., 2011). Now largely transplanted by HMD-VR, they are still a viable interface model for some use cases for the Metaverse, particularly if there is a need for spectators, and any metaverse should probably be flexible enough to support CAVEs and similar dome type displays, and perhaps even immersive projection venues such as London's Lightroom and New York's Lightbox.

360° Video VR and Stereoscopic Video VR

360° Video VR and Stereoscopic Video VR are alternative ways to use a VR headset. Rather than being in a 3D world where they can move anywhere they want, the user instead is just watching, and possibly interacting with, a movie – even if it is one which is all around them. A lot of current HMD-VR content is actually 360 VR, where the user can look around within the video, but they have no agency within it. Stereoscopic Video VR again uses video but is filmed with twin video cameras to produce a stereoscopic video pair which, when viewed through the VR headset, gives a real sense of depth to the video and a greater sense of immersion – the result is that there is a far more visceral reaction to what is being viewed. The technology can be used to provide structured inter-personal training as it delivers more emotional engagement than simple 2D video or 3D avatars. However, Video VR experiences are really just a tool for a set of specific use cases, rather than an inherent part of the metaverse since they lack the interactivity and agency that a modelled 3D environment provides.

Video Streaming

Video streaming, also called cloud gaming, delivers virtual world (and gaming) experiences to devices with reduced processing power – such as mobile phones. By doing the rendering of the scene on a central server and then just sending a resultant video feed to the user device, the virtual world or game can be made more accessible as the end-user device just has to show the video and capture and transmit any player interaction. *Second Life* experimented with the concept in 2012 (IGN, 2012). Google offered the Stadia service to support video game streaming from 2019 to 2023 (Carrascosa & Bellalta, 2022), and whilst a number of cloud gaming services are currently on offer, the reception has been mixed (e.g. Perry, 2023). As the power of smartphone processors increases, there is an increasing debate around the need for such an approach other than for all but the most demanding games (e.g. Coleman, 2023). As noted elsewhere, there is not necessarily a link between the Metaversal experience and the level of resolution, and ideally a metaverse should be able to natively support clients running at whatever level of resolution and detail they can support.

Haptics

Haptics is the way of making the user feel the things that they are touching in a virtual world. Computer games often have "haptic" controllers that vibrate when driving a vehicle or being shot at. Of more interest though are haptic gloves for use in VR, such as those from HaptX (https://haptx.com/). Here, actuators in the glove provides some force-feedback to give the user the sense of actually feeling, touching, or holding something in the virtual world. One of its most interesting use cases is that it lets the user replicate the physical world behaviour of looking at where something is, but then turning away to return visual focus on something else whilst using touch alone to reach out and pick the object up. Haptics can also extend to the whole body. Teslasuit (https://teslasuit.io/) has made an eponymous whole-body haptic suit which can simulate shocks or touch across the user's entire body, whilst OWO Games' Skin (https://owogame.com/) is a t-shirt equivalent.

A simpler approach to haptics, particularly with HMD-VR, is providing users with a physical controller that represents the physical device – ideally a version of the actual physical device which has simply been instrumented for VR use (e.g. Saghafian et al., 2020). This approach is already being used in military, medical, fire, and construction VR training, providing instrumented guns, surgical instruments, fire extinguishers, and hoist controllers for users to train on in the virtual world.

Locomotion

One area where the sense of immersion often falters in virtual worlds is with movement. Controlling an avatar by joystick, cursor keys, or the ASDF keys of a keyboard seems clunky. In DesktopVR, and even more so in HMD-VR, point and-click, where the user clicks on a destination and the avatar then navigates itself there, can be a more reliable way to navigate but can break the connection between a user and their avatar. In HMD-VR in particular, watching your avatar move, whether on auto-pilot or under joystick control, whilst your physical feet are firmly fixed to the floor just doesn't seem right. With the advent of room-scale tracking, users can now naturally walk around a space in HMD-VR, assuming they have an equivalent empty space in the physical world, but for other situations, alternative solutions are required.

Over the past decade or so, there has been significant research into the use of devices such as 360° treadmills, slippy shoes, and other technologies in order to allow users to "walk" in VR whilst staying in the same physical location. A useful overview of the research and a proposed taxonomy for VR locomotion has been presented by Boletsis (2017). However, cost, space, reliability, ergonomics, and other issues have so far kept solutions from the mass market (Hooks et al., 2020).

Flying in virtual worlds avoids the leg locomotion problem but is typically more suited to longer distance travel. There have been some amusing projects to investigate the use of arm-flapping and wind generators to enhance the flying experience (e.g. https://birdlyvr.com/). Bicycle simulators have also been explored (e.g. https://virzoom.com/vzfit-2/), particularly with respect to the exercise and fitness markets.

Another approach has been to use a brain-computer interface (BCI) to control avatar movement (Alchalabi et al., 2021), but until the brain can also be supplied with the sensation of the actual movement, this is as much a half-solution as many of the others.

Augmented and Mixed Reality

Both AR and MR devices are valid interfaces to the Metaverse, and the Metaverse should be able to support whatever interface device the user has and display relevant information in an appropriate way. AR tends to be single user and relatively passive, so it is MR that is more relevant.

MR displays – implemented by a headset, which may eventually reduce in form-factor to a set of glasses or even contact lenses – overlay 3D objects and information onto the user's view of the physical world. This can provide complex information to support navigation, or place virtual models in front of the user to play with or learn about, or annotate physical equipment to help in maintenance, and in both cases put virtual colleagues, friends, or tutors in the room with the user. MR could also re-write reality, re-interpreting almost everything the user sees and overlaying it with something out of a fantasy world or a science-fiction setting (Vinge, 2006). With the appearance of colour video pass-through on VR headsets (e.g. the Meta Quest Pro, Meta Quest 3, Varjo XR-3, Apple Vision Pro) enabling MR-like capabilities, the distinction between VR and MR headsets is slowly blurring, and HMD-XR may be a more useful descriptor for the hardware, although the HMD-VR and HMD-MR experiences remain distinct, even if instantly switchable.

Brain-Computer Interfaces

Whilst each generation of HMD-VR devices is improving, the approach of using purely visual and audio display and externalized body tracking has significant issues and limitations – not least the locomotion and sense challenges identified above. Researchers are working on BCIs for virtual environments, but these are currently limited to tracking electroencephalogram (EEG), electrocardiogram (ECG), and similar brain signals in order to add additional discrete control capabilities through an HMD-VR headset (e.g. Cassani et al., 2020). Putze (2019) discriminates between active BCI which "allow users to issue commands to devices or to enter text without physical involvement of any kind" and passive BCIs which "monitor a user's state (e.g., workload level, attentional state) and can be used to proactively adapt the VR/AR interface". Another useful distinction is between invasive (where electrodes and similar devices are implanted through the skull through surgery) and non-invasive (where sensors sit on the surface of the skin) BCIs (Zhao et al., 2023).

In terms of generating the VR experience directly in the brain research is at a very early stage (e.g. Morris, 2018), but organisations such as DARPA are already beginning research into "high-performance, bi-directional brain-machine interfaces" (DARPA, 2019). Technology may be many decades away from the sort of "holoband" interface device and experience shown in *Caprica* (Aubuchon & Moore, 2010), but it may be that it is not until there is a neural interface to the Metaverse that will give the user the ultimate in technical immersion that the fullest promise of the Metaverse will be delivered, and it becomes a truly everyday service.

Artificial Intelligence and the Metaverse

The recent advances in AI, particularly in neural networks, generative adversarial networks and large language models, are all having an impact on how AI can contribute to the creation of metaversal experiences. Some of the principal uses of AI for the Metaverse are in:

- Conducting the edge and object detection in an HMD-XR headset in order to build the model of the physical world with which digital objects will exist (Rokhsaritalemi et al., 2020);
- Speech recognition to support voice interaction with NPC avatars (already in GOXR) and the metaverse application itself (Siyaev & Jo, 2021);
- Natural language communications and chatbot development (already in Frame) using systems such as ChatGPT without the need to hard-code responses (Lv, 2023); and
- Generating virtual scenes either procedurally at scale prior to need (e.g. Deitke et al., 2022) or on demand from the user (e.g. Viviani, 2023) – a basic version is already in Hiberworld, and for skyboxes in Frame.

A survey of metaverse applications of AI is provided by Huynh-The et al. (2023).

Blockchain, Cryptocurrencies, and NFTs

Many of the newer proto-metaverses such as *Decentraland* and *Somnium Space* are based on the blockchain and cryptocurrencies, so it is important to understand the potential role of these technologies in any future metaverse.

A blockchain is fundamentally a distributed, secure, and digital ledger – a way of recording transactions and information in a way that cannot be changed, and which shows complete traceability for every transaction. A cryptocurrency, such as Bitcoin or Ethereum, is essentially just the use of a blockchain to implement a currency system, recording who owns what and who has given what to whom (Nakamoto, 2008). A NFT, such as being used to market art works and GIFs, is simply a token (i.e. a piece of information) tracked on a blockchain which links to an image or object, and of which there are typically only a limited number of copies. Useful introductions to the blockchain, cryptocurrencies, and NFTs are provided by Vasquez (2021) and Tysver (2023).

One of the key problems of blockchain systems is the excessive computing power needed to generate new tokens or coins (called "mining") and to update the encrypted ledger entries. One estimate in this hotly debated area is that 36% of the energy requirements of a blockchain-based metaverse could come from the blockchain transactions (Liu et al., 2023). This will be further considered in Chapter 5, along with some potential solutions to the problem.

A second issue is that the blockchain is only as secure as its user interface, and the media is full of reports of cryptocurrency systems and users accounts being hacked and people's savings lost from attacks against the periphery of the infrastructure. An estimated $88 billion has been lost through Bitcoin hacks alone (at 2021 pricing) between 2011 and 2021 (Charoenwong & Bernardi, 2021).

Thirdly, cryptocurrencies and NFTs are being treated by many as get-rich-quick schemes, where the physical world price of an NFT, a crypto-coin or a piece of virtual land or even clothing bought with a cryptocurrency, seems out of all kilter with any reasonable value. Of course, any art (and even to an extent currency system) is only worth the price that people are prepared to pay for it, but the blockchain, cryptocurrency, and NFT markets do seem to have taken this to a level reminiscent of the South Sea Bubble. A telling statistic in terms of cryptocurrency is the percentage of cryptocurrency holders who are actually using it for payment rather than investment. For example, a 2023 US Federal Reserve report showed that whilst in 2022 10% of Americans surveyed held cryptocurrency (down from 12% in 2021), only 2% had used them in payments for goods or services (Federal Reserve, 2023).

Opinion on the relationship between blockchain technologies and the future of the Metaverse is somewhat divided. Ball (2022) identifies a spectrum of five different levels of a relationship between the Metaverse and blockchain, ranging from it being wasteful and irrelevant to being an absolutely essential requirement. At the latter end of the spectrum, some see that "the Metaverse will not function without blockchain technology at its core on an economic level" (Rosa, 2023). Narula also sees blockchain technologies and cryptocurrencies as "integral to any efforts to build and maintain a bridge for the transfer of value within the metaverse". In contrast, Au notes that none of the current proto-Metaverse platforms based on the blockchain have "succeeded in terms of mass growth. Or really, hardly any growth at all" (Au, 2023, p. 152).

The core concept of the blockchain is undoubtably valid and will likely be more accepted as a practicable system for wider employment if some of its computing requirements and climate impacts can be mitigated. It may well be that it has a role in the Metaverse, particularly if cryptocurrency and blockchain concepts are more widely adopted within consumer finance and other industries. However, in its current form, it is probably doing more harm than good to the evolution of the Metaverse by restricting access to some otherwise imaginative proto-metaverses to those who are willing to buy-in to the cryptocurrency and NFT investment craze.

Summary

This chapter has provided an introduction to the technologies that are required to create a metaverse. It has covered eight broad areas, including the creation of 3D environments, navigation and land models, multi-user enablers, avatars, interactivity, ecosystem tools, user interfaces, and block-chain technologies.

The core of any metaverse is how it is presented and navigated as a spatial environment, that it operates as a multi-user space, is populated by avatars, and that those avatars have interactivity with each other and with the environment, and have the ability to freely and readily create within that environment. Game servers, eco-system tools, and particularly the sharing of user-generated content and common standards are vital enablers. Only after these comes the actual user interface, be it HMD-VR, DesktopVR, mobile, MR, AR, or even neural, and as stated, the Metaverse should be able to support all modes – and interaction between people using different modes. Only then should considerations such as blockchain come in – and largely as a technical enabler for the ecosystem tools.

The next chapter will consider some of the broader, and mostly non-technical issues that the idea of a metaverse raises, and which are, in most cases, far harder to resolve than the technical challenges.

Note

1 We have used the terms Minority World and Majority World to describe the "have" and the "have not" parts of the globe as these seem the most accurate and least pejorative of the terms available. See https://www.ncbi.nlm.nih.gov/pmc/articles/PMC9185389/

References

3DAce. (2021). Physically-based rendering: Using PBR for games, animations, and more. 3D Ace. https://3d-ace.com/blog/physically-based-rendering-using-pbr-for-games-animations-and-more/

Alchalabi, B., Faubert, J., & Labbe, D. R. (2021). A multi-modal modified feedback self-paced BCI to control the gait of an avatar. *Journal of Neural Engineering, 18*(5), 056005.

Aoyama, K. (2020, February 4). Galvanic taste stimulation method for virtual reality and augmented reality. *Human interface and the management of information. Designing information: thematic area, HIMI 2020, held as part of the 22nd international conference, HCII 2020, Copenhagen, Denmark, July 19–24, 2020, proceedings, part I* (pp. 341–349). Springer International Publishing.

Apostolakis, K. C., & Daras, P. (2015). Natural user interfaces for virtual character full body and facial animation in immersive virtual worlds. *Augmented and virtual reality: Second international conference, AVR 2015, Lecce, Italy, August 31–September 3, 2015, proceedings 2* (pp. 371–383). Springer International Publishing.

Au, W. J. (2023). *Making a metaverse that matters: From Snow Crash & Second Life to a virtual world worth fighting for.* John Wiley & Sons.

Aubuchon, R., & Moore, R. D. (Creators). (2010). *Caprica* [TV series]. Syfy.

Ball, M. (2022). *The metaverse: And how it will revolutionize everything.* Liveright Publishing.

Billington, P. (2018). *Wolves in the walls.* Fable Studios and Third Rail Projects. https://thirdrailprojects.com/wolvesinthewalls

BISim. (2023, May 12). *BISim's thermal imaging improvements* [Bohemia Interactive Simulations]. YouTube. https://www.youtube.com/watch?v=k63RzxVqk3w&ab_channel=BohemiaInteractiveSimulations

Boletsis, C. (2017). The new era of virtual reality locomotion: A systematic literature review of techniques and a proposed typology. *Multimodal Technologies and Interaction, 1*(4), 24.

Burden, D. (2011). A semantic approach to virtual world standards. *IEEE Internet Computing, 15*(6), 40–43.

Burden, D. J. H., & Savin-Baden, M. (2019). *Virtual humans: Today and tomorrow.* CRC.

Burden, D. J., Savin-Baden, M., & Bhakta, R. (2016). Covert implementations of the Turing Test: A more level playing field? In *Research and development in intelligent systems XXXIII: Incorporating applications and innovations in intelligent systems XXIV 33* (pp. 195–207). Springer International Publishing.

Campbell, S. (2023). *VR headset sales and market share in 2023 (How Many Sold?).* The Small Business Blog. https://thesmallbusinessblog.net/vr-headset-sales-and-market-share/

Campbell, A. G., Holz, T., Cosgrove, J., Harlick, M., & O'Sullivan, T. (2020). Uses of virtual reality for communication in financial services: A case study on comparing different telepresence interfaces: Virtual reality compared to video conferencing. *Advances in information and communication: Proceedings of the 2019 future of information and communication conference (FICC)* (Vol. 1, pp. 463–481). Springer International Publishing.

Carrascosa, M., & Bellalta, B. (2022). Cloud-gaming: Analysis of Google Stadia traffic. *Computer Communications, 188*, 99–116.

Cassani, R., Moinnereau, M. A., Ivanescu, L., Rosanne, O., & Falk, T. H. (2020). Neural interface instrumented virtual reality headsets: Toward next-generation immersive applications. *IEEE Systems, Man, and Cybernetics Magazine, 6*(3), 20–28.

Charoenwong, B., & Bernardi, M. (2021). *A decade of cryptocurrency 'hacks': 2011–2021.* Leibniz Information Center for Economics.

Chow, A. R. (2023, January 27). Why the AI explosion has huge implications for the Metaverse. *Time Magazine.* https://time.com/6250249/chatgpt-metaverse/

Coleman, T. (2023, June 8). Is cloud gaming the future for video games? *The Week*. https://theweek.com/talking-point/1023972/is-cloud-gaming-the-future

DARPA. (2019). *Six paths to the nonsurgical future of brain-machine interfaces*. DARPA. https://www.darpa.mil/news-events/2019-05-20

Deitke, M., VanderBilt, E., Herrasti, A., Weihs, L., Ehsani, K., Salvador, J., Han, W., Kolve, E., Kembhavi, A., & Mottaghi, R. (2022). ProcTHOR: Large-scale embodied AI using procedural generation. *Advances in Neural Information Processing Systems*, 35, 5982–5994.

Erl, J. (2023, March 22). 10.1 Million units: Short-term lower demand for VR and AR headsets. *Mixed News*. https://mixed-news.com/en/vr-and-ar-market-growing-slower-than-expected/

Federal Reserve. (2023). *Report on the economic well-being of U.S. households in 2022–May 2023*. US Federal Reserve. https://www.federalreserve.gov/publications/2023-economic-well-being-of-us-households-in-2022-banking-credit.htm

Felnhofer, A., Martinek, D., Pazour, P., & Riva, G. (2023). PAIN-EX: Probing alternative interventions for neutralizing pain EXperiences via embodiment in virtual reality. *Cyberpsychology, Behavior, and Social Networking*, 26(8), 662–664.

Gallagher, A. (2022). *What is a game server? Everything you need to know*. OneQode. https://www.oneqode.com/what-is-a-game-server/

Gilbert, R. L., & Forney, A. (2015). Can avatars pass the Turing test? Intelligent agent perception in a 3D virtual environment. *International Journal of Human-Computer Studies*, 73, 30–36.

Glassner, A. S. (Ed.). (1989). *An introduction to ray tracing*. Morgan Kaufmann.

GSMA. (2023). *The mobile economy: 2023*. https://www.gsma.com/mobileeconomy/

Havig, P., McIntire, J., & Geiselman, E. (2011). Virtual reality in a cave: Limitations and the need for HMDs? *Proceedings of SPIE—The International Society for Optical Engineering*, 8041. https://doi.org/10.1117/12.883855

Heeter, C., Day, T., & Cherchiglia, L. (2020). Interoceptive awareness: The 'being' dimension of 'being there' in virtual worlds. *Interacting with Computers*, 32(1), 1–16.

Hooks, K., Ferguson, W., Morillo, P., & Cruz-Neira, C. (2020). Evaluating the user experience of omnidirectional VR walking simulators. *Entertainment Computing*, 34, 100352.

Huynh-The, T., Pham, Q. V., Pham, X. Q., Nguyen, T. T., Han, Z., & Kim, D. S. (2023). Artificial intelligence for the metaverse: A survey. *Engineering Applications of Artificial Intelligence*, 117, 105581.

Ibáñez-Martinez, J., & Delgado-Mata, C. (2006). A basic semantic common level for virtual environments. *International Journal of Virtual Reality*, 5(3), 25–32.

Improbable. (2021). *Improbable and Midwinter Entertainment bring more than 4000 Scavengers players together in a single game world*. Improbable. https://www.improbable.io/blog/scavengers-scavlab-4000-players-in-a-single-game-world

IGN. (2012). *Vollee debuts Second Life on mobile*. IGN. https://www.ign.com/articles/2008/06/04/vollee-debuts-second-life-on-mobile

Ihrke, I., Restrepo, J., & Mignard-Debise, L. (2016). Principles of light field imaging: *Briefly revisiting 25 years of research*. *IEEE Signal Processing Magazine*, 33(5), 59–69.

ITU. (2023). *FG-MV D.WG1-01 exploring the metaverse: Opportunities and challenges*. ITU. https://www.itu.int/dms_pub/itu-t/opb/fg/T-FG-MV-2023-PDF-E.pdf

Jamil, R. (2023). *Comparing Three.js and Babylon.js: Which JavaScript 3D Library is Right for You?* Medium. https://mohammadrahi.medium.com/comparing-three-js-and-babylon-js-which-javascript-3d-library-is-right-for-you-7196ef21949e

Jijiashvili, G. (2021). *Omdia research reveals 12.5 million consumer VR headsets sold in 2021 with content spend exceeding $2bn.* Game Developer. https://www.gamedeveloper.com/blogs/omdia-research-reveals-12-5-million-consumer-vr-headsets-sold-in-2021-with-content-spend-exceeding-2bn

Kara, P. A., Tamboli, R. R., Adhikarla, V. K., Balogh, T., Guindy, M., & Simon, A. (2023). Connected without disconnection: Overview of light field metaverse applications and their quality of experience. *Displays, 78,* 102430.

Kerruish, E. (2019). Arranging sensations: Smell and taste in augmented and virtual reality. *The Senses and Society, 14*(1), 31–45.

Kleinermann, F., De Troyer, O., Mansouri, H., Romero, R., Pellens, B., & Bille, W. (2005). Designing semantic virtual reality applications. *Proceedings of the 2nd Intuition International Workshop,* Senlis, France.

Lang, B. (2022). *Tech Demo shows the real power of quest pro face tracking.* Road to VR. https://www.roadtovr.com/quest-pro-face-tracking-tech-demo-aura/

Lebaredian, R., & Kass, M. (2022). *Universal scene description as the language of the metaverse.* NVIDIA. https://developer.nvidia.com/blog/universal-scene-description-as-the-language-of-the-metaverse/

Lindquist, M., Maxim, B., Proctor, J., & Dolins, F. (2020). The effect of audio fidelity and virtual reality on the perception of virtual greenspace. *Landscape and Urban Planning, 202,* 103884.

Lin, H., & Wang, H. (2014). Avatar creation in virtual worlds: Behaviors and motivations. *Computers in Human Behavior, 34,* 213–218.

Liu, F., Pei, Q., Chen, S., Yuan, Y., Wang, L., & Muhlhauser, M. (2023). *When the metaverse meets carbon neutrality: Ongoing efforts and directions.* https://doi.org/10.48550/arXiv.2301.10235

Lv, Z. (2023). Generative artificial intelligence in the metaverse era. *Cognitive Robotics, 3,* 208–217.

Makin, S. (2023). *Virtual reality system lets you stop and smell the roses.* Scientific American. https://www.scientificamerican.com/article/virtual-reality-system-lets-you-stop-and-smell-the-roses/

Messaoud, M., Cherif, F., Sanza, C., & Gaildrat, V. (2015). An ontology for semantic modelling of virtual world. *International Journal of Artificial Intelligence & Applications, 6*(1), 65–74.

MetaQuest. (n.d.). *Intro to scripting.* MetaQuest. https://www.oculus.com/horizon-worlds/learn/tutorial/intro-to-scripting/

Milevo, G. (2020). *OVR technology creates first-of-its-kind virtual reality experiences with scents.* AR Post. https://arpost.co/2020/06/19/ovr-technology-virtual-reality-scents/

Mori, M. (1970). The uncanny valley. *Energy, 7*(4), 33–35.

Morris, A. (2018, April 30). Scientists project holograms into the brain to create experiences. *Forbes.* https://www.forbes.com/sites/andreamorris/2018/04/30/scientists-project-holograms-into-the-brain-to-create-experiences/?sh=2967869b1460

Moustakas, N., Floros, A., Rovithis, E., & Vogklis, K. (2019). *Augmented audio-only games: A new generation of immersive acoustic environments through advanced mixing.* Audio Engineering Society Convention 146. Audio Engineering Society. https://www.aes.org/e-lib/browse.cfm?elib=20336

Muhanna, M. A. (2015). Virtual reality and the CAVE: Taxonomy, interaction challenges and research directions. *Journal of King Saud University-Computer and Information Sciences, 27*(3), 344–361.

Muttik, I. (2008). *Securing virtual worlds against real attacks.* McAfee Inc.

Nakamoto, S. (2008). *Bitcoin: A peer-to-peer electronic cash system*. Decentralized business review. https://assets.pubpub.org/d8wct41f/31611263538139.pdf

Nesson, R., & Nesson, C. (2008). The case for education in virtual worlds. *Space and Culture, 11*(3), 273–284.

Neustaedter, C., & Fedorovskaya, E. A. (2009). Presenting identity in a virtual world through avatar appearances. *Proceedings of graphics interface 2009* (pp. 183–190). Canadian Information Processing Society.

Novotny, A., Gudmundsson, R., & Harris, F. C., Jr. (2020). A unity framework for multi-user VR experiences. *Proceedings of 35th international conference on comput-ers and their applications* (Vol. 69, pp. 13–21). International Society for Computers and Their Applications (ISCA).

Ordano, E., Araoz, M., Jardi, Y., & Meilich, A. (n.d.). *Decentraland white paper*. Decentraland. https://decentraland.org/whitepaper.pdf

Parger, M., Mueller, J. H., Schmalstieg, D., & Steinberger, M. (2018). Human upper-body inverse kinematics for increased embodiment in consumer-grade virtual reality. *Proceedings of the 24th ACM symposium on virtual reality software and tech-nology* (pp. 1–10). Association for Computing Machinery.

Perry, H. (2023, June 29). The best cloud gaming services aren't great (yet). *New York Times*. https://www.nytimes.com/wirecutter/reviews/best-cloud-gaming-services/

Peters, J., & Weatherbed, J. (2023, August 3). Why Apple bet on Pixar tech to make the metaverse work. *The Verge*. https://www.theverge.com/2023/8/3/23818718/apple-pixar-3d-tech-alliance-openusd-metaverse

Putze, F. (2019). Methods and tools for using BCI with augmented and virtual reality. In A. Nijholt (Ed.), *Brain art: Brain-computer interfaces for artistic expression* (pp. 433–446). Springer Nature Switzerland AG.

Riva, G., Di Lernia, D., Sajno, E., Sansoni, M., Bartolotta, S., Serino, S., Gaggioli, A., & Wiederhold, B. K. (2021). Virtual reality therapy in the Metaverse: Merging VR for the outside with VR for the inside. *Annual Review of Cybertherapy & Telemedicine, 19*, 3–8.

Rokhsaritalemi, S., Sadeghi-Niaraki, A., & Choi, S. M. (2020). A review on mixed real-ity: Current trends, challenges and prospects. *Applied Sciences, 10*(2), 636.

Rosa, N. (2022). *Understanding the metaverse: A business and ethical guide*. John Wiley & Sons.

Saghafian, M., Laumann, K., Akhtar, R. S., & Skogstad, M. R. (2020). The evaluation of virtual reality fire extinguisher training. *Frontiers in Psychology, 11*, 593466.

Scerbo, M. W., & Dawson, S. (2007). High fidelity, high performance? *Simulation in Healthcare, 2*(4), 224–230.

Siyaev, A., & Jo, G. S. (2021). Neuro-symbolic speech understanding in aircraft main-tenance metaverse. *IEEE Access, 9*, 154484–154499.

Smart, J., Cascio, J., Paffendorf, J., Bridges, C., Hummel, J., Hursthouse, J., & Moss, R. (2007). A cross-industry public foresight project. *Proceedings of the metaverse roadmap pathways 3D Web* (1–28). Acceleration Studies Foundation. https://www.metaverseroadmap.accelerating.org/MetaverseRoadmapOverview.pdf

Soto, M., & Allongue, S. (1997, June). A semantic approach of virtual worlds interoper-ability. *Proceedings of IEEE 6th workshop on enabling technologies: Infrastructure for collaborative enterprises* (pp. 173–178). IEEE.

Takahashi, D. (2021). *RP1 debuts a scalable platform for the 'shardless' metaverse*. VentureBeat. https://venturebeat.com/games/rp1-debuts-a-scalable-platform-for-the-metaverse/

Truly, A. (2023, July 1). Meta makes big advances in Quest full-body motion capture. *Mixed News*. https://mixed-news.com/en/meta-makes-big-advances-in-quest-full-body-motion-capture/

Tysver, D. A. (2023). *Introduction to blockchains*. Bitlaw. https://www.bitlaw.com/blockchain/intro-to-blockchains.html

Valori, I., McKenna-Plumley, P. E., Bayramova, R., Zandonella Callegher, C., Altoè, G., & Farroni, T. (2020). Proprioceptive accuracy in immersive virtual reality: A developmental perspective. *PLoS One, 15*(1), e0222253.

Vasquez, G. (2021). An introduction to blockchain. *The CPA Journal, 91*(6/7), 52–55. https://www.cpajournal.com/2021/08/18/an-introduction-to-blockchain/

Vinge, V. (2006). *Rainbow's end*. Tor Books.

Viviani, M. (2023, March 30). How ChatGPT and GPT-4 can be used for 3D content generation. *Medium*. https://medium.com/@nvidiaomniverse/chatgpt-and-gpt-4-for-3d-content-generation-9cbe5d17ec15

Vivo, P. G., & Lowe, J. (2015). *The book of shaders*. The Book of Shaders. https://thebookofshaders.com/

Waldo, J. (2008). Scaling in games and virtual worlds. *Communications of the ACM, 51*(8), 38–44.

Wihl, L., Varshney, M., & Kong, J. (2010). Introducing a cyber warfare communications effect model to synthetic environments. *The interservice/industry training, simulation & education conference (I/ITSEC)*. https://www.researchgate.net/profile/Jiejun-Kong/publication/228676783_InterserviceIndustry_Training_Simulation_and_Education_Conference_IITSEC_2010_Introducing_a_Cyber_Warfare_Communications_Effect_Model_to_Synthetic_Environments/links/02e7e5272c7286f5e3000000/Interservice-Industry-Training-Simulation-and-Education-Conference-I-ITSEC-2010-Introducing-a-Cyber-Warfare-Communications-Effect-Model-to-Synthetic-Environments.pdf

Zhao, Z. P., Nie, C., Jiang, C. T., Cao, S. H., Tian, K. X., Yu, S., & Gu, J. W. (2023). Modulating brain activity with invasive brain–computer interface: A narrative review. *Brain Sciences, 13*(1), 134.

5

Opportunities and Challenges

Introduction

This chapter provides a critique on the promises and dangers of the Metaverse, taking a broader perspective than previous chapters. It examines a number of competing pressures and dichotomies within the concept of a Metaverse, working from those which are more focused on the platform (and those who create it) to those where the primary concern is the individual, and ultimately to those which are about society as a whole. The topics are represented graphically in Figure 5.1. In most of these, the concept of a single, monolithic Metaverse is likely to face more challenges than that of a Multiverse.

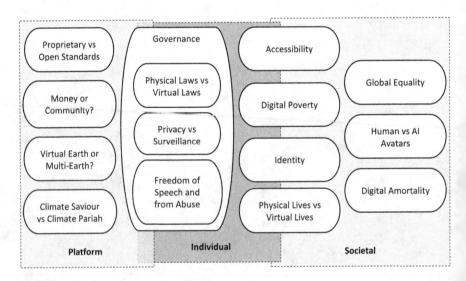

FIGURE 5.1
The Metaverse – opportunities and challenges.

DOI: 10.1201/9781003395461-6

Proprietary versus Open Standards

Perhaps the biggest tension in considering the future form of the Metaverse, and one which has an implication for many of the other topics in this chapter, is whether the Metaverse is something that is based on proprietary standards and corporate control, or is a ground-up, open-standards-based undertaking.

A spectrum of approaches already exists. Most of the current crop of metaversal worlds are based on the corporate/proprietary model – such as *Fortnite* and *Roblox*. In comparison, *Minecraft* tightly controls its public world, but developers can set up their own *Minecraft* servers where they have far more freedom to create what they want, although it is still proprietary code. Further down the spectrum, *Hubs* is open-source code which enables users to run their own servers. Cryptoworlds such as *Somnium Space* and *Decentraland* are largely following a Web3 model and so support both being open-source and decentralised. *Second Life* itself is proprietary and centralised, but with a fairly lenient by-exception curation model, whereas the *OpenSim* derivative is open-source and decentralised. Neal Stephenson's forthcoming *Lamina1* virtual world (https://www.lamina1.com/) is supporting an open-source model (Sparkes, 2022). Table 5.1 summaries the approach of some of the more popular virtual worlds but is a very subjective assessment.

Perri et al. (2023) argue that "The open standards and open source code are essential for the metaverse's growth and sustainability. The developers and policymakers should prioritize these principles to ensure the development of [an] inclusive and open virtual environment". The Metaverse Standards Forum (2022), whose members include companies such as Epic, Meta, Microsoft, Sony, and Unity, says that "Multiple industry leaders have

TABLE 5.1

Comparing Virtual World Models

	Decentralisation	Open Source	UGC Freedom
Fortnite			●●
Horizon Worlds			●●
Roblox			●●●
Minecraft	●		●●●
VRChat			●●●
Hubs	●●	●●●●●	●●●●
Frames			●●●●
Decentraland	●●●	●●●●●	●●●●●
Somnium Space	●●		●●●●●
Second Life		●	●●●●●
Open Sim	●●●	●●●●●	●●●●●

stated that the potential of the metaverse will be best realized if it is built on a foundation of open standards. Building an open and inclusive metaverse at pervasive scale will demand a constellation of open interoperability standards". The various metaverse standards initiatives were described in Chapter 4, but, as discussed, similar previous attempts have failed – will they be more successful this time around?

Driven by Money or Community?

Related to the debate about governance and centralised versus decentralised approaches is whether the Metaverse will ultimately be created and developed through a concern primarily for money or community. Ball (2022) appears to take the view that the Metaverse will most likely arise from a world or worlds taking a corporate, money-driven approach. "The most likely outcome is indeed that a handful of vertically and horizontally integrated platforms collect a significant share of total time, content, data, and revenues in the Metaverse" (Ball, 2022). Ball describes corporate executives as believing that the metaverse will be worth "multiple trillions of dollars" (whilst accepting that they can't agree on what it actually is yet) and quotes Jensen Huang of Nvidia as predicting that the value of metaverse "will eventually 'exceed that' of the physical world" (Ball, 2022). Au (2023) takes almost the opposite view, barely mentioning revenues (except where they relate to creator share) or investment in his book. Instead, he sees the Metaverse as a ground-up, community endeavour – "community creates value – not the other way around" (Au, 2023). Whilst Au expects metaverse platforms to be (at least initially) game-led, he considers that user-generated content with an independent purpose is the litmus test for a successful metaverse platform – i.e. whether "you will find a subset of content creators who create not primarily for profit, but for the benefit of the user community. And social recognition by that community" (Au, 2023).

The example of the World Wide Web is again salutary. Through gifting the underlying hypertext transfer protocol (HTTP) and hypertext markup language (HTML) standards, and browser and server code, to the global community, Sir Tim Berners-Lee enabled a ground-up, community growth of the Web, without anybody initially having any real concerns for revenue, investment, or profit. Some, such as Fodor (2020) from Mozilla, believe that this is how the Metaverse should evolve, along with being based on open source code. However, over time, corporate interest (and with that revenues, profit, and investment) became ever more significant, and the large corporate players, from Amazon to Google and Meta, came to dominate the Web. A key question, to be explored in Chapter 6, is whether the Metaverse will go through a similar process, or whether it is already at a situation of corporate dominance (e.g. Meta/Oculus, Epic/Fortnite), or whether there is a way to develop and maintain a high level of community involvement whilst also meeting the costs of creating, operating, and maintaining the technologies that underpin it.

Virtual Earth or Multi-Earth?

Linked to debate about the Metaverse or Multiverse is the extent to which any metaverse should actually be a digital twin of the Earth (and/or any other world) – or at least follow its basic geography. The Digital Earth Vision, developed by the International Society for Digital Earth (http://www.digitalearth-isde.org/), takes a literal digital twin approach, with a "digitally-formatted Earth accessible directly through the internet-connected citizens of the planet and supports facilitating data and information provision to others", one able to support social, cultural, and economic activity, and has spent almost 20 years supporting global collaboration in this area.

However, as discussed in Chapter 2, the Metaverse is almost certainly going to be an interconnected series of metaversal spaces in the short-to-medium term – partly because there are too many people who want "their" digital twin of a location which is at odds with other people's digital twin of the same space. Also, if there is just one digital earth, then all the issues of land ownership and rights, and extending physical world control into the virtual world, will come into play. More likely, there will be complementary (or even competing) digital twins of the Earth, hopefully drawn from common geospatial data, each with its own set of guidelines as to how it should be used. So, it may be that one world enforces a "physical world analogue" mandate – you can only build what physically exists, whilst another might be focused on environmental or global equality issues, and yet another on global tourism. But since these are, hopefully, all on the same interconnected infrastructure, users can readily teleport between each and even overlay data from them all in mixed reality, or even in yet another virtual reality (VR) space.

Of course, none of this prohibits any metaverse from also basing its geography on the whole solar system, a totally imagined world or universe, or a literature or movie-based one.

Climate Saviour or Climate Pariah

As with any technology that supports remote working, there seems to be a natural argument that the Metaverse can be good for climate change by reducing the environmental impacts of commuting and business travel (Le et al., 2020), and even through the development of virtual tourism (De-la-Cruz-Diaz et al., 2022; Gursoy et al., 2022). One study optimistically predicts that "increasing metaverse adoption can reduce the global surface temperature by up to 0.02°C before the end of this century and lower the greenhouse gas emissions by 10 Gt CO2e ... and saving 10% of nationwide energy use by 2050" (Zhao & You, 2023).

However, Kshetri and Dwivedi (2023) highlight that "a fierce debate is brewing over whether the metaverse will be an environmental sustainability disaster or if it will make the world cleaner and greener", since against any savings must be set against the environmental cost of running the servers and networks that are required to support a metaverse. Liu et al. (2023) have estimated the climate cost of the metaverse in 2030 against three main elements: the underlying infrastructure (accounting for about 20% of CO_2 emissions and energy consumption), computing and display devices (c.45%), and blockchain-based trading and economy services (c.35%). They summarise that "The metaverse will account for as high as 0.5% of the global carbon emissions by 2030 unless we take effective preventive measures from now on", before providing an analysis of potential carbon and energy saving measures for metaverse developments, but one still predicated on the blockchain (Liu et al., 2023).

As this analysis suggests, a key environmental issue is the impact of any blockchain and related cryptocurrency systems within a metaverse. The Bitcoin network's energy consumption has been described as comparable to Ireland's (De Vries, 2018) and Malaysia's or Sweden's (Carter, 2021). Whilst these comparisons have been challenged (e.g. McCausland, 2018), there is no doubt that the energy needs of current approaches to the blockchain are very significant. Improvements have been proposed which could reduce energy consumption by around 75% (Zhang & Chan, 2020), and making more use of renewable energy sources is another potential step (Ibañez & Freier, 2023). However, there still remain other significant environmental issues such as around the production and disposal of mining computing hardware (De Vries, 2019).

The Metaverse must be developed in a way that is cognizant of its environmental impact, optimising computer and communications resources wherever possible, ensuring that servers, communications, and access devices are all powered from renewable energy, and ensuring that any savings by using the Metaverse are not cancelled out by the environmental impact of running the Metaverse. Consideration must also be given to the use of finite and/or hard-to-get resources, such as lithium batteries found in most consumer electronic devices.

More positively, one potential contribution of the Metaverse to the climate agenda is in giving everyone a better understanding of climate change issues and building a greater global perspective. Astronauts talk about the "overview effect" – the way that political borders are not seen from space and that there is a "renewed sense of responsibility for taking care of the environment" (Voski, 2020). The Metaverse is a way to build this view on the ground – not just by providing large scale simulations of viewing the Earth from space (e.g. Stepanova et al., 2019), but also within the Metaverse itself, where people and places are linked by communities and ideas, not by nation-states. This is also an argument for the single Metaverse (or a coherent Multiverse), as against a series of unconnected virtual spaces, so that everyone lives on the same virtual planet and is very much aware of doing so, and so can readily experience and understand the issues that local communities are facing as a result of climate change, and more readily access and share the research which is going into understanding and (hopefully) solving, or at least mitigating it.

However, what it actually means for Barbados to open an embassy in the Metaverse (Thurman, 2021), in their case on *Decentraland*, just as the Maldives did in *Second Life* in 2007 (Sydney Morning Herald, 2007), or for Tuvalu to declare that it is replicating itself in the Metaverse (Fainu, 2023), is moot, and people should certainly be wary of any naïve futurism (Guiao, 2022). However, bringing global issues to a global audience through the Metaverse is likely to become more commonplace, and the Metaverse should be designed to enable and encourage this – whether it's virtual embassies, country digital twins, immersively experiencing droughts or floods, or collaboratively analysing climate impact data and stories in order to better communicate the risks to a wider audience in a more engaging and impactful way.

Governance

If the Metaverse is essentially a whole new world (only digital), then how should it be governed, and how should the governance of the Metaverse relate to national and supra-national governance? The models for this are to some extent tied to whether the Metaverse is one or more centralised, tightly controlled corporate spaces – in which case, corporate governance can be expected to rule – or a more decentralised, open-source model with the Metaverse being the sum of a larger number of parts, possibly with some "federation agreement" when linking from one to another to ensure that some shared standards of privacy, legality, and acceptable use are maintained. The proponents of Web3 are promoting the concept of decentralised autonomous organisations (DAOs) (Tse, 2020) to run virtual worlds, and they are already being used to run *Decentraland* (https://dao.decentraland.org/).

Governments, inter-governmental organisations, and non-governmental organisations are considering their role. The European Union has initiated reports and consultations to "develop a vision for emerging virtual worlds (e.g. metaverses), based on respect for digital rights and EU laws and values" such that "open, interoperable and innovative virtual worlds … can be used safely and with confidence by the public and businesses" (Choi et al., 2023). One such research project to develop a new ethical framework that can be used to help draft future EU legislation for the Metaverse is being led by respected ethicist Professor Luciano Floridi of the Digital Ethics Center, Yale University (Holden, 2022). In 2023, the European Union released an interim report on *Next Generation Virtual Worlds: Societal, Technological, Economic and Policy Challenges for the EU* in 2023 (Hupont Torres et al., 2023) and also the same year released a report on *An EU initiative on Web 4.0 and virtual worlds: a head start in the next technological transition*, looking at both economic and governance issues. This identified Web 4.0 as "the expected fourth generation of the World Wide Web. Using advanced artificial and ambient intelligence, the internet of things, trusted blockchain transactions, virtual worlds and XR capabilities, digital and real objects and environments are fully integrated and communicate with each other, enabling truly intuitive, immersive experiences, seamlessly blending the physical and digital worlds" (EU, 2023).

The IEEE's Global Initiative on Ethics of Extended Reality is looking at establishing a legalistic framework, similar to GDPR legislation in the European Union (Stephens, 2022). The World Economic Forum launched an initiative to build an equitable, interoperable, and safe metaverse in 2022, and their 2023 briefing paper on *Interoperability in the Metaverse* covered jurisdictional interoperability alongside technical and usage interoperability, as well as offering some initial guidance on composing "a governance framework that considers privacy, security, identity, safety and interoperability" (WEF, 2023).

Physical Law or Virtual Law

Part of the debate around governance is the issue of what laws apply within the world. Who does a user appeal to if robbed, groomed, abused, swindled, or worse? What counts as blasphemy or slander or illegal pornography in the world – and if they are transgressed, who prosecutes? There are similar issues with social networks on the Web – is it the physical location of the operator, the servers, the victim, or the abuser that counts? And where are the boundaries between anti-social behaviour and abuse – griefing (transgressive behaviour) being common across many, if not all, virtual worlds (Jenkins, 2010). A useful survey of the legal implications of the Metaverse, and of a Web3 approach to it, is provided by Garon (2022).

The assumption is probably that the virtual world should be subject to the same rules and laws as the physical world. However, physical world laws and rules vary by jurisdiction, organisation, and even culture – so which should be chosen for a virtual world or metaverse? Does the UN Declaration Human Rights apply in the Metaverse? Should operators and virtual landowners be able to enforce their own laws as long as they don't violate those basic rights? And who, in the Metaverse, will have the authority to establish laws and enforce them?

There are already debates about what legal jurisdictions apply to situations on the Internet where the provider, servers, and users may all be in different jurisdictions (e.g. Reidenberg, 2005), and the situation will be no different, and potentially worse in the Metaverse (Kostenko et al., 2022; Kalyvaki, 2023). Whilst a room-based metaverse might be a close analogue to the website/application situation, if the Metaverse is implemented as one or more spatial models, then do the same rules apply across the whole of the connected space, or just within certain areas of it? Could one area erect billboards on its borders that were viewable from another area where their content would be viewed as blasphemous or illegal? Could the avatar citizens of one area seek asylum on the servers of another area?

Law around intellectual property (IP) – whether manifest as builds, scripts, objects, or clothing – will also need some harmonisation across the different parts of the Metaverse. The European Union is already looking at how EU IP laws may apply across the Metaverse (Choi et al., 2023), and the World Intellectual Property Organisation, an agency of the United Nations, is looking at the global IP issues of the Metaverse (WIPO, n.d.).

Freedom of Expression versus Freedom from Abuse

Another aspect of governance is how to ensure user freedoms. Virtual worlds are places where the tension between freedom of expression and freedom from abuse has been evident from the very beginning – as in the Dibbell rape in cyberspace case mentioned in Chapter 1. The Guardian reported on a case of alleged gang rape in VR in 2022 and noted that there have reportedly been several sexual assaults in *Horizon Worlds* (Sales, 2024). The United Nations Interregional Crime and Justice Research Institute (UNICRI) report on *Gaming and the Metaverse: The Alarming Rise of Online Child Sexual Exploitation and Abuse within the New Digital Frontier* warns that as the use of "virtual platforms increases, so too will the scale and complexity of the potential harm to children" and that "children ... may be exposed to sexual exploitation and abuse, if proper safeguard measures are not in place" (UNICRI, 2022).

In contrast, Johnson (2010) describes how "For transgendered residents, Second Life allows for an expansive view of gender and political activism", providing a safe and supportive place to meet, and generally providing a "world of possibilities that allows one to experiment with 'sexual ideation' and ... begin to create links between 'the actual and the virtual'". The use of virtual worlds for political campaigning and demonstration has also already been described.

Interpol is working on how to police the Metaverse (Cieslak & Gerken, 2023), and Headleand et al. (2020) have proposed virtual community support officers drawn from within the virtual communities as a way of policing virtual spaces. The Centre for Long-Term Cybersecurity published a report in 2022 on community guidelines for the Metaverse that highlighted the importance of clarity, comprehensiveness, specificity, and transparency (Lazeron, 2022).

Greater centralised control could be expected to reduce abuse but could also impact political, gender, and other freedoms of expression, particularly where the world is being managed (or even accessed) from a country with authoritarian leanings. Finding the right balance will be as challenging in the virtual worlds of the Metaverse as it is in the physical world.

Privacy versus Surveillance

A linked consideration is that metaverse technologies provide significant opportunities for their operators, and potentially any controlling nation-state, to enact almost total surveillance on their users/citizens. Monitoring the game servers would allow the total monitoring of every user in a way that a combination of phone and CCTV surveillance could never hope to achieve in the physical world. The Snowden Papers revealed how Western intelligence agencies had console monitoring operations and plans for virtual world data collection back in 2008 (NSA, 2008), and Chapter 3 has described the potential issues around "fingerprinting" users and capturing their biometric data through their headset-mounted VR display (HMD-VR) use, and identifying emotional triggers, all of which could be exploited with hostile, or manipulative, intent (Rosenberg, 2022).

The Metaverse needs to ensure that user privacy is at least as good as that in the physical and cyber worlds. Whilst there are features that can improve the perceived privacy of the user (e.g. area access controls, zone of audio silence), these do not ensure absolute privacy from the platform operator or any malfeasant agent. Greater decentralisation, explainable artificial intelligence (AI), blockchain, global regulation, and more use of open source have all been proposed to help address privacy concerns (Fernandez & Hui, 2022; Sandeepa, n.d.), as well as considering the issues through a human rights lens (Heller, 2020).

Accessibility

If the Metaverse is to open up a wide range of possibilities across almost the whole gamut of a person's life, then it is vital that everyone, regardless of ability or disability, can participate in it to the same degree. A useful overview of the opportunities that virtual worlds and the Metaverse provide for disabled people is provided by Stendal et al. (2011). Stendal (2012) also provides a more detailed literature review and highlights the (then, and probably still current) lack of research in the area of virtual worlds for people with disabilities.

There are already lots of examples of disabled people using virtual spaces as a way of communicating, celebrating, or overcoming their disability. David remembers helping the BBC interview disability activist and virtual world entrepreneur Simon Stevens in *Second Life,* and the interviewer was taken aback both by the fact that Simon was still in a wheelchair and wearing a protective helmet in *Second Life* – when neither were obviously necessary, and by the fact that he was then trampolining and skydiving in said wheelchair! Simon has been interviewed by many others (e.g. Headstar, 2012;

Mollman, n.d.), and it is clear that there is not the simple *Avatar* film style "virtual worlds let you walk again" experience for those with disabilities, but rather it gives everyone new ways to express who they are and what they want to do.

One study using *Second Life* found that disabled users who used a virtual world showed "significantly improved on measures of affective states (depression, anxiety, positive emotion, life satisfaction, and feelings of loneliness) and self-evaluation (self-esteem)" (Gilbert et al., 2013). Another study of disabled users, using the *Gather.Town* 2D virtual world (2020, https://www.gather.town/), found that "participants' interpersonal relationships, problem-solving abilities in the workplace, and online interview skills were significantly improved" through training inside of the virtual world (Lee et al., 2023).

Disabled users will always be making a conscious decision as to whether they reveal their disabilities to fellow users or not – as in the case of *World of Warcraft* players studied by Lim and Nardi (2011) and *Second Life* users studied by Stendal et al. (2012). A study by Smith (2010) identifies disabled virtual world users as having two different motivations:

- **augmentationists** – who see the virtual world as a way of extending their physical world existences – and who may have avatars that embrace their physical selves; and

- **immersionists** – who see the virtual world as a distinct and alternative parallel to their existence in the physical world.

Of course, motivations may be very context dependent, and any metaverse should support users in exploring either mode at any time.

In order to be usable, particularly for those with motor control issues, the user interfaces for the Metaverse need to be designed with a high level of accessibility in mind – not all users can manage the fine movements required to control an avatar, or feel comfortable wearing a VR headset. The biggest challenge for the visual metaverse is of course for those with visual impairments, and it's one of the reasons that the axioms of the Metaverse in Chapter 2 try to avoid talking about a "visual" experience. It is certainly a spatial experience, and the interface needs to be designed to cope with blind and partially sighted users as well as those with good sight. As far back as 2009, a virtual guide dog was being developed in *Second Life*, which could help its owners navigate and identify objects and people (Anderson, 2009). The same audio guide technology being deployed in the physical world to help visually impaired people (e.g. Parker et al., 2021) could be applied to virtual worlds to help them navigate, typically through audio or haptic assistance. In addition to using voice, games developed or adapted for blind users such as *Shades of Doom, AudioQuake*, and *Terraformers* have also used sonar style "blips", directional timbres, and musical "earcons" to help create a rich soundscape for visually impaired users to interact with (Folmer, 2018).

Fernandes and Werner (2022) provide a useful overview of the human-interface challenges and potential solutions across the five senses. Politis et al. (2017) highlight the importance of involving people with disabilities in the design of games and virtual worlds from the beginning in order to help ensure their usability. Broad agendas on accessible design and inclusivity of the current generation of metaverse platforms have been described by Zallio and Clarkson (2022) and Parker et al. (2023), and XRAccess (https://xraccess.org/) is a research consortium aiming to make extended reality (XR) inclusive for all.

Digital Poverty

A more general case of the accessibility debate, and related to that of global equality discussed below, is that of how the Metaverse can respond to the issue of digital poverty. Digital (or data) poverty refers to the mostly financial, technical, social, and economic challenges that some people have in accessing digital services (Cáceres, 2007). The push of governments and organisations to go digital-first, and even digital-only, risks disenfranchising a significant proportion of the population. A 2015 study (Leidig et al., 2016) established a Data Poverty Index and found that about half the countries of equatorial Africa had high data poverty, and most other countries in Africa and most in Southeast Asia had above average data poverty. Digital poverty, sometimes measured as digital exclusion, also exists in Minority World countries. In 2020, the UK Office of Communications (Ofcom) reported that in the United Kingdom, "approximately 9% of households with children lacked access to a laptop, desktop, or tablet; 2% had no access to the internet and 4% had smartphone only access" with figures almost doubled for lower earning households (Coleman, 2021). A 2022 Ofcom report put the percentage of households without Internet at 6%, with a further 5% relying on mobile Internet (Ofcom, 2022).

If the Metaverse is to become a vital component of people's lives, then it must be designed and delivered to minimise the disenfranchisement of potential users. One of the most basic steps is to ensure that any VR experience or service is available as DesktopVR rather than just through an HMD, and for mixed reality (MR) experiences to also be available in AR, so that even smartphone users should be able to access them. The bandwidth required by a service should also be considered, although as noted in Chapter 4, XR experiences can require less bandwidth than video chat or streaming a film or TV program. This is also a reason why centralised rendering and video streaming as a way of accessing VR content should possibly be avoided.

A further consideration is, of course, that of cost. The Web in general costs nothing to access once a user has a smartphone or PC and broadband or mobile connection, and ideally the same should be true of the Metaverse. Certain areas and applications in the Metaverse may have a cost associated with them, just as places in the physical world and on the Web do, but any charges should be collected through a payment system which doesn't further exclude people. This is one of the big issues of current cryptoworlds. Quite apart from the volatility in the pricing, the ownership of cryptocurrencies is not at a level to make them available to all – for instance, a 2023 UK survey suggested that only around 10% of UK adults held crypto (FCA, 2023) – and based on earlier surveys, this is likely to be heavily biased towards well-off, mid-age males (Jones, 2021). The figures are higher in the United States where one study reports 17% of adults having invested in, traded, or used a crypto-currency, and again biased to better-off men (Faverio & Sidoti, 2023).

Even with access to technology and money to spend, some users may also be uncomfortable with being an avatar or find navigating an avatar through first or third person controls difficult. Ways of both educating people to be more comfortable in a virtual world and of providing technical solutions to any enduring metaverse-phobia should be considered. Technology adoption models have been used to study such issues (e.g. Wu & Yu, 2023), and these problems are in addition to those related to cybersickness (and its possible gender bias) already discussed. One approach to addressing all these issues is the concept of "design justice", putting all users at the centre of the design process:

> This means centring marginalised communities who are most at risk from Web2 and gaming's self-seeded sins, listening to them and integrating their lived experiences into the foundations of the metaverse's design. Through this we have a chance to make the new virtual world more accessible and equitable than that of its forefathers.
>
> **(Fusco-House, 2022).**

Identity

Whilst there has been significant work on identity in digital spaces (e.g. Haraway, 1991; Hayles, 1999; Ito et al., 2010), less has been done on people in virtual worlds. One useful approach, though, has been to examine how student learners act within virtual worlds to develop a typology of learner identity (Steils, 2013, pp. 242–250), which may be more generally applicable. The typology showed how students seek to manage their identity through their avatar and portrays identity across five dimensions:

- **Dislocated avatars**: The first dimension concerns the utilisation of default avatars. In this dimension, the avatar is positioned as merely functional. No emotional attachment to the avatar is indicated; participants basically ignored the appearance of the avatar.
- **Representative avatars**: The second dimension considers an understanding of the avatar as a representation of oneself in functional

terms, although the avatar's appearance seems closely connected to (or at least an approximation) the physical world appearance of the user. The students described the relationship with the avatar in terms of functional representation and rendered the avatar as an object or tool.

- **Avatars as toys and tools**: The third dimension portrays an understanding of the avatar as a tool and an object for playful engagement, as well as a status object. The avatar is positioned as an object that can be customised and played with to take on varied appearances.
- **Avatars as extensions of self**: The fourth dimension regards students who declared their respective avatars as an extension of themselves, both visually as well as emotionally. In their narratives, the avatar was described as closely related to the user not only in corporeal appearance and, possibly, by name, but the students also mentioned being emotionally and psychologically attached to their avatars.
- **Avatars as identity extensions**: In this dimension, students engaged with their avatars and the virtual world in terms of "laboratories for the construction of identities" (Turkle, 1996, p. 184). Thus, the avatar in this dimension ventured into dimensions of exploring notions of potential, new, or alternative identities for oneself both in the context of the virtual world and as a testing ground for the physical world, as well as exploring possibilities beyond its boundaries.

There still remain many debates about the nature of identities in cyberspace, with a wide diversity of opinions. For example, some scholars suggest that it is important to have a clear conceptual understanding of who we are in cyberspace, since without it, we risk being confused (e.g. Floridi, 2011). Those such as Floridi who argue for such a stance seem to suggest that by separating and being honest about identities brings with it some kind of honesty or morality, yet this would seem misplaced.

Understanding identities in relation to users and their avatars is complex. A new set of s/pl/ace identities are required which reflect squashed polarities, chaotic overlaps, and new configurations of space and place, as well as an appreciation of VR and metaversal spaces.

Physical Lives versus Virtual Lives

Alongside fashion, homes are a common focus of virtual world activity. Even though people are in a world where it never rains or is cold, and where complete security and privacy can be provided by a couple of mouse-clicks, people still like somewhere to call "home" and to be able to personalise it. This may be as simple as the home "den" in Oculus Quest or *Rec Room*, or a

Linden Home in *Second Life* in the finest ranch-style tradition, or something you fashion out of blocks in *Minecraft*. The need for a virtual, secure "home-base" seems an almost primeval urge (Goetz, 2017). The COVID pandemic drove millions to a housebound existence and a working-from-home model. Almost all of the virtual worlds showed a spike in usage as people used the virtual world as a way of escaping their physical home and extending their existence into a larger virtual space (Somoza Medina & Somoza Medina, 2023). Whilst most remote business meetings still tend to be on video conferencing systems, if metaversal models and all of the collaboration tools mentioned earlier become more common, then there may be a similar extension of the physical office into the virtual (something that companies like IBM tried in the early *Second Life* days).

Does the Metaverse offer a further opportunity to blend the physical and the digital/virtual, so that, rather than virtual homes becoming (often) idealised versions of the homes people would like to have in the physical world, they become a part of a more symbiotic relationship? One where physical and virtual homes are interconnected, bleeding through and into each other, and supporting the development of a Metaverse that encompasses all of people's lives – both physical and digital. And does this same discussion also apply at a city level – how might cities be redesigned if they exist as viable and effective entities in both the physical and virtual worlds, and if their citizens are likewise existence-fluid? Mitchell (2003) talked about Me++, how the then emerging digital world was letting us extend our existence beyond our physical selves, so that we were defined by both (physical) boundaries and (mostly digital) networks. In the era of the Metaverse, are we also defined by the virtual worlds we inhabit?

Broadening this discussion out, a key consideration is how the physical world and the virtual world of the Metaverse will co-exist – with many (e.g. Narula, 2022; Hackl, interviewed in Alaghband, 2022) seeing the physical and virtual as all part of the same Metaverse. Science fiction has often presented the danger of people being completely seduced by the virtual to the exclusion of their physical health, relationships, and environment – as in the film *WALL-E* (Stanton, 2008). What can be done to avoid that, and are there ways by which the virtual can actually enhance the physical – as has already been discussed in the context of climate change and global equality?

The potentially addictive nature of computer games and their effects have long been recognised (Aziz et al., 2021), and the Chinese have even tried to limit the amount of time that children play video games – although reportedly to little effect (Stokel-Walker, 2023). Time compression (i.e. losing track of real time) has also been well studied in DesktopVR and HMD-VR experiences (e.g. Mullen & Davidenko, 2021) – although it can be even more of an issue in HMD-VR since the user has no sense of the change in daylight in the physical world.

There is an obvious tension between promoting the metaverse as something that people use regularly as part of their everyday existence, and not wanting people to become so addicted to it that they neglect their physical world and existence.

The types of features that would enable users to be more connected into their non-metaverse digital existence whilst in the Metaverse, such as the virtual mobile phone shown by Meta at their Connect 2021 event (Burden, 2021), could actually help to maintain a connection between the virtual and physical world, similar to a virtual assistant who can keep track on a user's in-world time, or even the simple expedient of an alarm on the HUD or virtual tablet within a virtual world. It may be that by making the Metaverse more a part of people's everyday lives, bringing in the bad and the good, that, for the most part, it loses that sense of escapism and is something that users attend to in the same way that they do to any physical world task – although escapist environments are always likely to have a place in the Metaverse.

Perhaps the future is one where – particularly with the sort of augmented/ mixed reality overlays envisaged by Rainbow's End (Vinge, 2006) – the boundary between the physical and the virtual becomes increasingly blurred. Indeed, Narula (2022) sees the Metaverse as "a network of consequences and meaning between multiple worlds and which people are simultaneously engaged and invested. One or more of these worlds is made of ideas, the other one is the physical world". And philosopher David Chalmers argues strongly for the "reality" of virtual experiences (Chalmers, 2022), so does it even matter if there is blurring?

Liminality

There is often a sense of being confused or displaced in a virtual world which is not just troublesome in itself, in terms of what occurs in people's lives, but also as concepts. When people engage with knowledge and virtual spaces they find troublesome, they experience disjunction – a sense of becoming stuck. Such disjunction prompts people to reconsider beliefs about who they are and the way they operate in a metaversal space, and results in a state called liminality.

Liminality tends to be characterised by a stripping away of old identities, an oscillation between states and personal transformation. Liminality is a term first coined by van Gennep (Gennep, 1960) who described a psychological or metaphysical subjective state of being at the threshold of two existential planes. Although the term was originally applied to rites and rituals in small human groups, it was extended to whole societies by writers such as Jaspers (1953). Turner later described people in a liminal state as "a realm of pure possibility whence novel con- figurations of ideas and relations may arise" (1969). He suggested that those in liminal states were often ritually, symbolically, or metaphorically removed in order not to threaten the social order while they experience transition, transformation, or "in-betweenness".

In the transition from what has been traditionally a largely analogue delivery of information and knowledge from human to human without digital inter-mediation, people interacting in a new, uncharted territory often have a sense of being stuck and moving into a liminal space. Transition through liminality can bring with it not only new knowledge and understanding for the individ-ual, but also often a new sense of identity. Ball (2022) argues that understand-ing and aligning one's internal and external worlds in the face of disjunction present a variety of challenges to emotional, material, and social resources – something which needs to be considered in relation to the Metaverse.

Global Equality

Many of the arguments for a Metaverse to help with climate change also apply to a Metaverse to help with global equality. At worst, this can be an argument for the "moral imperative" – where the virtual experience is seen as a sop for people who cannot access or afford the physical experience of living in a stylish beach side house or driving the latest fast car (Au, 2023). At best, the Metaverse could, like the mobile phone, be considered as a way by which Majority World nations can potentially leap-frog a generation of busi-ness and infrastructure development and become more "metaverse-native" than many of their counterparts in the Minority World (Koomson, 2018). Of course, VR/MR headsets are currently less robust, and more expensive, than mobile phones, and these are issues that can be addressed, but, as has been discussed, the Metaverse should be accessible from a wide range of devices, including mobile phones, so this should not be a real problem.

Language has often been a barrier to high-technology access in the Majority World (Ejiaku, 2014), but the Metaverse is primarily a visual, audio, and social experience, and most of the content should be user-generated, so anyone should be able to enter the Metaverse and start using it, and even creating in it.

A potential approach to help develop global equality within the Metaverse is to ensure that metaverse developments are orientated around the United Nations' Sustainable Development Goals (SDGs) (https://sdgs.un.org/goals). Two key questions are (Umar, 2022a):

- Can the Metaverse be used to accelerate the advancement of SDGs; and
- What challenges could the Metaverse raise for SDGs, and what type of policies will be needed to address these challenges?

Umar (2022b) also provides a high-level mapping of metaverse applications and approaches to the SDGs. The UN's Internet Governance Forum (IGF) ran a workshop on the "Joint efforts to build a responsible & sustainable Metaverse" based on the SDGs (IGF, 2022), and others have looked at how the Metaverse addresses specific SDGs – for instance, Goal 4: Quality Education (Nilashi & Abumalloh, 2023). In a systematic review of the Metaverse and sustainability, Jauhiainen et al. (2022) identify that:

> The metaverse as a global platform will become one important arena in which SDGs can be addressed. The metaverse could play an important role in the achievement of various SDGs, not only addressing them in the digital realm, but also by transforming the material word connected to SDGs. However, the metaverse's development, construction, and implementation can create challenges to sustainability.

Human versus AI Avatars

At present, most of the avatars that a user meets in a social virtual world will be controlled by other humans. Automated (i.e. computer-controlled) avatars may be present in a world as helpers, guides, or non-player characters, and some worlds (e.g. gaming experiences) may have more automated avatars (sometimes called robotars) than human avatars, but human-controlled avatars still generally dominate in virtual worlds. But will this situation persist?

First, it should be noted that automated avatars need not be synonymous with AI-driven avatars – although that may increasingly be the case. Most current automated avatars are driven by very simple scripts. The games industry has been a significant player in developing ever more complex behaviours in their non-player characters (e.g. da Silva & de Souza Ribeiro, 2021), but virtual worlds have also been identified as a useful (and perhaps ideal) environment in which to explore the development of grounded and embodied AI (e.g. Burden et al., 2016).

A key element of a virtual world is that when confronted by another avatar, a user has no initial way of knowing whether the other avatar is human or computer-controlled – the engagement instantly becomes a variation on the Turing Test (Shah et al., 2016). As a result, virtual worlds are ideal places to hold covert Turing Tests in order to see whether, when not even prompted that another avatar may be computer-driven, a human can spot whether the avatar they are engaging with is human- or computer-controlled. As mentioned in Chapter 5, in one test that David helped staged, even when prompted, only 22% of participants correctly identified an avatar as being computer-controlled (Gilbert & Forney, 2015).

Apart from purely computer-controlled avatars increasingly being found in service, support, and assistant/companion roles in virtual worlds, the idea of avatars which are optionally computer-controlled might be a possibility. Many people have dreamed about sending a copy of themselves to a meeting they don't want to attend, and this is far more feasible in the Metaverse than in the physical world. Indeed, if you have a computer application which is working as your virtual assistant and metaphorically sitting on your shoulder and watching (and recording and analysing) everything that you do and say then giving that virtual assistant temporary control of your metaverse avatar for specific meetings may be a logical next step (Burden, 2019).

Digital Amortality

If you have a virtual assistant that knows everything you do, the key question then is what happens if you get hit by a (very physical) bus, or otherwise die? Can the virtual assistant continue to operate your avatar in your now-perpetual absence? Is that assistant (and avatar) owned by you, or your employer or your next-of-kin? Can it continue to earn on your (or your employer or your spouse's) behalf? And what legal status does it have anyway? The situation is even more vital when one considers not a virtual assistant which has a secondary role of standing in for the user but where the user has created a digital twin of themselves for the express purpose of both standing in for them during their life (e.g. during holidays or sickness, or just as a way of multiplying their earning power) and even after it.

The terms digital amortality for the concept and digital amortal for the entity were coined in Neal Stephenson's *Fall; or, Dodge in Hell* (Stephenson, 2020). They are perhaps better than digital immortality/immortal given the significant technical and economic challenges in keeping such an entity operational forever (Burden, 2020). Amortality implies a state where the entity can decide if and when it wants to terminate its life. Whilst such ideas might seem like science fiction, in their most basic form, such systems are already possible (Savin-Baden & Burden, 2019). The technologies that support them are developing rapidly – *Somnium Space* has already previewed a "Live Forever" mode (Somnium Times, 2023) – so the ethical implications need to be considered now.

As a final aspect of this concept, whilst media explorations such as *Upload* (Daniels, 2020) have shown the living and the virtual dead existing in (relative) harmony (albeit in divided worlds), it may be that such a positive outcome is not realistic. Arthur C. Clarke wrote in *2001: A Space Odessey* that the dead outnumbered the living by 30:1 (Clarke, 1968) – although current estimates put that number at more like 13:1 (Routley, 2022). What if, in a few decades time, everyone was leaving (possibly multiple) copies of their own digital amortal? Perhaps one outcome might be a "thanoverse" – a part of the wider Metaverse but which is (largely) inhabited by the avatars of the dead. The concept of a thanoverse might even overlap with the role of the Metaverse within interstellar exploration to be described in Chapter 6. It may be that the humans who explore the stars are not just virtual ones but also dead ones.

Summary

This chapter has examined 15 different areas in which tensions exist in how the Metaverse may develop. Those tensions range from relatively technical ones such as whether it is closed and centralised or open and decentralised through wider issues that matter to the individual such as privacy, legality, identity, and accessibility to global issues around climate change, global equality, and the impacts on society as a whole. The next, and final, chapter will take a broad look at the future development of the Metaverse and examine seven different scenarios as to how the Metaverse could develop, each charting a different course through these challenges and delivering a very different set of issues and opportunities.

References

Alaghband, M. (2022, March 29). *What is the metaverse—And what does it mean for business?* [Podcast]. McKinsey. https://www.mckinsey.com/capabilities/mckinsey-digital/our-insights/what-is-the-metaverse-and-what-does-it-mean-for-business

Anderson, P. F. (2009). *Max, the (Second Life) guide dog.* Emerging Technologies Librarian. https://etechlib.wordpress.com/2009/06/22/max-the-guide-dog-in-second-life/

Au, W. J. (2023). *Making a metaverse that matters: From snow crash & second life to a virtual world worth fighting for.* John Wiley & Sons.

Aziz, N., Nordin, M. J., Abdulkadir, S. J., & Salih, M. M. M. (2021). Digital addiction: Systematic review of computer game addiction impact on adolescent physical health. *Electronics, 10*(9), 996.

Ball, M. (2022). *The metaverse: And how it will revolutionize everything.* Liveright Publishing.

Burden, D. J. H. (2019, July 15). *Developing conversational AI solutions for the MOD.* CogX2019 [Video]. YouTube. https://www.youtube.com/watch?v=SQj8kTpN7Iw

Burden, D. J. H. (2020). Building a digital immortal. In M. Savin-Baden & V. Mason-Robbie (Eds.), *Digital afterlife.* CRC.

Burden, D. J. H. (2021). *Facebook (aka Meta) Connect2021.* Daden's Blog. https://daden-blog.blogspot.com/2021/10/facebook-aka-meta-connect2021.html

Burden, D. J., Savin-Baden, M., & Bhakta, R. (2016). Covert implementations of the Turing test: A more level playing field? *Research and development in intelligent systems XXXIII: Incorporating applications and innovations in intelligent systems XXIV 33* (pp. 195–207). Springer International Publishing.

Cáceres, R. B. (2007). *Digital poverty: Concept and measurement, with an application to Peru.* Helen Kellogg Institute for International Studies.

Carter, N. (2021). *How much energy does bitcoin actually consume.* Harvard Business Review.https://hbr.org/2021/05/how-much-energy-does-bitcoin-actually-consume

Chalmers, D. J. (2022). *Reality+: Virtual worlds and the problems of philosophy.* WW Norton.

Choi, S. J., Cooper, D., & Szewczyk, B. (2023). *Regulating the Metaverse in Europe.* Global Policy Watch. https://www.globalpolicywatch.com/2023/04/regulating-the-metaverse-in-europe/

Cieslak, M., & Gerken, T. (2023, February 4). Interpol working out how to police the metaverse. *BBC News.* https://www.bbc.co.uk/news/technology-64501726

Clarke, A. C. (1968). *2001: A space odyssey.* Longman.

Coleman, V. (2021). *Digital divide in UK education during COVID-19 pandemic: Literature review.* Research Report. Cambridge Assessment. https://www.cambridgeassessment.org.uk/Images/628843-digital-divide-in-uk-education-during-covid-19-pandemic-literature-review.pdf

da Silva, G. A., & de Souza Ribeiro, M. W. (2021). Development of non-player character with believable behavior: A systematic literature review. *Anais Estendidos do XX Simpósio Brasileiro de Jogos e Entretenimento Digital* (pp. 319–323). Brazilian Computing Society.

Daniels, G. (2020). *Upload* [TV series]. Deedle-Dee Productions.

De Vries, A. (2018). Bitcoin's growing energy problem. *Joule, 2*(5), 801–805.

De Vries, A. (2019). Renewable energy will not solve bitcoin's sustainability problem. *Joule, 3*(4), 893–898.

De-la-Cruz-Diaz, M., Alvarez-Risco, A., Jaramillo-Arévalo, M., Lenti-Dulong, M. F., Calle-Nole, M., de las Mercedes Anderson-Seminario, M., & Del-Aguila-Arcentales, S. (2022). Virtual tourism, carbon footprint, and circularity. *Circular economy: Impact on carbon and water footprint* (pp. 245–263). Springer Singapore.

Ejiaku, S. A. (2014). Technology adoption: Issues and challenges in information technology adoption in emerging economies. *Journal of International Technology and Information Management, 23*(2), 59–68.

EU. (2023). *An EU initiative on Web 4.0 and virtual worlds: A head start in the next technological transition.* European Commission. https://eur-lex.europa.eu/legal-content/EN/TXT/?uri=CELEX%3A52023DC0442

Fainu, K. (2023, June 27). Facing extinction, Tuvalu considers the digital clone of a country. The Guardian. https://www.theguardian.com/world/2023/jun/27/tuvalu-climate-crisis-rising-sea-levels-pacific-island-nation-country-digital-clone

Faverio, M., & Sidoti, O. (2023). *Majority of Americans aren't confident in the safety and reliability of cryptocurrency.* Pew Research Center. https://www.pewresearch.org/short-reads/2023/04/10/majority-of-americans-arent-confident-in-the-safety-and-reliability-of-cryptocurrency/

FCA. (2023). *FCA introduces tough new rules for marketing cryptoassets.* Financial Conduct Authority. https://www.fca.org.uk/news/press-releases/fca-introduces-tough-new-rules-marketing-cryptoassets

Fernandes, F., & Werner, C. (2022). Accessibility in the metaverse: Are we prepared? *Anais do XIII workshop sobre aspectos da interação humano-computador para a web social* (pp. 9–15). SBC.

Fernandez, C. B., & Hui, P. (2022). Life, the metaverse and everything: An overview of privacy, ethics, and governance in metaverse. *2022 IEEE 42nd international conference on distributed computing systems workshops (ICDCSW)* (pp. 272–277). IEEE.

Floridi, L. (2011). The construction of personal identities online. *Minds and Machines*, *21*(4), 477–479.

Fodor, G. (2020). *The secret Mozilla Hubs master plan*. Medium. https://gfodor.medium. com/the-secret-mozilla-hubs-master-plan-2c1364033bec

Folmer, E. (2018). Video games for users with visual impairment. In R. Manduchi & S. Kurniawan (Eds.), *Assistive technology for blindness and low vision* (pp. 359–382). CRC Press.

Fusco-House, C. (2022). *We must learn from our mistakes*. WPP. https://www.wpp.com/ en/wpp-iq/2022/11/we-must-learn-from-our-mistakes

Garon, J. M. (2022). Legal implications of a ubiquitous metaverse and a Web3 future. *Marquette Law Review*, *106*, 163.

Gennep, A. (1960). *The rites of passage*. University of Chicago Press.

Gilbert, R. L., & Forney, A. (2015). Can avatars pass the Turing test? Intelligent agent perception in a 3D virtual environment. *International Journal of Human-Computer Studies*, *73*, 30–36.

Gilbert, R. L., Murphy, N. A., Krueger, A. B., Ludwig, A. R., & Efron, T. Y. (2013). Psychological benefits of participation in three-dimensional virtual worlds for individuals with real-world disabilities. *International Journal of Disability, Development and Education*, *60*(3), 208–224.

Goetz, C. (2017). Securing home base: Separation-individuation, attachment theory, and the "virtual worlds" paradigm in video games. *The Psychoanalytic Study of the Child*, *70*(1), 101–116.

Guiao, J. (2022, November 21). *The metaverse will be a digital graveyard if we let new technologies distract us from today's problems*. The Guardian. https://www.theguardian. com/commentisfree/2022/nov/21/the-metaverse-will-be-a-digital-graveyard-if-we-let-new-technologies-distract-us-from-todays-problems?CMP=fb_a-technology_b-gdntech.

Gursoy, D., Malodia, S., & Dhir, A. (2022). The metaverse in the hospitality and tourism industry: An overview of current trends and future research directions. *Journal of Hospitality Marketing & Management*, *31*(5), 527–534.

Haraway, D. (1991). A cyborg manifesto: Science, technology, and socialist-feminism in the late twentieth century. *Simians, cyborgs and women: The reinvention of nature* (pp. 149–181). Routledge.

Hayles, K. (1999). *How we became posthuman: Virtual bodies in cybernetics, literature and informatics*. University of Chicago Press.

Headleand, C. J., Free, J., Farndale, S., & Hall, M. (2020). Virtual community support officers: Community policing in the digital space. *2020 International conference on cyberworlds (CW)* (pp. 121–124). IEEE.

Headstar. (2012). *Profile feature—Simon Stevens: A high flyer in two worlds*. Headstar E-Access Bulletin Live. http://www.headstar.com/eablive/?p=758

Heller, B. (2020). *Reimagining reality: Human rights and immersive technology*. Carr Center for Human Rights Policy, Harvard Kennedy School, Harvard University.

Holden, K. (2022). *Digital Ethics Summit 2022* [2022]. Tech UK. https://www.techuk. org/resource/digital-ethics-summit-2022.html

Hupont Torres, I., Charisi, V., de Prato, G., Pogorzelska, K., Schade, S., Kotsev, A., Sobolewski, M., Duch Brown, N., Calza, E., Dunker, C., & Di Girolamo, F. (2023). *Next generation virtual worlds: Societal, technological, economic and policy challenges for the EU*. Publications Office of the European Union. https://doi.org/ 10.2760/51579

Ibañez, J. I., & Freier, A. (2023). Bitcoin's carbon footprint revisited: Proof of work mining for renewable energy expansion. *Challenges, 14*(3), 35.

IGF. (2022). *IGF 2022 WS #217 Joint efforts to build a responsible & sustainable Metaverse.* Internet Governance Forum. https://www.intgovforum.org/en/content/igf-2022-ws-217-joint-efforts-to-build-a-responsible-sustainable-metaverse

Ito, M., Baumer, S., Bittanti, M., Boyd, D., Cody, R., Herr-Stephenson, B., Horst, H. A., Lange, P. G., Mahendran, D., & Martínez, K. Z. (2010). *Hanging out, messing around, and geeking out.* MIT Press.

Jaspers, K. (1953). *The origin and goal of history.* Yale University Press.

Jauhiainen, J. S., Krohn, C., & Junnila, J. (2022). Metaverse and sustainability: Systematic review of scientific publications until 2022 and beyond. *Sustainability, 15*(1), 346.

Jenkins, H. (2010). *Watching the watchers: Power and politics in Second Life (Part One).* Henry Jenkins. https://henryjenkins.org/blog/2010/04/watching_the_watchers_power_an.html

Johnson, P. (2010). *Second Life, media, and the other society.* Peter Lang.

Jones, R. (2021, June 17). About 2.3m Britons hold cryptocurrencies despite warnings of risk. *The Guardian.* https://www.theguardian.com/technology/2021/jun/17/about-23m-britons-hold-cryptocurrencies-despite-warnings-of-risk

Kalyvaki, M. (2023). Navigating the metaverse business and legal challenges: Intellectual property, privacy, and jurisdiction. *Journal of Metaverse, 3*(1), 87–92.

Koomson, W. K. (2018). Leapfrog technologies: Can Mobile technologies competes successfully with traditional learning management systems? *Advances in Social Sciences Research Journal, 5*(8), 234–250.

Kostenko, O., Furashev, V., Zhuravlov, D., & Dniprov, O. (2022). Genesis of legal regulation web and the model of the electronic jurisdiction of the metaverse. *Bratislava Law Review, 6*(2), 21–36.

Kshetri, N., & Dwivedi, Y. K. (2023). Pollution-reducing and pollution-generating effects of the metaverse. *International Journal of Information Management, 69,* 102620.

Lazeron, R. (2022). *A secure and equitable metaverse: Designing effective community guidelines for social VR.* Centre for Long-Term Cybersecurity. https://cltc.berkeley.edu/wp-content/uploads/2022/11/Secure_Equitable_Metaverse.pdf

Le, D. A., MacIntyre, B., & Outlaw, J. (2020, March). Enhancing the experience of virtual conferences in social virtual environments. *2020 IEEE conference on virtual reality and 3D user interfaces abstracts and workshops (VRW)* (pp. 485–494). IEEE.

Lee, S., Lee, Y., & Park, E. (2023). Sustainable vocational preparation for adults with disabilities: A metaverse-based approach. *Sustainability, 15*(15), 12000.

Leidig, M., Teeuw, R. M., & Gibson, A. D. (2016). Data poverty: A global evaluation for 2009 to 2013-implications for sustainable development and disaster risk reduction. *International Journal of Applied Earth Observation and Geoinformation, 50,* 1–9.

Lim, T., & Nardi, B. (2011, June). A study of raiders with disabilities in World of Warcraft. *Proceedings of the 6th international conference on foundations of digital games* (pp. 161–167). Association for Computing Machinery.

Liu, F., Pei, Q., Chen, S., Yuan, Y., Wang, L., & Muhlhauser, M. (2023). *When the metaverse meets carbon neutrality: Ongoing efforts and directions.* https://doi.org/10.48550/arXiv.2301.10235

McCausland, P. (2018, May 18). Study claims Bitcoin uses as much energy as Ireland. Not so fast, experts say. *NBC News.* https://www.nbcnews.com/tech/tech-news/study-claims-bitcoin-uses-much-energy-ireland-not-so-fast-n875211

Metaverse Standards Forum. (2022). *Leading standards organizations and companies unite to drive open metaverse interoperability.* Metaverse Standards Forum. https://

metaverse-standards.org/news/press-releases/leading-standards-organiza-tions-and-companies-unite-to-drive-open-metaverse-interoperability/.

Mitchell, W. J. (2003). *Me++: The cyborg self and the networked city*. MIT Press.

Mollman, S. (n.d.). Online a virtual business option for disabled. *CNN*. https://edition.cnn.com/2007/BUSINESS/07/10/virtual.disabled/index.html

Mullen, G., & Davidenko, N. (2021). Time compression in virtual reality. *Timing & Time Perception*, 9(4), 377–392.

Narula, H. (2022). *Virtual society: The metaverse and the new frontiers of human experience*. Currency.

Nilashi, M., & Abumalloh, R. A. (2023). The metaverse and its impacts on sustainable development goals 4: Quality education. *Journal of Soft Computing and Decision Support Systems*, 10(4), 1–8.

NSA. (2008). *Exploiting terrorist use of games & virtual environments*. NSA. https://www.theguardian.com/world/interactive/2013/dec/09/nsa-files-games-virtual-environments-paper-pdf

Ofcom. (2022). *Digital exclusion: A review of Ofcom's research on digital exclusion among adults in the* UK. Ofcom. https://www.ofcom.org.uk/__data/assets/pdf_file/0022/234364/digital-exclusion-review-2022.pdf

Parker, A. T., Swobodzinski, M., Wright, J. D., Hansen, K., Morton, B., & Schaller, E. (2021). Wayfinding tools for people with visual impairments in real-world settings: A literature review of recent studies. *Frontiers in Education*, 6, 723816.

Parker, C., Yoo, S., Lee, Y., Fredericks, J., Dey, A., Cho, Y., & Billinghurst, M. (2023). Towards an inclusive and accessible metaverse. *Extended abstracts of the 2023 CHI conference on human factors in computing systems* (pp. 1–5). Association for Computing Machinery.

Perri, D., Simonetti, M., Tasso, S., & Gervasi, O. (2023). Open metaverse with open software. *International conference on computational science and its applications* (pp. 583–596). Springer Nature Switzerland.

Politis, Y., Robb, N., Yakkundi, A., Dillenburger, K., Herbertson, N., Charlesworth, B., & Goodman, L. (2017). People with disabilities leading the design of serious games and virtual worlds. *International Journal of Serious Games*, 4(2), 63–73.

Reidenberg, J. R. (2005). Technology and internet jurisdiction. *University of Pennsylvania Law Review*, 153(6), 1951–1974.

Rosenberg, L. (2022, December 28). Mind control in the metaverse. *Medium*. https://medium.com/predict/mind-control-in-the-metaverse-48dfbd88c2ae

Routley, N. (2022). *This is how many humans have ever existed, according to researchers*. World Economic Forum. https://www.weforum.org/agenda/2022/04/quantifying-human-existence/

Sales, N. J. (2024, January 5). A girl was allegedly raped in the metaverse. Is this the beginning of a dark new future? *The Guardian*. https://www.theguardian.com/commentisfree/2024/jan/05/metaverse-sexual-assault-vr-game-online-safety-meta?CMP=Share_iOSApp_Other

Sandeepa, C., Wang, S., & Liyanage, M. (n.d.). *Privacy of the metaverse: Current issues, AI attacks, and possible solutions*. ResearchGate. https://www.researchgate.net/profile/Madhusanka-Liyanage/publication/369331696_Privacy_of_the_Metaverse_Current_Issues_AI_Attacks_and_Possible_Solutions/links/64151c8f66f8522c38b3ca9e/Privacy-of-the-Metaverse-Current-Issues-AI-Attacks-and-Possible-Solutions.pdf

Savin-Baden, M., & Burden, D. (2019). Digital immortality and virtual humans. *Postdigital Science and Education*, 1, 87–103.

Shah, H., Warwick, K., Vallverdú, J., & Wu, D. (2016). Can machines talk? Comparison of Eliza with modern dialogue systems. *Computers in Human Behavior, 58*, 278–295.

Smith, K. (2010). *The use of virtual worlds among people with disabilities.* Proceedings of the International Conference on Universal Technologies, Oslo, Norway.

Somoza Medina, X., & Somoza Medina, M. (2023). Video games and the COVID-19 pandemic: Virtual worlds as new playgrounds and training spaces. *COVID, 4*(1), 1–12.

Somnium Times. (2023). *Why Somnium Space's Live Forever Mode Just Makes Sense.* Somnium Times. https://somniumtimes.com/2023/04/06/why-somnium-spaces-live-forever-mode-just-makes-sense/

Sparkes, M. (2022). *Sci-fi author Neal Stephenson wants to build a metaverse open to all.* New Scientist. https://www.newscientist.com/article/2339401-sci-fi-author-neal-stephenson-wants-to-build-a-metaverse-open-to-all/

Stanton, A. (2008). *WALL-E* [film]. Walt Disney Pictures.

Steils, N. (2013). *Exploring learner identity in virtual worlds in higher education: narratives of pursuit, embodiment, and resistance* (Doctoral dissertation). Coventry University, Coventry, UK.

Stendal, K. (2012). How do people with disability use and experience virtual worlds and ICT: A literature review. *Journal for Virtual Worlds Research, 5*(1).

Stendal, K., Balandin, S., & Molka-Danielsen, J. (2011). Virtual worlds: A new opportunity for people with lifelong disability? *Journal of Intellectual and Developmental Disability, 36*(1), 80–83.

Stendal, K., Molka-Danielsen, J., Munkvold, B., & Balandin, S. (2012). Virtual worlds and people with lifelong disability: Exploring the relationship with virtual self and others. *ECIS 2012: Proceedings of the 2012 information systems European conference*, Association for Information Systems, Barcelona, Spain, pp. 156–179).

Stepanova, E. R., Quesnel, D., & Riecke, B. E. (2019). Space—A virtual frontier: How to design and evaluate a virtual reality experience of the overview effect. *Frontiers in Digital Humanities, 6*, 7.

Stephens, M. (2022). *Metaverse and its governance.* IEEE. https://standards.ieee.org/wp-content/uploads/2022/06/XR_Metaverse_Governance.pdf

Stephenson, N. (2020). *Fall; or, dodge in hell.* William Morrow & Company.

Stokel-Walker, C. (2023). *China's video-game limits haven't cut heavy gaming.* New Scientist. https://www.newscientist.com/article/2387005-chinas-video-game-limits-havent-cut-heavy-gaming/

Sydney Morning Herald. (2007, May 23). *Maldives opens first virtual embassy on Second Life.* Sydney Morning Herald. https://www.smh.com.au/national/maldives-opens-first-virtual-embassy-on-second-life-20070523-gdq7im.html

Thurman, A. (2021). *Barbados to become first sovereign nation with an embassy in the Metaverse.* Coindesk. https://www.coindesk.com/business/2021/11/15/barbados-to-become-first-sovereign-nation-with-an-embassy-in-the-metaverse/

Tse, N. (2020). Decentralised autonomous organisations and the corporate form. *Victoria University of Wellington Law Review, 51*(2), 313–356.

Turkle, S. (1996). *Life on the screen: Identity in the age of the Internet.* Weidenfeld & Nicolson.

Turner, V. (1969). Liminality and communitas. *The ritual process: Structure and anti-structure* (pp. 94–130). Walter de Gruyter.

Umar, A. (2022a). *Metaverse for UN SDGs—An exploratory study. Science-policy brief for the multistakeholder forum on science, technology and innovation for the SDGs, May 2022.* United Nations. https://sdgs.un.org/sites/default/files/2022-05/2.1.4-27-Umar-Metaverse4SDG.pdf

Umar, A. (2022b). Metaverse for public welfare and the United Nations sustainable development goals. *2022 International conference on cloud computing, big data and internet of things (3CBIT)* (pp. 160–165). IEEE.

UNICRI. (2022). *Report on gaming and the metaverse: The alarming rise of online child sexual exploitation and abuse within the new digital frontier.* UNICRI. https://unicri.it/sites/default/files/2022-11/Gaming%20and%20the%20Metaverse.pdf

Vinge, V. (2006). *Rainbow's end.* Tor Books.

Voski, A. (2020). The ecological significance of the overview effect: Environmental attitudes and behaviours in astronauts. *Journal of Environmental Psychology, 70,* 101454.

WEF. (2023). *Interoperability in the Metaverse.* World Economic Forum. https://www3.weforum.org/docs/WEF_Interoperability_in_the_Metaverse.pdf

WIPO. (n.d.). *The metaverse and intellectual property.* World Intellectual Property Organisation. https://www.wipo.int/about-ip/en/frontier_technologies/metaverse-and-ip.html

Wu, R., & Yu, Z. (2023). Investigating users' acceptance of the metaverse with an extended technology acceptance model. *International Journal of Human–Computer Interaction.*

Zallio, M., & Clarkson, P. J. (2022). Designing the metaverse: A study on inclusion, diversity, equity, accessibility and safety for digital immersive environments. *Telematics and Informatics, 75,* 101909.

Zhang, R., & Chan, W. K. V. (2020). Evaluation of energy consumption in blockchains with proof of work and proof of stake. *Journal of Physics: Conference Series, 1584*(1), 012023.

Zhao, N., & You, F. (2023). The growing metaverse sector can reduce greenhouse gas emissions by 10 Gt CO_2e in the United States by 2050. *Energy & Environmental Science, 16*(6), 2382–2397.

6

The Future of the Metaverse

Introduction

Having looked at the past and present of the Metaverse, and given some consideration to the factors that might be shaping the Metaverse, this final chapter looks to the future of the Metaverse. The chapter is divided into two parts. The first uses two lenses to look at the idea of the Metaverse and considers what needs to be done to encourage the development of a compelling, ubiquitous metaverse or multiverse environment, and what some of its implications might be. The two lenses are considered:

- The ReLive 2011 Delphi Study; and
- Marshall McLuhan's Tetrad.

The second part of the chapter presents seven different future scenarios, each examining a possible way in which the Metaverse might develop – for good or ill.

It should be noted that, just as for the rest of this book, this chapter does not talk about projections for "metaverse market growth" or "metaverse market value". Such discussions make little sense when people cannot even agree on what the word Metaverse actually represents. Also, as discussed earlier, the true value of the Metaverse is more likely to come from the people using it, and how they use it. In terms of market size, global internet access is around 50% (United Nations, 2021), global mobile smartphone penetration is at around 80%, and mobile phone penetration is at around 90% (Deloitte, 2017). The aim should surely be for every one of these people to have access to the Metaverse, and of course to support actions to raise all of these to as near to 100% as possible. Access to the Metaverse should also not be dependent on access to (or sales figures of) a head-mounted display XR (HMD-XR) headset. The Metaverse should be an integral part of the on-line experience for everyone.

DOI: 10.1201/9781003395461-7

The ReLive Study

Back in 2011, the Open University held its second Research Into Learning in Virtual Environments (ReLive) conference, which both Maggi and David attended – Maggi being on the Academic Committee. The conference conducted a Delphi poll to ask attendees about what they thought the short-, medium-, and long-term challenges and opportunities of virtual worlds were (Burden, 2011). The study identified the following goals (which are shown graphically in Figure 6.1):

- **Short Term (c.2011–2013)** – Make virtual worlds seamless and desirable;
- **Medium Term (c.2013–2020)** – Provide mobile access and unify virtual worlds; and
- **Long Term (c.2018 onwards)** – Embrace novel interfaces devices (e.g. head-mounted display VR [HMD-VR]) and respond to and create societal change.

Note where HMD-VR was placed.

Having already revisited this forecast in 2020 and 2022 (Burden, 2022), it still offers a useful lens through which to examine the development of the Metaverse, over 13 years after its initial creation.

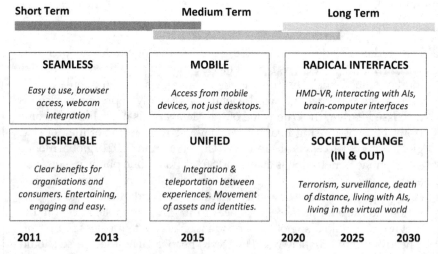

Short Term	Medium Term	Long Term
SEAMLESS *Easy to use, browser access, webcam integration*	**MOBILE** *Access from mobile devices, not just desktops.*	**RADICAL INTERFACES** *HMD-VR, interacting with AIs, brain-computer interfaces*
DESIREABLE *Clear benefits for organisations and consumers. Entertaining, engaging and easy.*	**UNIFIED** *Integration & teleportation between experiences. Movement of assets and identities.*	**SOCIETAL CHANGE (IN & OUT)** *Terrorism, surveillance, death of distance, living with AIs, living in the virtual world*
2011 2013	2015	2020 2025 2030

FIGURE 6.1
The ReLive 2011 forecast.

Seamlessness

Even back in 2011, the barriers to entry of a social virtual experience were seen as too hard. Key issues considered were making these spaces accessible in the browser, and whether users would be faced with one "world" through which all spaces could be accessed, or whether there would be a plethora of virtual worlds, all catering to different audiences (a forerunner of the Metaverse vs. Multiverse argument) – audiences often being as much dissuaded by choice as attracted by it. Linked to these was the challenge of discovery and direction. Were virtual worlds environments that people discovered – through word of mouth or the media, or were they places they would be directed to – by retailers, entertainers, search results, educators, and so on? Essentially, would a push or pull model dominate, or would it be a combination.

The need to integrate webcams and desktops into the virtual experience was also identified, enhancing the productivity of virtual worlds for "serious" use and more personal interactions. Even the ability to trigger avatar gestures and facial expressions from webcam inputs was being discussed.

The need to integrate with (rather than be dominated by) social media platforms was identified. Why create one profile on each virtual world when they could all (if the user wished) share an existing social media profile.

Finally, the different needs of users, creatives (or more generally creators), and professionals were highlighted. It might be one virtual world, but each user was likely to want a different set of features and functionality and different ways to access, manage, and share experiences.

Even now, this still doesn't seem like a bad to-do list for people trying to enhance the development of the Metaverse. Of the specific items discussed:

- Browser access has arrived, principally through WebXR, *Hubs*, and *Frames*, but in doing so, much of the feature set of virtual worlds has initially been lost;
- We are still in the plethora of virtual worlds state, with no sign of a single point of access;
- The challenges of discovery and direction remain. Metaversal experiences aren't a tab on the search page, and there is often no URL to pass around to bring people into the same space;
- Webcams and desktop sharing are being integrated, although access to Desktop apps is only slowly coming;
- Triggering avatar gesture and facial expression from webcam inputs is technically proven but still not a common feature;
- Integration with social media platforms is happening (at least for Meta/Oculus/Facebook) but is from a dominant position, and not helping with seamless access across platforms; and

- The different needs of users are still being addressed through completely different platforms, not through different User interfaces (UIs) and feature sets.

The important message at ReLive11, and for now, is that users (rather than tech-enthusiasts) just want things to work. The whole experience needs to be easy and seamless, and until this is sorted (and it's debatable whether it even has been with the Web and web applications), gaining users will always be an uphill battle.

Desirability

Returning to the theme of push versus pull, the second ReLive strand revolved around how to make virtual worlds desirable – a recognition in itself that the existing pull wasn't enough. Apart from reinforcing the message above that virtual worlds needed to be easy to access (and fun and engaging to be in), several areas were identified where case studies needed to be assembled and arguments clearly communicated, including:

- Learning benefits for educators;
- Business benefits and cost savings for industry and government;
- Revenue generation opportunities; and
- Social benefits for consumers and family.

As Chapter 3 showed, there are ample case studies from across the widest range of industries and public life that show the benefit of XR technologies – but communicating these to organisations and the public at large remains a challenge. At present, there may be a danger that by too closely allying the Metaverse with HMD-VR technologies, which as discussed have a range of issues, that the DesktopVR (and especially mobile) approach to the Metaverse is being at best forgotten or at worse ignored. DesktopVR (in its broadest sense) is the lowest barrier to entry into the idea of the Metaverse and its benefits, and perhaps along with better communicating the benefits of metaversal approaches, there should be more focus on non-HMD-VR methods to access the Metaverse.

DelSignore (2022) identifies two barriers to desirability with HMD-VR, the form-factor of headsets, and the disconnectedness that people feel when using HMD and VR applications. Each iteration of HMDs is improving on the first issue, and the Quest 3 is vastly better than the DK1, and whilst the Apple Vision Pro does away with the controllers, it also adds a cumbersome cable and battery pack – we are a long way yet from the holoband of *Caprica*. The disconnect issue is possibly one which the Metaverse solves which the metaverses don't. With greater interoperability and commonality between metaversal spaces, more of us will be in them more of the time, and bringing our two-dimensional (2D) web tools with us, and able to communicate across spaces and applications in a way that just isn't possible at the moment.

One reason why the take-up of metaversal experiences has not been as high as expected may be linked to the concept of lean-forward and lean-back media (Picone, 2007). Lean-back experiences are those involving minimal input from the user – they are passively consuming the content, and as such, the user does not need to invest much thought in accessing the content and can attend to other things at the same time. In contrast, lean-forward media, such as games and of course virtual worlds and the Metaverse, require users' almost complete attention and to forgo what is happening in the physical world around them. This means that lean-forward media have a significantly higher barrier to entry – doing something in a virtual world is never going to be as easy and undemanding as watching a TV programme. Even many Zoom calls can become predominantly lean-back activities. As a result, virtual worlds and the Metaverse, particularly when thought of as an entertainment or even a collaboration or learning environment, need to provide a higher level of proof of worth and reward than some competing media if the user is going to see the participation as worth the higher investment. It also suggests that barring some of the pathologies discussed in Chapter 5, we should not be expecting people to spend their whole time in the Metaverse, since it is a tool to be used across your work, family, and recreational lives, sharing time with mobile, TV and more traditional computer screen time, but only slowly shifting some other physical activities from the physical to the virtual.

Mobile

Back in 2011, the advantages of getting the virtual world experience off of the desktop and into the literal hands of users through mobile devices were well recognised. There were some early experiments with video streaming and 2D clients, but a decade or so later, having a mobile metaverse experience is almost a done deal. Many massively multi-player online games (MMOs) and metaverse apps run natively on mobiles, WebGL worlds run in mobile browsers, and Facebook even made mobile access to *Horizon Worlds* one of the highlights of its Connect 2023 event (IGN, 2023). This is probably the only one of the six issues raised at ReLive that can be marked as essentially done – but it needs to be done for every metaversal platform.

Standards and Integration

If there was not going to be a single, monolithic Metaverse, then even in 2011, it was recognised that the metaverses that do exist should be interoperable to a high degree so that identity, assets, and even functionality can be moved between them. Three approaches were discussed, all of which are still highly relevant to today's debate about how to integrate different

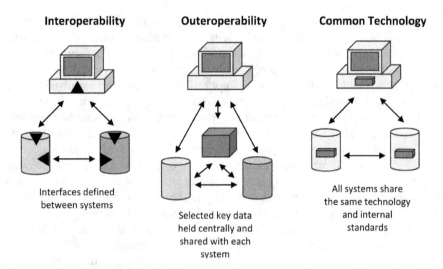

Interoperability   **Outeroperability**   **Common Technology**

Interfaces defined
between systems

Selected key data
held centrally and
shared with each
system

All systems share
the same technology
and internal
standards

FIGURE 6.2
Three different models of integration.

metaversal spaces into a coherent multiverse. The three models (represented in Figure 6.2) are:

- **Interoperability** – Each constituent metaverse runs on its own software, with its own internal data standards, but there are agreed interfaces between the systems (for instance, the exchange format of a three-dimensional [3D] model or a packet of account information). These interfaces should ideally be based on open standards so that anyone can participate.

- **Outeroperability** – There is a central repository of the core information which applies across multiple environments (for instance, account information, avatars, etc.), and each environment then makes use of these to inform its own operation. This is the model that is being seen with services such as ReadyPlayerMe where the user's avatar is defined and stored in a third-party application, and then accessed and realised by individual platforms. Again, this should be based on open standards, and ideally the software driving the central services should be open source.

- **Common Technology** – Each constituent is running on effectively the same code, although there may be some local enhancements (e.g. in security, functionality, or performance). However, anyone can run a component of the infrastructure, and the code should be open source. This is the model implemented by *OpenSim* and also *Mozilla Hubs* server edition. It is also fundamentally the model used in the early days of the Web.

There is also a good discussion of interoperability for the Metaverse in *Interoperability in the Immersive Web* (E, 2022).

Whilst the Metaverse remains based on proprietary technology and walled gardens, with minimal interoperability, there is a high chance that the Metaverse will never reach its full potential and may well fail as users become frustrated with different accounts, different capabilities, and redundant assets. However, beyond the core web page functionality, we need to bear in mind that these problems haven't really been solved for the 2D Web either.

Radical Interfaces

In 2011, the radical interface that people mainly had in mind was the HMD-VR. This was in the period between Virtuality, which gave many people their first taste of HMD-VR, and the launch of the Oculus DK1 which finally delivered an HMD-VR at a price that most developers could afford – and in 2013, so almost two time bands early! Since then, Meta's Quest series has steadily improved the capabilities of an affordable, stand-alone HMD-VR headset, and with the Quest 3 being an affordable HMD-XR headset.

Another novel interface considered was that of using webcams and audio to interact to the physical world with virtual characters in the virtual world – typified by Lionhead Studio's Project Milo demonstration (Chung, 2010). The already mentioned Lucy from Fable Studio's *Wolves in the Walls* (Billington, 2018) is probably the closest so far to that demo, although all in VR, but the general developments around artificial intelligence (AI) characters suggest that this sort of interactivity between virtual avatars and physical people, whether in games, virtual worlds, between worlds, or through smartphones will become increasingly common.

The final interface considered was that of the brain computer interface (BCI). As discussed in Chapter 4, this technology may actually be what moves the Metaverse from a could-have to must-have for a variety of reasons, but the technological progress towards it remains slow.

Societal Change

The Metaverse as concept will only be safe from failure once it becomes embedded in society, in the same way that the TV, mobile phones, and the World Wide Web have. The two aspects of societal change considered at ReLive were:

- How will virtual world (aka metaverse) development will be impacted by developments in the physical world? and
- What impact will virtual world/metaverse use have on society itself?

Chapter 5 has considered a variety of issues such as the ongoing tensions between privacy and surveillance, the variation in cultural norms across the globe, the push towards home working, and other societal and global factors that may both encourage the development of the Metaverse and give cause for challenge. The chapter also looked at how the Metaverse could impact global society. This could be just by contributing to the "death of distance", supporting homeworking and virtual team-working and maintaining global links with family and friends. Or it could be more profound, making us more aware of global issues (especially climate change), enhancing the overview effects, and making us more open to different cultures, viewpoints, lifestyles, and sexual and gender choices through a greater ability to directly and indirectly experience these for ourselves. Looking further to the future, the Metaverse might give rise to new societal forms which pay far less attention to physical locations and polities and may also become the place where we interact with advanced AIs and even digital amortals.

Whether we have a firmer idea, 13 years after ReLive11, as to what societal change may be possible through the Metaverse is probably another moot point.

A New Timeline?

Based on the progress that has, or hasn't, been made since the original 2011 ReLive Delphi study, Figure 6.3 shows a possible future timeline, based on the analysis above, of how the development of the Metaverse concept could be focussed.

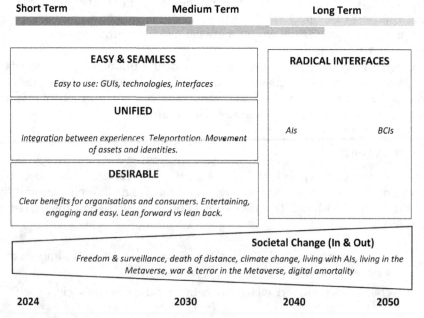

FIGURE 6.3
An updated ReLive-style plan.

Marshall McLuhan's Tetrad

Marshall McLuhan's Tetrad (McLuhan & McLuhan, 2017), shown in Figure 6.4, was originally developed to consider changes in the media but is a useful tool to analyse any new technology or phenomena – such as the Metaverse. It consists of four questions:

- What does a technology, medium, or any human artefact enhance?
- What does it obsolesce?
- What does it retrieve that had been obsolesced earlier?
- What does a medium flip into when pushed to the limits of its potential?

What Does the Metaverse Enhance?

The Metaverse effectively gives us superpowers. It enables us to go anywhere, see anything and do anything – as long as it's in the virtual realm. Through MR, it also enables us to enhance reality, bringing in information and even new virtual objects in order to better see things as they were, as they are, or as they might be.

What Does the Metaverse Obsolesce?

The Metaverse *should not* obsolesce the 2D Web or the mobile phone; the Metaverse is about subjective experience – not objective experience. The

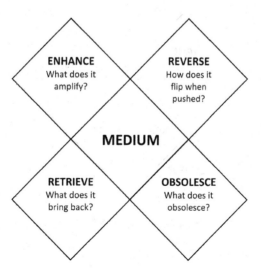

FIGURE 6.4
Marshall McLuhan's Tetrad (after McLuhan & McLuhan, 2017).

Metaverse *may* obsolesce some types of travel (particularly air travel), which would be good for the climate, and potentially does so whilst enabling a better sense of "being there" than the webcam or TV travel show. The Metaverse *might* help obsolesce some old-fashioned attitudes towards different cultures and lifestyles and could even help obsolesce some of the issues around global inequality and cultural divisions. It may even, through the emergence of new forms of society and governance, help obsolesce the nation-state.

What Does the Metaverse Retrieve That Had Been Obsolesced Earlier?

The Metaverse retrieves the campfire. It brings global technology back to a group of people sat around a (virtual) fire chatting. It should retrieve storytelling, giving people the tools to tell their own stories and have their own adventures, rather than passively consuming high-gloss media. It may even retrieve imagination.

What Does the Metaverse Flip into When Pushed to the Limits of Its Potential?

It may be that the Metaverse becomes an unsavoury world populated by griefers, con-men, sex-pests, criminals, and terrorists; a virtual slum. Worse still though, it becomes a siren's song, somewhere that is so nice, where we feel so good, that we neglect our physical selves, physical relationships, and physical planet.

These are summarised in Figure 6.5.

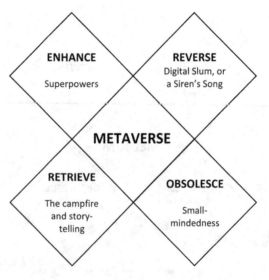

FIGURE 6.5
A Tetrad for the Metaverse.

Scenarios of the Future

Trying to predict a specific future for the Metaverse is probably a pointless challenge. Not only do people and companies still have different ideas as to what the Metaverse is, but the underlying technologies, and society's attitudes towards them, are constantly evolving. However, it is important to have some view about what the future might bring. Having some possible scenarios of the future can provide a set of landmarks in a map of the future and help us to identify in which direction the real future is heading as it unfurls. This is especially important if the aim is to try and guide development in some directions and avoid developments in others. This section looks at seven possible future scenarios (illustrated graphically in Figure 6.6):

- **The Failed Metaverse** – where the Metaverse never becomes more than a niche interest;
- **The Corporate Multiverse** – where the future is all about walled gardens and single-purpose worlds;

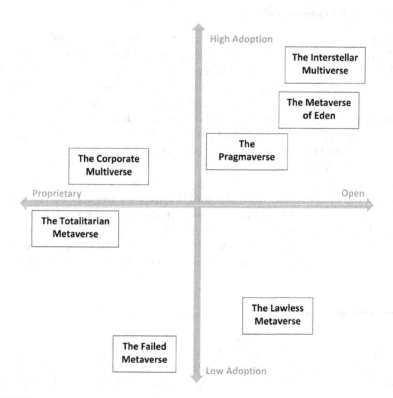

FIGURE 6.6
Seven future scenarios for the Metaverse.

- **The Lawless Metaverse** – where we have a Metaverse, but it becomes so lawless and uncontrolled that most people avoid it;
- **The Totalitarian Metaverse** – where one organisation (or group) runs it as a fiefdom;
- **The Pragmaverse** – a more likely medium-term future;
- **The Metaverse of Eden** – an idealised medium-term future; and
- **The Interstellar Multiverse** – a possible long-term future.

For each, consideration is given as to what the steps might be towards their emergence, the positive and negative aspects of each scenario, and what could be done to encourage or discourage its realisation. For alternative views, read *The Metaverse in 2040* report by the Pew Research Centre which canvassed the opinions of a variety of experts across different fields of the Metaverse (Anderson & Rainie, 2022).

The Failed Metaverse

If this book was being written about 10 or 12 years ago, then this might well be the scenario that was seen as having come to pass. After *Snow Crash* initiated the discussion about the Metaverse, the early 3D worlds of the late 1990s rapidly explored the idea, and then in *Active Worlds* and *Second Life*, platforms were released that actually fulfilled many of expectations of what the Metaverse should be. The hope at the time was that we would see a steady improvement in the capabilities of platforms like *Second Life*, more and more successful case studies emerging, and a gradual but steady adoption of this version of the Metaverse.

But somehow it all went wrong. Pricing and policy changes at *Second Life*, ongoing user frustration, and minimal progress on integrating the different platforms all helped to frustrate the expected growth. The nail in the coffin, ironically, was possibly the release of the Oculus DK1 HMD-VR, and from 2013 onwards, it seemed that anything that didn't promote HMD-VR was dead in the water. The first great experiment in the Metaverse had failed.

How We Get There

The question has to be, will there be a failure in this second wave of the Metaverse? The way that the Metaverse has become aligned in some quarters with the speculation and profiteering of cryptocurrency and non-fungible tokens (NFTs) would seem to make a metaverse crash more likely. The sales of HMD-VR headsets look good on the face of it, but market penetration is still very low. Issues such as cybersickness, having the space to use the devices (especially in European homes), and the isolation and vulnerability that using a headset brings all seem to mitigate against a sudden uptick in adoption. Indeed, during the writing of this book, we have seen a shift away from "metaverse" and towards "spatial computing". The ongoing lack of integration between platforms (as in the 2010s) doesn't help, and we've still never really delivered on those first two "short-term" priorities of ReLive 2011 – desirability and ease of use. Ironically, and perhaps a reflection of the technology push rather than societal pull, industry has actually done a lot better on achieving the medium- (mobile access) and long-term (HMD-VR) goals. This technology focus perhaps lies behind the rebranding of many technology and businesses metaverse activities as spatial computing – a tech term if ever there was one, and one which, as discussed earlier, seems to eliminate the human.

What Is It Like?

In this scenario all of these frustrations build, there is a big crypto/NFT crash (or at least investors decide that cryptoworlds aren't the place to be), and by soon, the whole Metaverse bubble has burst, and people have moved on to something else. A few die-hards are still using the social virtual worlds such as *Second Life, OpenSim,* and *Frame,* and most of the business collaboration platforms have gone bust as users found their cost-benefit calculus didn't work out, although some of the large event platforms such as *VirBela* and *AmazeVR* may struggle on. The two bright spots are that there is a slow continued growth in the use of DesktopVR and HMD-VR for learning and training (but "metaverse" is now a dirty word and vendors have stuck with "spatial computing" or gone back to "virtual experience"), and MMO games such as *Fortnite* that make the Metaverse fun, and those that offer the user a degree of agency such as *Minecraft* and *Roblox* continue to do well, reborn in a different form for each new generation.

There probably aren't any really specific pros and cons to this scenario – other than a broad failure to capitalise on the possibilities of the Metaverse, so what can be done to avoid ending up in this scenario (assuming that there is no wish to work for failure).

Discouraging the Failed Metaverse

One of the key drivers in creating The Metaverse Series was an awareness that a lot of the debates around the idea of the Metaverse had already been going on since the early 2000s, or even earlier – and not just discussion but practical implementation , experience and real research. However, a lot of the current debates around the Metaverse seem to be taking place in ignorance of them. The metaverses of the 2000s largely failed, and many of the roots of that failure are in the issues identified in the ReLive conference in 2011. If history is not to be repeated, and the Failed Metaverse scenario is to be avoided, then all involved in the consideration and development of today's metaverses would do well to heed these discussions from the past and to address the problems and challenges identified throughout this book.

The Corporate Multiverse

In the absence of any other major drivers, and assuming that at least some of the actions described above are taken in order to discourage the Failed Metaverse, the Corporate Multiverse seems like it may be the default destination.

How We Get There

Companies like Meta and Epic in the West, and Baidu, Alibaba, and Tencent in China continue to expand on their fledgling early steps into VR and MR space and slowly build out the Metaverse. Meta's *Horizons* is perhaps an example, starting as just your "welcome page" when you put on your headset, then becoming *Venues* and a place to view streamed content, then *Horizon Home* where you can customise your home experience, before finally becoming *Horizon Worlds* where you can socialise with other people and build experiences and share them. Backed by large marketing budgets, these worlds have a sense of safety and are the default experience on popular hardware. As long as the range of experiences and features is keeping track with what the majority of users enjoy, these corporate worlds could retain a default position in the consumer space. Entertainment and game brands might partner with these companies or feel big enough to develop their own brand worlds. In the business space, a similar model develops, with leading business solution providers developing worlds focused on business collaboration and training and learning providers establishing go-to training and education worlds, and so on.

What Is It Like?

Whilst there might be some commonality in terms of the underlying technology, and some worlds may even feel quite similar, each world is its own ecosystem, with minimal ways of moving identity, assets, or experiences between them. This is very much a collection of separate metaverses, rather than a single Metaverse or a federated Multiverse. A possible analogy is the pre-World Wide Web days when the "information superhighway" was dominated by discrete systems such as Prodigy, AOL, and Compuserve. Strict corporate control probably also means that stability and security are favoured over creativity and imagination, so user agency, particularly in terms of in-world building and especially scripting, may be limited. User-generated content (UGC) is only encouraged where it meets corporate guidelines and can improve the corporate bottom line. The worlds may look very pretty, but they could be seen as gilded cages.

Affecting the Evolution

Whilst some might be happy with such a future, our assumption is that most users would like more freedom, agency, flexibility, privacy, and ownership than this scenario provides. The key to this is probably in ensuring that it is as easy for someone to establish their own metaverse space – at both the server and experience level – as it is for them to buy web hosting and build their own website. This in turn suggests ensuring that the key technologies that drive the metaverse are open source and based on open standards – encouraging innovation and exploitation.

There is also a need to demonstrate to less engaged users that the potential of the Metaverse far outstrips the sanitised and restrained version being promoted by corporate organisations – encouraging them to move to other providers to take the full advantage of the potential of the Metaverse.

The Lawless Metaverse

If the Failed Metaverse shows what happens if things go wrong at the very beginning, then the Lawless Metaverse shows what happens if they go wrong along the way.

How We Get There

Metaverse developments might begin in a very promising direction. The software and hardware required are steadily developed and adopted, multiple worlds, or even a few dominant worlds become established within the Metaverse, and for a while, things look good. But just as social media has become something of a troll's playground, and scammers and hackers abound on the web and the Internet, so too will the less savoury parts of society recognise the opportunities for money, mayhem, and maliciousness in the Metaverse. Having an avatar in your face, shouting abuse, or using some hack to disable your movement, or even force your movement whilst shouting obscenities or waving a giant pixel penis at you (or worse) is likely to dissuade many users from engaging with the environment, and it rapidly sinks to a lowest common denominator space. As Chapter 1 related, at least one high-profile proto-metaverse (Google's Lively) closed partly as a result of in-world abuse and, as discussed, abusive uses of metaverse spaces continue to be an issue, as do concerns over privacy, illegal activities and even hostile action.

What Is It Like?

In this scenario, the Metaverse becomes more-or-less a part of the so-called Dark Web. It's a place that people only tend to visit if they're participating in activities which are dubious or outright illegal. Pornography, theft, violent images, and extreme abuse are commonplace. Countries with age verification programmes might restrict access to it, or it may be somewhere that you can only get to through a Metaverse version of the Tor browser. Given the user and operator concerns over security, it is more likely to be a Multiverse rather than a singular Metaverse, with lots of discrete servers loosely linked into a network of worlds, with blockchain or similar technology controlling access, asset ownership, and transfers between worlds.

Avoiding the Lawless Metaverse

Probably the biggest requirement to try and avoid a Lawless Metaverse is to ensure that safety and security features and tools are present in every metaverse development, that users are not only aware of their existence but are also comfortable with their use, and that there is good but fair governance.

Whilst some might object, having each account linked to a traceable real-world identity is probably a basic step – although that is not to suggest that users cannot operate anonymously within the world as far as other users are concerned. What does it mean, though, is that if a user transgresses the platform or community guidelines or applicable laws, then appropriate sanctions (including not only banning of current accounts and future access but also physical world legal action) can be taken. There are of course civil liberty issues here, and how these are dealt with within a multi-national context are of prime concern. Also, if the Metaverse becomes essential to daily life, then lifetime bans might not be feasible – and a fool-proof electronic means of restricting capabilities and freedoms (perhaps the virtual equivalent of an electronic tag) may be required.

At a lesser level, virtual worlds have long included a variety of personal safety features, such as the zones of safety described in Chapter 2. Many worlds allow you to mute aurally and visually specific users who are annoying you, along with being able to report them for abuse. Privately owned areas can establish their own ban lists for people who transgress local bye-laws. Automated and AI surveillance can also be used to enforce things like content guidelines for imagery, chat, and potentially even 3D models. Some worlds (e.g. *Second Life*) require users to flag privately held areas with content classification ratings similar to films, so that areas could be rated U (for anyone), A (advisory or accompanied), 15 (age 15 or over), 18 (18 or over), or X (deliberately explicit material). Age verification on accounts could then help ensure that accounts are matched to classifications – but a child using an adult's account may be hard to prevent (although the same cameras that enable facial expression detection might also be able to implement identity or even age detection within the headset or from the webcam – but again create new privacy issues).

Whatever route is taken to the future, there are likely to be unsavoury areas in any metaverse, just as there are in the physical world. That they exist is not necessarily a completely bad thing, as long as basic rights are protected. The challenge is to ensure that they remain a small part of the experience, that people are aware of when they are straying into them, and that protection and help are available even in the depths of them.

The Totalitarian Metaverse

If the Lawless Metaverse represents a failure of the Metaverse at an individual level, the Totalitarian Metaverse represents a failure at a corporate or national/governmental level.

How We Get There

This probably starts like the Corporate Multiverse scenario, but one company wins big. In countries that already have a control-orientated government, it may be that the government only allows one company (its own) to establish the "national metaverse" and that access to other metaverses is blocked. Either way, as far as any user is concerned, they only have one metaverse option, and that metaverse is controlled by one entity which may not have the user's best interests at heart.

What Is It Like?

The Totalitarian Metaverse is another digital dystopia. The ability to use VR to track not only user identity but also potentially their emotional behaviours and triggers as well as their interests and usage have already been discussed. If the Metaverse becomes a large part of daily life, then the potential abuse of that level of information, along with an equal level of control, is very concerning. *Second Life* abandoned its reputation management early on, but implementing a Chinese-style "social credit" system in a metaverse is not only easier but also far more encompassing than trying to implement it in the physical world. In the Totalitarian Metaverse, you behave, or else.

Affecting the Evolution

If the critical path to the Totalitarian Metaverse is the emergence of a monopolistic platform, then as with the Corporate Multiverse enabling anyone to set up a metaverse has to be a key defence against it. A monopolistic metaverse may be an extreme outcome of the Corporate Metaverse scenario, and that monopoly may even be benign, but before we let such an entity emerge, we need to be absolutely sure that is the right thing to do and that there is always an opportunity to back out and set up an alternative metaverse.

Whilst in the discussion about the Lawless Metaverse, the Tor-browser-enabled metaverse was the villain, and here it may even be the saviour, allowing even those within totalitarian regimes to gain safe access to more liberal metaverses.

The Pragmaverse

As intimated earlier, one Metaverse to rule them all may have its own issues as different stakeholders want and expect different things, quite apart from the challenges in getting some universally adopted standards to stick (although again, we managed that with the Web). Perhaps the most pragmatic scenario for the future is something which is more of a "mixed fleet", where an open-standards metaverse/multiverse co-exists with more proprietary technologies or spaces.

How We Get There

As organisations explore the commercial potential of the Metaverse, a wide variety of use cases are emerging. These are already supported by a variety of dedicated technologies and systems, such as training worlds, entertainment worlds, conferencing worlds, meeting and collaboration worlds, and even military worlds. Is it realistic that all of these will converge on the same set of technologies and standards – let alone just become parcels within one all-encompassing Metaverse?

In the Pragmaverse, there is likely to be some consolidation. A key element is the HMD-XR headset. People are unlikely to want different headsets for different uses, so standardising on the presentation element of the metaverse stack is something that we have already seen – particularly with standards such as WebXR. At the other end of the pipeline, there are obvious economies if developers can use the same 3D models and avatars across multiple platforms – glTF and services like ReadyPlayerMe are already helping here. Even the game engines that drive these worlds have seen significant consolidation, with Unreal and Unity tending to dominate. It is in the applications themselves that the differentiation occurs and will likely continue to occur.

Whilst there is always an incentive to "stick to your knitting", it may be that platforms gradually extend to cover related topics – why shouldn't a training world also offer collaboration and conference facilities, or a collaboration space offer training facilities? In parallel with this, there may be growing user pressure for UGC worlds where they can be creative and do-their-own-thing.

And if people then find that they can offer services using UGC that rival some custom environments (as happened in *Second Life*), then perhaps that might provoke further consolidation. So, within this scenario, it may that there are two sub-scenarios, one where the "corporate" platforms are the dominant form, but where the UGC worlds are a lively force, and a second one where the UGC worlds are actually the dominant form, with corporate platforms just handling the most specialist use cases.

It may also be that ultimately there is a joining of islands, as different metaverses and microverses find benefit in linking up into a more coherent multiverse.

What Is It Like?

As a user, you are more conscious of the existence of different systems than in most of the other scenarios. You use the same XR headset for all of the different applications, but it may be that some need different login identities, and you may have different profiles, avatars, and assets in different worlds. If you are having a virtual meeting and then need to go to some training, you'll probably have to log out and then log in to a different world. If you're then moving onto another task and think that it would be useful to bring in that interactable from the training session, you probably can't. And at 5 o'clock, you log out of your corporate world and into a boardgame world to play *Root* with friends, and then go into yet another world to virtually attend a concert on the other side of the globe. You finish the day in a UGC-led world where you hang out with another group of friends or work on a pet project.

Affecting the Evolution

Whilst the Pragmaverse may not be the default future, it is probably the most likely outcome if the more negative scenarios can be avoided. The key influencing activities are around implementing those ReLive observations. As the narrative above shows, the biggest user issue is likely to be the fragmentation – which doesn't help with making the experience seamless, but having broadly adopted standards at all levels may help address that.

Where the balance falls between the corporate and UGC worlds will probably depend on the power and flexibility of the worlds that support UGC – if a user can do something better in a UGC world than a corporate one, then the pressure for corporates to embrace that UGC world will increase. So, to encourage the UGC future, those UGC capabilities (and particularly scripting) need to be made available on both UGC-led worlds (and ideally other platforms), and people need to have the skills to use and exploit these new UGC tools to create the tools and experiences that they want in the Metaverse.

The Metaverse of Eden

When people traditionally talk about the "Metaverse" the vision is typically about a single virtual world to which everyone has access and which fulfils all of their metaverse-related needs and seamlessly integrates with their physical lives. Is that a realistic expectation?

How We Get There

If people pay heed to the points raised in the Failed, Totalitarian, and Corporate Metaverse scenarios and focus on the seamlessness of the experience, the open standards that support it, building services which meet real needs, and supporting societal change that embraces the Metaverse as a vital part of our lives going forward, then we could be well on the way towards the Metaverse of Eden. Society pretty much achieved this with the World Wide Web, and why shouldn't society also achieve it with the Metaverse?

What Is It Like?

The Metaverse of Eden is the metaverse of the marketing video and the Hollywood films. It is *Ready Player One*'s OASIS or *Caprica*'s V-World. Everyone can access the Metaverse through their smartphone/tablet or home computer or from an XR headset or glasses (although both of these worlds are, at least initially, corporate metaverses). Most locations have some form of "holographic projector" (as in *Blade Runner 2049*) to avoid local users from having to wear a headset in order to see virtual visitors. The world has some geographic sense of the Earth but may also include the planets of the solar system and even some fantastical and genre worlds, mixing a variety of public and private spaces. As in the axioms presented earlier, in the Metaverse of Eden, you can "learn, teach, earn, create, sell, buy, trade, collaborate, communicate, explore, make friends, play, have fun, entertain, and be entertained, have relationships, have new experiences and leave a legacy". This Metaverse will also be home to millions or even billions of AI-controlled avatars, some little more than virtual sales and support assistants, some the digital amortals (DAs) of the dead, and perhaps a few the verge of (or even achieving) artificial general intelligence (AGI). The Metaverse of Eden will be a vital part of everyone's lives, and we will have almost no thought as whether something happens in physical or virtual space.

Affecting the Evolution

As stated above, to get to Eden, the focus needs to be on the seamlessness of the experience, the open standards that support it, matching services and experiences to real needs, and supporting any resulting societal change, all whilst avoiding the bear-traps of the Corporate and Totalitarian Metaverses.

Probably the biggest challenge will be that different people, and particularly organisations, and even countries and societies, have different needs and different norms. For example:

- The different societal and legal expectations of different countries and cultures may make their co-existence in the same Metaverse problematic (just as it can be in the physical world). Who's rules of dress apply, what financial models, and what rules of freedom of speech and expression?

- An organisation might not feel safe about trusting its trade secrets, confidential information and intellectual property (IP), and sensitive meetings to even a "private" space on a globally shared metaverse. Players in the defence and intelligence space may have even more concerns.

- Different organisations may have different views about how the same digital twin of a real-world location should be represented and potentially changed. The actual civic authorities may want a combined smart city and marketing representation, community groups might want to "make-good" or improve their own virtual districts, planners might want to fast-forward the city a decade out, the owning military might want to wargame defence plans, and hostile militaries might want to wargame attack plans. Whilst the idea of a single digital twin is attractive, it rapidly breaks down given these sorts of use cases.

Four broad solutions exist:

- The solution is the same as the physical world – each piece of virtual land has its own protections and rules, and users are expected to follow the local rules. In this case, a single metaverse may suffice – although this doesn't meet the security or digital twin challenge.

- A very technical solution could be that whilst there is only instance of each point on the Earth, you can choose between different layers of virtual reality to display and interact with whilst you are there – a combination of virtual reality and mixed reality – a mixed virtual reality as it were!

- A more likely solution is that the Metaverse is actually some form of Multiverse. There may be some form of common core world, but people and organisations are able to create their own constituent metaverses (or multiverses), which can be accessed from the core space, are built using the same software to the same standards, are subject to local rules, have their own access controls, and run on their own hosting. Digital twins in each of these worlds could be different, but with links between them and possibly linked to some "master" for updating.

- In a more extreme case, countries and societal groups may run metaverses or multiverses which, whilst possibly sharing common code,
  are only accessible through specific portals and have limited connectivity to the rest of the Metaverse – akin to the Great Firewall of China.

The Interstellar Multiverse

Finally, what does a possible long-term future look like? The development (or
failure) of the Metaverse is happening concurrently with significant strides in
space exploration. By the 2030s/2040s, there will likely to be bases on the Moon,
and around 2040, the first Mars landings might take place. In parallel with this,
the first AGIs may emerge sometime this century. By the 2100s, humankind and
AIs may begin to reach for the stars. The Metaverse may be at the heart of all of
this and even accompany those first travellers beyond the solar system.

How We Get There

For simplicity, it is assumed that it is the Multiverse form of the Metaverse
of Eden that has eventually won out, and the Earth has a global Multiverse
(but called the Metaverse), which provides access and opportunities to all.
A key challenge is in how the Metaverse moves off planet. The significant
time delays even to the Moon and back (c.2.6 seconds) can make real-time
interactions of avatars in a shared world highly problematic, and such interactions become impossible with an average c.25-minute delay to Mars and
back. The solution is a Multiverse of Multiverses. Each moon or planet has
its own Multiverse, but some elements of this are synchronised with other
Multiverses, so common experiences can be shared. For human-to-human
communications, the advances in AI technology allow users to dispatch virtual versions of themselves to the other Multiverses as required (as they may
already be doing for multiple meetings) to have local conversations without
the time delay, and then report back. The future Metaverse becomes a fusion
of humans, virtual representatives, Digital Amortals, and AIs.

What Is It Like?

The Metaverse is populated not just by human-controlled avatars but also
by avatars controlled by people's virtual personal assistants (VPA), by both
simple AI and AGI avatars, and by the DAs of many of the deceased – who
spend most of their time working with AGIs in a large part of the Multiverse
called the Thanoverse.

Your avatar will access whichever is the local Metaverse, but compatibility
and interoperability between the Multiverses mean that all of your account
information and digital assets and funds follow with you. It may be that you

"rent" home or office space on the local 'verse in the same way that you might rent somewhere when you physically travel on the Earth (or even to Mars).

To visit someone "off-verse", you send a virtual personal representative (VPR) to make the visit for you. On its return, your VPR would not only update you but, in the absence of any memory-uploading breakthroughs, have its memories of the trip automatically incorporated into the memory graph of your persistent VPA. This means that the VPA could recall the memories, discussions, and key decisions of the trip whenever they become relevant to what you are doing, and over time, they might become so familiar to you that your recollection of whether you went or your VPR becomes blurred. And if the stage is reached where we have true digital amortality, your VPA can provide the foundation for a virtual, amortal, you.

Affecting the Evolution

The challenges of getting to the Metaverse of Eden, or even the Pragmaverse, and making that available to everyone on the planet are probably more than enough for people to be getting on with, without worrying about how the Metaverse gets taken to other planets. However, it may be that an off-earth metaverse is closer than expected. As scientists and explorers consider how to build bases on the Moon, how to manage the two to three years trip to Mars and back, and even to establish colonies on Mars, having an array of metaversal spaces on each world for the explorers to use to support planning, design, science, exploration, socialising, family-connectedness, and relaxation will almost certainly be essential.

And to the Stars?

The same discussions that apply to moving from the Earth to the Moon and planets also apply to reaching out to the stars. Current technologies suggest that any mission in the next century or so are likely to be without a human crew (Peck, 2023), and as discussed, it may be that metaversal spaces are essential in creating and sustaining grounded AIs (Burden & Savin-Baden, 2019; Gamez, 2023). Any DAs also on the trip will no doubt want to bring their piece of (virtual) home with them. One neat trick is that within a ship-board Multiverse, different worlds could run at different rates, so AIs or DAs whose main tasks are only on arrival could experience the journey at a dilution rate of 1:100, so a hundred-year trip only seems to take a subjective year – enough for them to analyse new information and adjust their planning as arrival approaches. Once they do arrive and two-way communication is established, a new stellar Metaverse can be linked to all the local multiverses back home – allowing all of humanity to experience the new worlds at first (virtual) hand. And new VPRs and DAs can be transmitted out to go and live and work in that distant new Multiverse.

With the new colony established, with its own network of planetary Metaverses, the robots can build the starships for the next wave of exploration and push on across the galaxy as an ever-expanding wavefront of avatar-crewed Von Neuman machines (Matloff, 2022). The Metaverse becomes truly interstellar, and possibly Galactic.

And of course, at some point, we may meet a group of alien intelligences, and an alien Metaverse, coming the other way. Once the technical challenges are dealt with, it may even be that the alien AIs and their DAs can visit our local Metaverse, and as the technical understandings grow, proper portals and portability between the two Metaverses might be established, and slowly alien spaces and avatars can propagate back through each race's interstellar Metaverse. As a result, the first experience that physical humanity might have of an alien race is when an alien portal is opened up within the Earth's Metaverse providing access to a local copy of the alien Metaverse, and the ability to meet and speak to alien avatars. For most physical humans, their first encounter with aliens may not be in a space suit on a rugged and hostile planet, but from the comfort of their own sofa.

Conclusion

The Metaverse is nothing without users, and there is still a huge challenge in making the Metaverse (and even virtual world) concept understandable, let alone desirable, for the average person. The ReLive-based analysis above begins to identify some concrete steps that could help with the growth of the Metaverse/Multiverse, and the seven scenarios provide some idea of what the future could hold – some futures to be avoided, and other to be worked towards.

There is a generation that has grown up on virtual experiences such as *Club Penguin*, *Animal Crossing*, *World of Warcraft*, and *Habbo Hotel*; and *Roblox* and *Minecraft* may be spawning a new generation of fans. But it's not yet obvious that these people are growing into a generation of avid VR and virtual world users, although some are taking virtual worlds into their adult life.

This is going to be a long haul, and we need to make sure that the Metaverse is meeting real needs, not technologist's fantasies, and that we are communicating and demonstrating the benefits in all the best ways that we can. We also need to be learning from the past. That period from the release of *Snow Crash* to Facebook's change of name to Meta, or even just to the release of Oculus DK1, wasn't a metaversal desert. It was full of developers creating rich proto-metaverse platforms, of users finding all sort of ways to use these spaces for family, recreation, work and learning, and of researchers studying and reporting on them. We need to learn from the wealth of experience that was generated, and largely documented, through those times.

When the new generation does enter the Metaverse, it must let them do whatever they want – that's what makes it different from a meeting app or a game or an event app. That was one of the real strengths (and yet for many a real weakness) of *Second Life* – once you were there, you could do whatever you wanted: have meetings, play games, build relationships, look at data, teach, relax, make money, or just hang out. A true Metaverse must also give us that flexibility – it's the physical world, just digital.

References

Anderson, J., & Rainie, L. (2022). *The Metaverse in 2040*. Pew Research Centre. https://www.pewresearch.org/internet/2022/06/30/the-metaverse-in-2040/

Billington, P. (2018). *Wolves in the Walls*. Fable Studios and Third Rail Projects. https://thirdrailprojects.com/wolvesinthewalls

Burden, D. J. H. (2011). *Virtual Worlds: A Future History* [Presentation]. https://www.slideshare.net/davidburden/virtual-worlds-a-future-history

Burden, D. J. H. (2022). *The Metaverse—A future history?* Medium. https://medium.com/@davidjhburden/the-metaverse-a-future-history-e6f18b080d15

Burden, D. J. H., & Savin-Baden, M. (2019). *Virtual humans: Today and tomorrow*. CRC.

Chung, J. (2010). *Microsoft's Milo: A virtual 4-year-old boy*. TechEBlog. https://www.techeblog.com/microsofts-milo-a-virtual-4-year-old-boy/

Deloitte. (2017). *Global mobile consumer trends* (2nd ed.). Deloitte. https://www2.deloitte.com/content/dam/Deloitte/us/Documents/technology-media-telecommunications/us-global-mobile-consumer-survey-second-edition.pdf

DelSignore, P. (2022). *The challenges of virtual reality*. Medium. https://medium.com/blockchain-biz/what-is-wrong-with-virtual-reality-1955dafdf21

E, L. (2022). *Interoperability in the Immersive Web, Parts 1 & 2*. Mozilla Hubs. https://hubs.mozilla.com/labs/interoperability-in-the-immersive-web/; https://hubs.mozilla.com/labs/interoperability-in-the-immersive-web-part-2/

Gamez, D. (2023). *Which properties and structures must a virtual world have to enable the successful creation of human-level artificial intelligence?* davidgamez.eu. http://www.davidgamez.eu/papers/Gamez23_PropertiesVirtualWorld CreationIntelligence.pdf

IGN. (2023, September 27). *Meta Quest 3 revealed: Meta Connect 2023 keynote live-stream* [Video]. YouTube. https://www.youtube.com/watch?v=q09j-y05Prw&ab_channel=IGN

Matloff, G. L. (2022). Von Neumann probes: Rationale, propulsion, interstellar transfer timing. *International Journal of Astrobiology, 21*(4), 205–211.

McLuhan, M., & McLuhan, E. (2017). *The lost tetrads of Marshall McLuhan*. OR Books.

Peck, M. (2023). Robots, people, or some combination—What or whom should we send to the stars? *Interstellar travel* (pp. 83–100). Elsevier.

Picone, I. (2007). Conceptualising online news use. *Observatorio, 3*, 93–114.

United Nations. (2021). *Achieving universal connectivity by 2030*. United Nations. https://www.un.org/techenvoy/content/global-connectivity

Epilogue

We hope that this book has provided you with a (relatively) concise and critical introduction to the concept of the Metaverse, its history, technology, potential benefits and challenges, and some idea of how the Metaverse might evolve over the coming years, decades, and even centuries.

If you would like to explore further any of the ideas presented in this book, then we refer you to the rest of the books that are being published in this series. Books already underway have been listed at the front of this book, but we are actively identifying and commissioning new authors as we go to press, and for long after this initial book is published. Some of the other ideas that we have for potential books in the series are listed below.

Accessibility

Arts and Fashion

Blockchain and Cryptocurrency

Business and Collaboration

Climate Change

Cybersecurity

Digital Amortality

Economics

Entertainment and Gaming

Global Equality

Governance

Health & Care

Identity & Sexuality

Law

Literature and the Media

Marketing

Philosophy & Ethics

Politics, Campaigning and Extremism

Society and Anthropology

If you think that you are qualified to write on one of these topics, or have a different aspect of the Metaverse to suggest, then please get in contact with the CRC/Taylor & Francis series editor, Randi Slack, at Randi.Slack@taylorandfrancis.com.

Bibliography

Whilst some of these have been specifically mentioned in the text, this is a summary list of key books, media, and websites that are of relevance to any discussion of the Metaverse. An updated list is also available on the Metaverse Series website at http://www.themetaverseseries.info.

Non-Fiction Books

Au, W. J. (2009). *The making of Second Life: Notes from the new world*. Collins Business.

Au, W. J. (2023). *Making a metaverse that matters: From Snow Crash & Second Life to a virtual world worth fighting for*. John Wiley & Sons.

Ball, M. (2022). *The Metaverse: And how it will revolutionize everything*. Liveright Publishing.

Bartle, R. A. (2004). *Designing virtual worlds*. New Riders.

Blascovich, J., & Bailenson, J. (2011). *Infinite reality: Avatars, eternal life, new worlds, and the dawn of the virtual revolution*. Harper Collins.

Burdea, G., & Coiffet, P. (2003). *Virtual reality technology*. Wiley.

Burden, D. J. H., & Savin-Baden, M. (2019). *Virtual humans: Today and tomorrow*. CRC.

Burden, D. J. H., Savin-Baden, M., & Mason-Robbie, V. (2022). *Pedagogy for virtual reality training & education*. Free eBook. https://www.daden.co.uk/p4vr.

Carr, P., & Pond, G. (2007). *The unofficial tourist's guide to Second Life*. Pan Macmillan.

Chalmers, D. J. (2022). *Reality+: Virtual worlds and the problems of philosophy*. Allen Lane.

Ffiske, T. (2022). *The metaverse: A professional guide: An expert's guide to virtual reality (VR), augmented reality (AR), and immersive technologies*. Amazon.

Guest, T. (2007). *Second Lives: A journey through virtual worlds*. Random House.

Kannen, V., & Langille, A. (Eds.). (2023). *Virtual identities and digital culture*. Routledge.

van Kokswijk, J. (2007). *Digital ego: Social and legal aspects of virtual identity*. Eburon Academic Publishers.

Meadows, M. S. (2008). *I, avatar: The culture and consequences of having a second life*. New Riders.

Moore, D., Thome, M. & Haigh, K.Z. (2008). *Scripting your world: The official guide to second life scripting*. Wiley Publishing.

Narula, H. (2022). *Virtual society: The metaverse and the new frontiers of human experience*. Currency.

Rosa, N. (2023). *Understanding the metaverse: A business and ethical guide*. Wiley & Sons.

Rymaszewski, M., Au, J. W., Batstone-Cunningham, B., Ondrejka, C., Wallace, M. & Winters, C. (2007). *Second Life: The official guide*. Wiley & Sons.

Savin-Baden, M. (2010). *A practical guide to using Second Life in higher education*. Open University Press.

Savin-Baden, M., & Mason-Robbie, V. (Eds.). (2020). *Digital afterlife: Death matters in a digital age*. Chapman & Hall/CRC.

Savin-Baden, M., Tombs, C., Poulton, T., & Kavia, S. (2009). *Getting started with Second Life*. JISC.

Sinha, I. (1999). *The cybergypsies: A frank account of love, life and travels on the electronic frontier*. Scribner.

Weber, A., Platel, R. & Rufer-Bach, K. (2008). *Creating your world. The official guide to advanced content creation for Second Life*. Wiley Publishing.

Web Sites, Blogs and Podcasts

Active Player - https://activeplayer.io/category/live-player-count/
    A useful place to get up to date statistics on the usage levels of various games and many virtual world platforms.

Hypergrid Business - https://www.hypergridbusiness.com/
    A long-standing and respected source of virtual world and metaverse news.

Immersive Learning Research Network - https://www.immersivelrn.org/
    Research into learning and education across a range of virtual worlds and technologies.

Journal Metaverse - https://independent.academia.edu/JournalMetaverse
    A useful collection of academic papers on virtual worlds and the Metaverse

Journal of Virtual Worlds Research - https://jvwr-ojs-utexas.tdl.org/jvwr/
    An open-access journal on virtual worlds and the metaverse which ran from 2008 to 2020.

KZero Worldswide - https://www.linkedin.com/company/kzeroworldswide/
    Nic Mitham has been tracking virtual world data for almost 20 years and produces an excellent Metaverse Radar Chart.

New World Notes - https://nwn.blogs.com/nwn/
    Wagner James Au's long running blog on virtual world and metaverse matters.

The Next Billion Seconds - https://nextbillionseconds.com/a-brief-history-of-the-metaverse/
    Produced an excellent A Brief History of the Metaverse series.

Theo Prestley - https://medium.com/@theo
    One of the better Medium commentators on Metaverse issues.

Voice of VR Podcast - https://voicesofvr.com/
    A great source of VR and metaverse interviews.

Standards Groups and Industry Groups

Alliance of OpenUSD - https://aousd.org/
Augmented Reality for Enterprise Alliance - https://thearea.org/
Metaverse Standards Forum - https://metaverse-standards.org/
Open Metaverse Alliance - https://www.oma3.org/
Open Metaverse Foundation - https://www.openmv.org/
Open Metaverse Interoperability Group - https://omigroup.org/
OpenXR - https://www.khronos.org/openxr/
Virtual Worlds Education Consortium - https://www.vweconsortium.org/
VR/AR Association - https://www.thevrara.com/
XRAccess - https://xraccess.org/
XR Association - https://xra.org/

Fiction Books

Byrne, E. (1999). *ThiGMOO*. Earthlight.
Cline, E. (2011). *Ready player one*. Crown Publishing Group.
Egan, G. (2008). *Permutation city*. Gollancz.
Gibson, W. (1984). *Neuromancer*. Ace.
Gibson, W. (1996). *Idoru*. Viking Press.
Moggach, L. (2013). *Kiss me first*. Anchor Books. Picador.
Sharpson, N. (2021). *When the sparrow falls*. Solaris.
Stephenson, N. (1992). *Snow Crash*. Bantam Books.
Stephenson, N. (2020). *Fall; or, dodge in hell*. William Morrow & Company.
Taylor, D.E. (2016) We are legion (we are bob). Worldbuilders Press.
Vinge, V. (2007). *Rainbows end*. Tor Books.
Vinge, V. (2015). *True names and the opening of the cyberspace frontier*. Tor Books.

TV, Film and Audio Fiction

Aubuchon, R., & Moore, R. D. (Creators). (2010). *Caprica*. Syfy.
Brooker, C. (2011). *Black mirror* [TV series]. Channel 4.
Broughton, M., Dromgoole, J., Hoyle, S., & Robinson, J. (Creators), & Dromgoole, J. (Producer). *PlanetB*. (2009). BBC
Cline, E. (2018). *Ready player one*. Warner Bros. Pictures.
Daniels, G. (2010). *Upload*. Deedle-Dee Productions.
Elsley, B. (2018). *Kiss me first*. Channel 4.
Konaka, C. J. (writer). (1998). *Serial experiments lain*. TXN.
Roddenberry, G. (Creator & Executive Producer). (1987). *Star Trek: Next generation*. CBS Television.
Wachowskis. (1999). *The matrix* [Film]. Warner Bros.

Computer Games

Billington, P. (2018). *Wolves in the Walls* [VR]. Fable Studios and Third Rail Projects. Available at: https://thirdrailprojects.com/wolvesinthewalls

Role-Playing Games

Newton, S., & Snead, J. (2014). *Mindjammer*. Modiphius Entertainment.

Virtual Worlds and Proto-Metaverses

Active Worlds - https://www.activeworlds.com/
Alloverse - https://alloverse.com/
AmazeVR - https://www.amazevr.com/
Arthur - https://www.arthur.digital
Cryptovoxels - https://www.voxels.com/
Decentraland - https://decentraland.org/
Engage - https://engagevr.io/
Fortnite - https://www.fortnite.com/

Frame - https://learn.framevr.io/
Gather.town - https://www.gather.town/
Glue - https://glue.work/
Hiberworld - https://hiberworld.com/
Hyperfy - https://hyperfy.io/
Lamina1 - https://www.lamina1.com/
MeetInVR - https://www.meetinvr.com/
MetaVRse/TheMall - https://themall.io/
Meta Horizon Worlds - https://horizon.meta.com/
Microsoft Mesh - https://www.microsoft.com/en-us/microsoft-teams/microsoft-mesh
Minecraft - https://www.minecraft.net/en-us
Mozilla Hubs - https://hubs.mozilla.com/
Open Sim - http://opensimulator.org/
Rec Room - https://recroom.com/
Roblox - https://www.roblox.com/
Sansar - https://www.sansar.com/
Second Life - https://secondlife.com/
Somnium Space - https://somniumspace.com/
Spatial - https://www.spatial.io/
StellarX - https://www.stellarx.ai/
Vark - https://corp.vark.co.jp/
Virbela - www.virbela.com
Vircadia - https://vircadia.com/
Virtend - https://www.3dicc.com/
VISPA - https://www.vispa.io/
VR Chat - https://hello.vrchat.com/
Wonderland - https://wonderlandengine.com/
World of Warcraft - https://worldofwarcraft.blizzard.com/en-gb/
XRSpace/GOXR/PartyOn - https://www.xrspace.io/us

This list will age as worlds come and go. A more up to date list, together with world images and key data, is available through the Metaverse Series website at http://www.themetaverseseries.info.

Glossary

180VR: Stereoscopic video VR (q.v.) where only the forward view is shown in order to conserve bandwidth and memory.

3DOF: 3 degrees of freedom, i.e. the ability to look up/down, left/right, and tilt left/right.

360VR: Stereoscopic video VR (q.v.) where the full 720° around the camera (360° up/down and 360° left/right) is recorded.

6DOF: 6 degrees of freedom, that of 3DOF (q.v.) plus the ability to move forwards/backwards, left/right, and up/down.

augmented reality (AR): overlays digital information onto a viewscreen (typically a smartphone, but possibly a heads-up-display or a set of glasses) and supplements reality, rather than replacing it.

avatar: a user's (usually visual) representation of themselves in a virtual world, or a similar representation created and controlled by a computer programme.

blockchain: a distributed, secure, digital ledger – a way of recording transactions and information in a way that cannot be changed, and which shows complete traceability for every transaction.

CAVE: a room where a virtual world is shown on screens occupying the whole of at least three walls, either using projection or video screens.

chatGPT: the OpenAI implementation of a chatbot based on a large-language model approach, but increasingly being used as a generic term for such chatbots.

concurrency: the (typically maximum) number of users in a virtual world at any one moment in time.

confederated multiverse: a multiverse where the constituent metaverses have few services or even architectures in common and may operate on more of a peer-to-peer basis.

constituent metaverse: a metaverse which is connected to the larger multiverse, which may implement local rules and likely runs on its own infrastructure. May also be known as a satellite metaverse.

cryptocurrency: a currency based on a blockchain.

cryptoverse: a virtual world which is built on a blockchain and uses a cryptocurrency for all payments and receipts.

cybersickness: the nauseous feeling that some people get from using HMD-VR headsets.

de-rez: to remove an object from a virtual world and often place it back in your inventory, usually with the option to restore it at a later date.

desktopVR: refers to VR experiences delivered using a conventional 2D computer screen (desktop, laptop, tablet, or mobile), in either first person (the view out of the avatar's eyes) or third person (an "over the shoulder" view which includes the back of the avatar). A combination of mouse, keyboard, joystick, and touchscreen are used for control and interaction.

DOXing: revealing a virtual world user's physical world identity against their wishes.

extended reality (XR): the umbrella term used for all the technologies that create immersive experiences in which users interact with digital content which augment or replace the perceived physical world. As such, it includes VR, MR, and AR.

federated multiverse: a multiverse where the constituent metaverses share common services and even architectures.

game server: a computer whose job is to initially send a copy of a location to a user's computer, to get updates from the user about what they are doing, and then keep the computers of all users in that space up to date with the activities of every other user. Also called a reflection server.

glTF/glb: a new open standard for encoding 3D models which offers better portability between systems than previous standards such as .obj and .fbx.

griefing: anti-social and transgressive behaviour within a virtual world.

graphical user interface (GUI): graphical user interface – the controls that a user sees on a screen.

haptics: the sense of touch within a virtual environment, usually delivered through gloves, but can involve whole-body suits.

head-mounted display: a display that is strapped to your head and can typically also track your movements. Currently synonymous with HMD-VR, but increasingly should be taken as referring to HMX-XR.

head-mounted display VR (HMD-VR): VR delivered through a head-mounted display which fully covers the user's field of view, completely blocking out the physical world. Hand controllers and/or ordinary body movement are used for control and interaction.

head-mounted display XR (HMD-XR): an HMD capable of operating in both VR and MR modes, typically enabling MR through video pass-through rather than projecting onto a transparent screen.

inventory: the collection of objects, clothing, media, and scripts that a user or avatar owns in a virtual world.

javascript: a simple computer language widely used on the web to make web pages interactive.

massively multi-player online game (MMO): a game designed to be played by a large number of players at the same time, all of whom can potentially interact within the game world.

massively multi-player online role-playing game (MMORPG): a form of MMO which emphasises character, role-play, exploration, and adventure rather than combat.

material: in 3D graphics, the material is how rough or smooth something looks, more akin to what is called texture in the physical world.

mesh: the shape of an object defined typically in terms of points, vertices, and polygons. Essentially synonymous with wireframe (q.v.), but early versions of *Second Life* severely constrained the shape primitives which could be used.

metaverse: a persistent digital synthetic environment populated by a large number of avatars who have agency and can interact, for collaboration, work, recreation, learning, relationships, and/or play; and which may be accessible through a range of technologies including VR, MR, and possibly AR.

Metaverse: the ultimate manifestation of the metaverse concept, covering all metaversal features in a globally used and accessible system, which may be a singular metaverse, or a network of interconnected individual metaverses – i.e. a multiverse.

metaversal: exhibiting some or all of the features of a metaverse.

microverse: a small metaverse created for a very specific function – such as a training course, project, meeting, group, or entertainment event.

mixed reality (MR): overlays 3D digital visualisations onto a head-mounted screen or see-through visor, where the digital information is "aware" of the physical geometry of the world and the user's movement in it and can respond to both.

monthly active users (MAUs): the number of different users who use an application or service each month (c.f. concurrency).

multi-user dungeon (MUD): the first text-based virtual worlds, enabling large numbers of users to adventure in a fantasy dungeon, and later any space, through text descriptions, to take actions, and to interact with each other.

multi-user dungeon object-orientated (MOO): a second generation of MUDs which used an object-orientated approach to their design to make things easier for programmers and users.

multi-user virtual environment (MUVE): a term which is used within the education and learning sectors to describe virtual worlds.

multiverse: a network of interconnected individual metaverses. It may be that the Metaverse is actually a Multiverse – the capitalisation is again reserved for the fully developed manifestation.

non-fungible token (NFT): a token on a blockchain which represents a particular thing (e.g. an artwork) rather than a generic thing (e.g. an amount of money).

non-player character (NPC): an avatar which is controlled by the virtual environment rather than a user, and whose intent is to enhance the user experience. Originally found in game-based worlds, but now applied more generally.

not possible in real life (NPIRL): an old saying in *Second Life* to highlight the ability to do things within a virtual world which would just be impossible in the physical world.

physically-based rendering (PBR): rendering which tries to model some element of the physics of real lighting and illumination.

player character (PC): an avatar controlled by a user. Originally found in game-based worlds, but now applied more generally.

pocket metaverse: similar to a microverse but likely to be pinched out of a larger metaverse, such as by security and access controls.

proto-metaverse: a metaverse which shows many or most of the metaversal features but which is not fully enough developed to warrant the term Metaverse.

reflection server: another name for a game server (q.v.).

render: the process by which lights, textures, and materials (q.v.) are used to make an object in a virtual world something that a user can see.

rez: to place or make something appear in a virtual world – usually by placing it from a user's inventory.

robotar: an avatar controlled by a computer programme. A more general term than non-player character (q.v.).

roomscale: the ability to explore a 3D scene by physically moving around in your physical space rather than having to use a set of controllers to explicitly move your avatar.

scene graph: the totality of objects and avatars within a virtual scene, where they are, what they are, and how they relate.

semantic web: a version of the World Wide Web where pages and other assets carry meta-information about what they are and show in order to make them easier for code and computers to understand.

semantic metaverse: a version of the metaverse where objects carry meta-information about what they are, what they look like, and what they can do in order to make them easier for code and computers to understand.

skybox: a 360° image that typically surrounds a 3D build in order to give the impression of the sky and a distant horizon.

social virtual world (SVW): a virtual world which emphasizes social interaction, rather than, say, game playing or combat.

stereoscopic video VR: video which has been recorded with two cameras, separated by a typical inter-eye distance, so that when viewed in VR, it has the perception of depth.

streaming: in the virtual world sense, when the scene is rendered (q.v.) on a central computer and then the resulting imagery is streamed to the user's device – reducing the need for local processing but increasing the need for bandwidth.

synthetic environment: any environment that provides a synthetic or artificial sense of reality, usually taken to mean a digital synthetic environment.

teleport (TP): to move directly from one place to another in a virtual world without having to walk or fly.

texture: the colour and patterning of an object. Confusingly in 3D graphics, virtual textures are more akin to physical (visual) materials, whereas virtual materials are more akin to physical textures.

uncanny valley: the sense of unease someone gets when viewing a (typically) human avatar that is too "realistic" to be seen as a cartoon, but not realistic enough to look exactly like a person.

user-generated content (UGC): content created in a virtual world, or on the web, by users rather than the platform owners.

video pass-through: available on HMDs and uses forward facing cameras to show the user the physical world in front of them which they could not otherwise see as they are using an enclosed headset. Initially used for safety but now used to enable MR experiences.

virtual reality (VR): a 3D spatial, subjective, synthetic digital environment, which can be accessed through a smartphone, a tablet, or a conventional computer (DesktopVR) or a head-mounted display (HMD-VR). VR completely replaces physical reality in the user's view (and even other senses).

virtual reality markup language (VRML): one of the first computer languages to build 3D spaces with.

virtual world (VW): a VR environment which provides a space for users to interact, to have agency and (ideally) some ability to shape the world. Often interchangeable with "metaverse".

voxel: the 3D equivalent of a pixel, the smallest cube within a 3D scene. Many early 3D environments were based around voxels (e.g. Habbo Hotel), and some still are (e.g. Dual Universe), but most have moved away from the approach to meshes.

webGL: a web-based approach to building 3D scenes which runs in a browser.

webXR: a further development of webGL to allow the viewing of 3D scenes within an HMD-VR browser.

wireframe: the shape of an object defined typically in terms of points, vertices, and polygons. Essentially synonymous with mesh (q.v.).

XR: see Extended Reality.

Index

Note: Locators in *italics* represent figures and **bold** indicate tables in the text.

Printed in the United States
by Baker & Taylor Publisher Services